dmt

HEY WORLD
HERE ARE SOME SUGGESTIONS

tweet me harder   volume 1

KRIS STRAUB & DAVID MALKI !

BEARSTACHE BOOKS
VENICE, CA

Tweet Me Harder Volume 1: Hey World Here Are Some Suggestions™
©2010 Kris Straub & David Malki !
Illustrations by Kris Straub

Published by **Bearstache Books,** Venice, CA
2554 Lincoln Blvd #214 • Venice, CA 90291
BEARSTACHE.COM • TWEETMEHARDER.COM

Second Edition, June 2010.

ISBN-13: 978-0-9821671-1-3

10 9 8 7 6 5 4 3 2

Printed in the United States of America

"Say what you will about Tom,
but he knew how to commit
to a bit."

REPRINTED WITH PERMISSION FROM READER'S DIGEST, 1971

MORE BY KRIS STRAUB

Starslip Crisis: Volumes 1–3
Chainsawsuit: Volumes 1–3
How to Make Webcomics

starslip.com
chainsawsuit.com
krisstraub.com

MORE BY DAVID MALKI !

The Annotated Wondermark
Beards of our Forefathers
Clever Tricks to Stave Off Death
Dapper Caps & Pedal-Copters
Dispatches from Wondermark Manor

wondermark.com
areyouexpendable.com
machineofdeath.net

Contents

Foreword

Tweet Me Harder is a podcast in which the two of us spend about an hour a week describing a *better way of life*. Why does a podcast need a book? Why does *anything* need a book? Why do encyclopediae need books, or Bibleses or dictionari or thesauraux? For that matter, why do *telephones* need books? Telephones have been around for a hundred years and they *still* got massive books coming out like twice a year or something. So clearly *everything* needs books. It is a Government mandate. In compliance with the Books Act of Nineteen-Booky-Four, please enjoy the following grudgingly-compiled collection of our first ten episodes. *Are you happy now, Your Honor?*

—Kris Straub & David Malki !

Parka Car Wash

DAVID MALKI !: Hello, welcome to Tweet Me Harder, the world's first, best, only and last talkback-enabled interactive audio podblast.

[*THE THEME MUSIC CONTINUES TO PLAY UNABATED*]

KRIS STRAUB: This isn't the fade-out version.

DM: I'm David Malki !

KS: And I'm Kris Straub.

DM: Thanks for tuning in. This is how the show works: you can Twitter to us at any time. Our user is @TWEETHARD, and this is the very first show, so please use the hashtag #TMH1. Any Twitter that says #TMH1, we will be able to see, and we will be using for...who knows what. I don't know what. Maybe we're going to sell 'em! Maybe we're going to make shirts based on 'em.

KS: You know what, though? Shirts are so played. Why don't we put it on other merchandise, like thongs...

DM: Yes.

KS: Or clocks.

DM: Clocks?

KS: Not black shirts. Yeah, just cheap, kind of plasticky...

DM: Clocks that you wear around your neck, like Flavor Flav?

KS: You could.

DM: Or clocks that you put on the wall?

KS: You could. But you know, if you wear a clock with a tweet on it around your neck, why don't we just make you a shirt?

DM: ...If you wear a clock with a tweet? Because the clock is an accessory. You can wear that with anything. A shirt you have to wash in-between.

KS: Wear it with any color shirt! I like it!

DM: Yeah! It's modular.

KS: That's not bad.

DM: So here's the thing. What else can we put tweets on? We can put them on underwear. We can put them on shoes...

KS: Anything that's worn, is a given.

DM: Well, you wear shoes every day, for sure.

KS: Yeah. Hey, you could put it on—I got it, I got it, I got it.

DM: Tell me.

KS: You create a process...you'd have to know a little bit more about making soap. But you make it into soap, so when you wash your body...*subsequent tweets* are revealed.

DM: Oh, yes! I like this.

KS: Right?

DM: You know where I thought you were going to go: when you use the soap, it embeds tweets on your skin.

KS: I think it would just streak 'em.

DM: Well, that's where the technology comes into play.

KS: Oh, well, yeah. That sounds like a VC sort of a deal.[1]

DM: All right. So here's the thing about soap that reveals tweets over time. There's a similar sort of thing with toilet paper—have you seen this? Where it's like, the novels or whatever, they're written one square at a time on toilet paper, and as you unroll the thing, you get the whole story?

KS: No way. Is that a thing?

DM: In fact...I don't know how many people are doing novels. I think you typically see this on very...*ideologically extreme* websites, where they sell toilet paper with, like, the thing that they hate on it. Like the face of Osama, or...

KS: Sure, yeah, yeah.

DM: ...Or the pages of the Qur'an.

KS: Or I guess the story that they hate.

DM: Right. "Boy, I hate *War and Peace*, let's embed it on toilet paper."

KS: "Good thing, 'cause I had Taco Bell, and..."

DM: But really, it's almost like a Twitter feed, because of the revealed-slowly nature of it. You're not gonna unroll the whole thing and read the novel, you're just going to do it, you know, eight squares at a time, three times a day or whatever.

KS: Well that's what I was going to say, is that you have to figure out some optimal redundancy. Because I'm not going to use *a square*. I gotta take care of business.

DM: Well, sure. It's the same thing with Twitter: something can stand on its own or be part of a longer series, I suppose.

---

1 Are we referring here to "venture capital", the process by which investors fund promising new businesses, or "Viet Cong", the opposing force to the United States in the Vietnam War? It frankly works either way.

KS: What if it's a really good book and I gotta take that on, like, the train? And I'm just unrolling…I'm spooling it onto another roll.

DM: You have a pencil or something that you're re-spooling it onto, and basically you're making like a Talmudic scroll.

KS: Of toilet paper.

DM: So my question for you is: if the right-wing websites have the toilet paper with the Qur'an or with Osama's face, what would the left-wing websites have? I don't really think that any of them have actually done this, because it's such a horrible idea, and, you know. They're too *tolerant.*

KS: It's such a sour…yeah. Too tolerant.

DM: But what would that product be? Like, what would be on that toilet-paper roll for the super-liberal audience?

KS: Are you posing that to the listeners?

DM: Yes. Actually, yes. Tweet us—hashtag T-M-H-1—what is on the toilet-paper roll that the left-wing activists sell?

KS: I got an idea. How about pictures of flowers and the Earth? Because those need poop to grow. And that's just natural. That's just good.

DM: I like this, I like this. So what we're doing is subverting the whole idea of toilet paper as something to put poop on—

KS: "Why is that such a *bad* thing?"

DM: Yeah! So the first way of thinking is, "I hate this thing *so much,* I'm just gonna put poop *all over it!*" But the other guys are saying, "No, poop's *natural,* it's from our *body…*"

KS: "There's nothin' wrong with it!"

DM: Okay, this is what I like. Not just that, but what that suggests: recontextualizing the whole idea of toilet-paper literature.

KS: Well—

DM: Maybe the toilet paper is just the format, and you don't even put poop on it. Maybe there's some form of toilet-paper literature that…its ideal form is not even used in the bathroom. It just takes that format for some other reason.

KS: That's like super-microfiction. It's completely disposable fiction.

DM: Yeah, the whole idea of it is the fact that it's super-delicate.

KS: Let's see…@ALOHAAIRCARGO tweets: "The toilet paper would be made out of cloth, so you can wash and reuse it."

DM: I have heard of this. I have heard of the reusable toilet paper, where they have— it's almost like a Kleenex box, and they're cloth. And they have a little bin.

KS: But then what do you do with it when you've got a box full of this filthy…

DM: You wash it.

KS: *(sighing)* No. And you know what, though…that gets away from the idea of the story. Because that has to be a story you want to read again.

DM: Well, yeah. And so maybe that's—

KS: Or you know what? Maybe just a memorable...like, a parable. Or a quote from the Bible. Because people like to have that in their home all the time. They read it a million times.

DM: If it's going to be individual squares—because these things are not on a roll. Reusable toilet paper's format is wipes. It's not something you tear off of a roll.

KS: Sure.

DM: So each selection on the toilet paper has to be modular. It has to be, like you say—it's an aphorism. Maybe it's a poem.

KS: Maybe it's like that magnetic poetry.

DM: Wait, so what happens is, you use it and you stick it to your wall? And you build a large poem over time?

KS: Nah, you don't stick it to your wall, you just remember what the word was. Or you know what, maybe you take a picture of it, then string the pictures together digitally. You know. Be smart. This is the twenty-first century.

DM: All right. @DUSTINCORREALE says, "It's like 'Far Side' calendars." So there's something separate on every thing that is part of a greater theme, but you just get one little bite at a time.

KS: Oh, wow. That would really develop. That would really take a long time to get to the end of it.

DM: Well, a "Far Side" calendar is just a gag a day, it's not, you know...

KS: Oh, I see. You're saying they're not interconnected stories. It's just like a little laugh. It's like a "Ziggy" cartoon.

DM: ...I thought you said *laugh.*

KS: Oh, sorry.

DM: I could see someone taking this as a challenge. What's the thing that they could write that's so compelling in the toilet-paper medium, that people would want to go and reread it again every time they wash their toilet paper?

KS: I don't know, but just the sound of the phrase "wash your toilet paper"—

DM: It's probably not paper. It's probably "toilet wipes." I really don't know what the terminology is.

KS: "Ah, man, it's Sunday, the banks are closed, I can't get any quarters, but I gotta do laundry 'cause I gotta take a dump, and now...ah, geez."

DM: The "gotta do laundry because I gotta take a dump" is rough situation to get into.

KS: Ugh.

DM: But I mean, people use cloth diapers. It's the same idea, just applied to the whole household.

KS: Yeah, but somehow a baby's waste is like a more natural...*fun* thing. You know. It's *pleasant.* Even though it's really not.

DM: We don't have kids. This is not something I'm sure we're going to get a lot of agreement on from the child-rearing audience.

KS: It's almost *adorable.*

DM: There are also services—diapering services, I believe they're called—where you just have a bin, and you put all your diapers in them, and then some—

KS: What a friggin' *expense!*

DM: —You put it on your porch, and they come once a week, and they go and launder them. It's like a uniform service.

KS: What kind of left-wing guys *are* these, they got enough money to pay for an adult diaper service?

DM: Well, they do the tradeoff with the cost of buying disposable stuff, plus of course the environmental impact of all the waste that it generates, both in its manufacture and at the end product.

KS: That's true, they can rationalize it. Aww, I didn't expect to start with this.

DM: Well, what did you expect to start with? *Not*-poop?

KS: Not poop. Pretty much.

DM: So let's see...we asked everybody to respond to the question, "What's the worst topic for a talk show?"

KS: Hey, wait a minute.

DM: Oh yeah? What?

[KRIS TRIGGERS THE ACCORDION STING]

DM: *(laughs)* You're listening to Tweet Me Harder, the world's first, best, only and last talkback-enabled interactive audio podblast. We are now listening to what people say about the worst type of talk show. @PROFESSOR_D says, "Attempting to disprove every world religion as a valid belief system." I think that's the answer.

KS: That's pretty—I mean, it's offensive. But it could be interesting if you're open-minded enough.

DM: I like how he says "attempting to disprove." So the idea is not in your presenting an ironclad case, it's just the act of arguing.

KS: Well, he's got a bias. He's saying "clearly you can't."

DM: I don't know that he does or he doesn't, but the whole point of any kind of a talk show, ever, about religion is always going to be hearing different sides of the equation, and having them argue with each other. And in my experience, the listener is always listening to these kinds of shows just waiting for someone to say what *they* feel. And everyone has such divergent opinions about religion, I think that happens fairly rarely.

KS: Yeah. So is that just the ultimate troll show? Just 'cause nobody will ever be satisfied with anything that's uttered on that show?

DM: I think the only way anybody, from a listener standpoint, is going to be satisfied is if—all they want is their side to be heard. Everyone has their own little belief system that they've carved out for themselves that's either close to or far from, you know, any other person's belief system. So as long as they get someone on the show—if someone on the show says what *that listener* believes, then they feel like they've had their day in court. I think that's all they need, because no one is ever converted by listening to a radio show. Unless you're Johnny Hart, and you've watched eight hours of satellite—that has to be an apocryphal story. I'm sorry. That must be an apocryphal story. Do you know this story?

KS: He had a lot happening. I mean, I don't know what it is, but...

DM: Well, did you ever hear the story about how he was converted?

KS: No! I mean, I know that that's what happened, but...

DM: Well, Johnny Hart from "B.C.", he used to just be a regular old cartoonist. If you read the oldest "B.C." comics from...I guess he started in the sixties or seventies? I forget. But they're—

KS: Yeah, it's just workaday caveman gags.

DM: I think it's pretty interesting, because there were a lot of pretty wacky concepts in there: clams that walked around, and there was a guy making bubbles out of water that he carried around...

KS: Blasphemy. *Blasphemy!*

DM: No, this is before he had any sort of religious fervor. And what happened was, his wife had convinced him to install a satellite dish at the house. So the satellite-dish guy—on purpose or not—tuned the station to some religious, you know, preaching channel, saying "I have to leave it on this for two hours so we can tune in the signal." Because this is back in the days of a dish in the back yard, and it's eight feet wide.

KS: Oh, no.

DM: And so Johnny Hart's sitting there watching this TV preacher...and he's converted!

KS: Wow.

DM: And that's the story! And from then on, "B.C." is about Jesus.

KS: That's pretty good. Good on that cable-repair guy.

DM: I guess he's doing the Lord's work, right?

KS: ...What else we got?

DM: Someone says, "Turn down the tweeting-birds sounds." That's pretty good.[2]

KS: I could do that right now! I mean, provided that I'm the one to play it.

DM: Maybe we should turn it down. Everyone's...okay, here's the last, like, eighteen tweets: "Why are there bird noises constantly on the audio feed?" "Your Twitter client is too loud." "Is it a sound effect? What's going on?" "Dial-down the tweeting-bird sound." This is what we like about instant feedback.

KS: Don't worry! It's easily fixed, and I'm gonna try it right now. *(silence)* What do you say?

DM: I don't even hear that.

KS: Yeah, I can't hear it either.

DM: Perfect.

KS: Is it even playing? All right, this'll work.

DM: Sounds like the problem is solved.

KS: I guess we did it! Thanks to the Internet.

DM: Hey, so let me ask you this question. What's your feeling on the bikini car wash?

KS: Oh, wow! I was just looking at that today.

DM: Wait, what?

KS: Unrelatedly.

DM: Is that a thing?

KS: No, it's not.

DM: I'm talking about the concept. Is that like a site?

KS: No, it's not a site. It's many, many sites, my friend!

DM: I just want to make sure we're on the same page.

---

2 In the first epsiode, while we were still figuring out the sound effects, we'd play a chorus of tweet sounds every time we read a listener's tweet. And it went on for about fifteen seconds each time. Charming, eh?

KS: I feel like it's exploitational. Exploitative. I don't think I like it?

DM: Does it exist outside of pop culture? Have you ever seen a bikini car wash in real life?

KS: I've never seen one in real life. I've seen student car washes; I've seen church-group ones; I've seen, like, recovering drug-addict ones here in Dallas, believe it or not. Related to church groups. That's actually kind of a whole—it's like a Venn diagram, they all merge at some point.

DM: This is, or is not, involving bikinis? The drug-addict one?

KS: No bikinis, though.

DM: No bikinis?

KS: No bikinis.

DM: Some? Is it like half and half?

KS: You—nope.

DM: There's just *no* bikinis.

KS: That's just wishful thinking. Just not at all. I mean, maybe beneath what they're wearing. But probably not.

DM: I don't know anything about Texas. I'm just trying to guess. I'm trying to picture it.

KS: Well, how about in L.A.? They got any of that? It seems like an L.A. thing.

DM: You would think so! I did get my car washed not terribly long ago at some kind of a church youth-group thing. But yeah, I think the church youth-group and the bikini car wash are probably, sort of...the Venn diagram looks like Garfield's eyes. A sort of mutually-exclusive...

KS: They just kiss.

DM: The movie *Bring It On* has taught me that bikini car washes are a cheerleading thing. Like a school fundraiser?

KS: Yeah! I mean, I would assume.

DM: So *if* they happen, that's probably how they happen.

KS: They're not doing it because they love bikinis and washing cars. They're doing it for money!

DM: Well, here's the thing that I am not sure of, and this is what I wanted to get your opinion on. What do you think the quality of the car wash is? You think they get all the crevices? You think they actually get the windows streak-free?

KS: No! You know what? They don't do any detailing at all! I think that they've got a great system in place to obscure the quality of...you know, the level of attention that they pay to your vehicle.

DM: Right.

KS: They probably didn't even do the passenger side. 'Cause you're not looking.

DM: Yeah, because they're so busy *leaning sultrily* over the hood that they don't actually...they probably don't even pull the wipers up to get the windshield. To get the bottom of the windshield.

KS: Right, and you didn't care. You're just happy that they're talking to you.

DM: @ALOHAAIRCARGO on Twitter says, "Great if you're watching from the sidelines, but I want a good car wash, period." I think this is a very important thing to keep in mind. So the question is, the people that stop at bikini car washes, who're you going to have? You're going to have pervy uncles. You're going to have fundraising enthusiasts, people that want to support the booster club or whatever. Now here's the question: are *those* groups mutually exclusive? Are you attracting one at the expense of the other?

KS: Or both. Or maybe one is just an excuse for the other. Although I don't know why you would be a pervert in order to boost the academics club. It's more likely the other way around: that you, under the *guise* of supporting the school...

DM: Right, yeah. It's like, "Honey, I'm gonna go take the car to be washed, the school's having a fundraiser." "Oh, isn't that nice."

KS: There's this whole thing about perception-of-value that I always have a problem with, as far as...going to strip clubs, or this sort of thing with a bikini car wash, where it can go one of two ways in my head and both of them are negative. Number one, she's washing my car, and I'm looking at her, and she's like "He-e-ey, I hope you're enjoying the show!" and then I'm like "Ugh. Go to school. Enjoy your life." You know? "Have a nice family. I'm not this guy. This is awful." And then the other end of it is, if she looks like she's completely disappointed and sad to be there but she's doing it anyway because she's gotta.

DM: Right, because she's trying to get to summer camp.

KS: Yeah, and I've got the five bucks that's going to get her there. And I ain't lettin' her *have* it till she washes my entire car in the sun!

DM: How much of that is a ploy? I'm not saying that anybody who looks miserable in a bikini car wash/strip club is not actually miserable, I'm sure those things are miserable occupations. But by *looking* miserable, the onus is now put on the visitor, or the patron, to pay more. To make it so that they don't have to be out in the sun all day long.

KS: It's a guilt thing.

DM: Although those fundraiser things—I don't think they typically end with a dollar amount being hit. There's no threshold, it's just "we're gonna be here till six o'clock regardless."

KS: Let me ask you this, then. Do you think that—if it's a guilt factor—could you make more money with, like, Parka Car Wash? All the kids are wearing coats and blankets and they're just *miserable!* They are *all* getting heatstroke. And *your* money will get them out of there. And to safety. So tip 'em, for God's sake!

DM: Okay. So are you saying that when you tip them, they start taking *off* the clothes? So they become *more* comfortable?

KS: Umm...no! Because in that scenario it's too easy to say "why are you wearing that? Take it off! You're gonna die!" And I'd prefer that you'd install, like, a *dictator* of the car wash who's *making* them wear it, and you have to appease *him*. And they're like, "We're just pawns in his mad game; we have to wash a car while we're dying."

DM: Okay, so far I'm seeing a couple marketing problems with getting people into the car wash.

KS: Okay.

DM: One, the fact that you have children in parkas, soaking wet, in the hot sun.

KS: *Too* sexy!

DM: Number two, that they are being overseen by some sort of dictator, whom you have to pay to appease for the children's well-being.

KS: It's not real. It's not a *real* thing!

DM: Okay, so number three, it's people *play-acting* a *child-labor dictatorship*. And these are people that are asking for your support!

KS: Well, you know the story about the Dutch version of Santa Claus, right?

DM: What, the one where he beats you if you smoke pot?

KS: Yeah, he beats you up if you were bad that year. But then as we grew more civilized to now...he just *pretends* to kick you. You know? It has the intent, but not the actual brutality. So, you going to this car wash with the dictator, there's an *understanding* that there is play-acting going on here. And you do not *breach* that. You don't pierce that veil.

DM: You have to stay in character at all times.

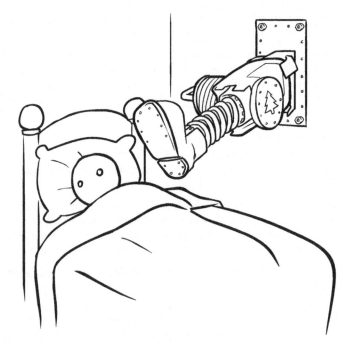

KS: Yeah. You have a contract with this group of kids.

DM: Okay. So this is what I want to know: How many dictatorship parka car-washes does it take before the public consciousness begins to understand the social contract inherent in the dictatorship parka car wash?

KS: You know what? I don't know. I don't think it's an unlimited number. It depends on how sadistic an area you live in, I guess.

DM: @ALINAPETE says, "Sketchiest bikini car wash I've ever seen also sold 50-cent hot dogs. Not good, not good at all."

KS: Wow.

DM: 50 Cent—now is this like the rapper? No, it's probably not.

KS: Which would be expensive, and really awesome.

DM: Right, they're probably gold-encrusted.

KS: I would think so.

DM: What about hot dogs with little scallops in them so that they don't dislodge the diamonds in your front teeth?

KS: Wow. Or like, they have optimal *pierced crescents* where you put your teeth. So you don't have to disturb your grill.

DM: Talk about niche marketing.

KS: That's pretty solid thinking. Although it'd be easy to machine.

DM: I was gonna say *pre-bitten* hot dogs because that way, you don't have to worry about the—you can still enjoy the chewing action. It's not a *milkshake* hot dog, where, you know, you have to *drink* it. You can still use your molars and everything. But you don't have to do the *incising* at all. Everything is bite-sized.

KS: You could kinda stick it in the corner of your mouth like a cigar. If you don't need the front of your mouth whatsoever. You don't need any knife action.

DM: Maybe what you'd end up doing is going to the market, picking up the little cocktail-weenie package—

KS: Yeah.

DM: —And then opening the package, and dumping it into a *new* package that says "Bling Bling Hot Dogs" and marking it up by double and reselling it.

KS: In practice, that's probably what you're gonna get. I don't think anybody's going to go to the trouble of, you know, machining hot dogs so they break off easily. Although when you first said "hot dogs with scallops in them," I thought you meant the sea creature. And I thought "What a *decadent* sausage! What a great treat."

DM: I do like the idea of *machining* hot dogs. Like there's a giant factory press that's just—you know, it's like a laser cutter, and the hot dog is being held by a vise on either side. And it's being moved around—like, rotated very precisely, so the laser can cut it into a very precise shape.

KS: It's like the robot arms at an auto mill.

DM: Yeah! Exactly.

KS: Spinning it elaborately in the air.

DM: Yeah, and then there's a giant robot that picks it up and sets it on the conveyor belt, or whatever. I mean, really it comes down to marketing. Most makeup is made in like three factories, and the label that they put on it is what determines the price that you pay for it.

KS: Right.

DM: Whether it's, you know, Macy's, or whether it's Nordstrom, or whether it's the really high-end Beverly Hills boutique, there's a whole scale at which it's the same makeup in different packaging and at different price points.

KS: Yeah. That's absolutely a given. I don't know how we got here from car washes...

DM: No, I'm talking about the hot dogs! I'm talking about, you're reselling those hot dogs marketed for different audiences. And this audience can only pay x amount, so you only charge x amount and you put it in the Food4Less. And then *this* audience, they—if you can put diamonds in your canines, you're going to pay a hundred dollars for a bag of hot dogs. You just have to market it appropriately.

KS: For a bag of hot dogs! The thing that kills me is like, be it hot dogs or the car-washing, any time you have a business that advertises with a sign that's written on the back of a refrigerator box, there's going to be a dearth of quality in the end product. I think.

DM: Wait, so—no, we wouldn't sell Rapper Hot Dogs on refrigerator boxes. *Ohhh! I* see what you're talking about. You're talking about getting *both* ends of the spectrum: *Pre*—like on their way *up* to multi-platinum album, *and* when they're destitute on the street! You gotta offer Homeless Hot Dogs, in a language that they speak!

KS: "You can chew these!" That's the slogan.

DM: Yeah! And instead of the little scoop-out so that your diamonds don't get caught in it, you just change the marketing. You make it a little bit less flashy and you say, "Look. We understand that you don't have teeth."[3]

KS: "You will not break your one tooth on *this* hot dog. That's *our* guarantee."

DM: The problem is, you might have to use pictograms. Depending on how literate these people are. I mean, I don't know. Maybe homeless people—I see one homeless guy who reads a lot of books.

KS: Oh. Well, I was gonna say, you split the difference. You invest a little money in one of those talking—those voice chips that go into stuffed animals. And it's just on the package.

DM: Oh yeah, like on greeting cards. I like that.

KS: And then there's just a picture of a thumb, and then they know to push it. And then it's gonna tell you. "Soft hot dogs."

---

3 We gave the transcript of this episode to Homeless Bob, our homeless-issues ombudsman, to make sure it could not in any way be construed as offensive to the noble homefree community. Other episodes, absolutely, but this one he said was all right.

DM: "These hot dogs are for *you!* They're not those fancy rich-man hot dogs. These hot dogs are made with your unique needs well in mind."

KS: Oh, man.

DM: @Posiduck says, "You have a nice male-patriarchal fantasy going on." You, in particular. I'm much more even-handed.

KS: Is that me?

DM: Clearly, yeah.

KS: Why? Because I want—I didn't say that the hot-dog car-wash dictator was a *man*.

DM: That's true!

KS: Change up their genders! Why did *you* assume that? I think *you're* the sexist!

DM: That's true. We have never once, on this entire show, *ever* insisted that the bikini car wash is women.

KS: Could be dudes. They make bikini thongs for dudes. To wear.

DM: And they even have bikini *briefs*. They're not even thongs, they actually have a little coverage. Right?

KS: Probably more decent. That's the kind the church group would wear.

DM: Okay, so Bikini *Man* Car Wash. The question is, who is the market for car washes? Typically it's people that—

KS: Guys with cars.

DM: In the way that more women buy greeting cards than men, do more men get their cars washed than women? I don't know. I would think it's fairly even.

KS: Oh, I don't know. I think you're already going to deal with a high-end clientle, just on the basis that their car is gonna be nicer and they're gonna want it to look nice. Because I have a Honda Fit, and I could care less when's the last time it was washed. I'm not going! I'm gonna wait for it to rain.

DM: So the people that are going to the bikini car wash are the kind of douchebags that also spent their money on a Porsche. Because they're not married—or they are married and they have a midlife crisis. Is that what you're saying?

KS: Yeah. They're having a lot of trouble. And that's my assumption. If you own a Porsche, and you're listening to the show, use the tag #TMH1 and we'll discuss it!

DM: Actually, I do want to put out a query. Use hashtag #TMH1 and tell us: What is the most expensive luxury item that you have ever bought—that you could have paid eight dollars for at the regular store? But you ended up paying a hundred dollars for at the fancy store.

KS: I got one, probably.

DM: Tell me.

KS: My sunglasses. My aviators. Here's what happened. We went to Sunglass Hut, and there they're like a hundred and twenty-five bucks. Put those on; all right, they're about what I expected, 'cause my dad owned a pair. And then we're like,

"Ah, we can't justify this cost, too expensive!" So we drove to, like, a Sav-On. I think we went to a gas station. We're like "these look exactly the same! They're exactly the same. Put 'em on." And there was just something innately, like...just didn't feel *right*. And what we should have done was put that one on first.

DM: Yeah, then you wouldn't have known.

KS: It was a total setup.

DM: That intangible—

KS: We ended up going back to buy the—Yeah. We bought the regular ones. We bought the *expensive* ones.

DM: I mean, if something costs more, it's usually better. That's a given—that's the default nature of the universe.

KS: I hope!

DM: The question is, in this case, if the difference between the hundred-dollar sunglasses and the $3.95 sunglasses at Sav-On was *enough*—if it was ninety-six dollars and five cents' worth of difference to you.

KS: Yeah!

DM: To justify that purchase. Right? I'm asking.

KS: Yeah, it was hefty. It was! I mean, there was an upper bound. If they had been three hundred dollars, I don't think I would have—there was no way I was gonna buy 'em. But you think about what you're paying for: you're paying for a little sliver of metal and some lenses. Oh, although I do—a little bit tangential, I do have a funny story related to the purchase of my *second* pair, some years later after my first pair was scratched.

I went to Sunglass Hut. I knew exactly what I wanted. But there was a young gentleman there who'd probably *just* started working there. He said "Can I help you out?" I said, "Nope, I kinda know what I'm looking for." But I was curious, because the pair I had, I recognized—but there was another pair that, on the lens, it said "P". I didn't know what "P" was. But they looked a little yellower than the other lenses. So I said "Yeah, actually, I have a question. What is the 'P' on these—what does that mean on that lens?"

And he says, "Oh, the 'P' stands for *polarized*. Once you wear a pair of polarized glasses, you're not gonna use the regular kind. And once you wear a pair of *Maui Jims,* you'll *never* go back to *any other brand!*"

DM: All right.[4]

KS: And I was thoroughly disgusted. Because I will not wear Maui Jims. And I felt really bad for him, because that's clearly a line that he's been given, and it's his twentieth time saying it. And him standing there wearing a pair of Maui Jims was not really a big sale to me. It didn't work.

DM: This is something that I've seen. Speaking of people having that *line*. I've seen this a lot recently. My office is on a sidewalk. Storefront office. So there's plenty

---

4　This is the point in this show where David starts feigning like he has any knowledge at all of Maui Jims. It's a brand of sunglasses apparently? He still does not really know.

of people walking up and down all day long. And we get solicitors fairly often. Until I put up a sign a couple days ago, we were getting solicitors at minimum once a week.

KS: Yeah.

DM: These were not people who were selling you a Thomas Guide door-to-door, or, like, an oversized calculator. Like you may have seen before. These are people who are trying to promote businesses. And their promotional strategy is to just go to every other business in the area and drop off a flyer. The owner of a sign shop came by; there was a guy in a three-piece suit, full-on business attire, from some local bank, you know, "we offer financial blah-blah-blah, can I leave you with a flyer, blah-blah-blah."

KS: Yeah.

DM: So anyway, the last guy and the one who broke the camel's back and made me put up the sign, was this really gangly guy in a long suit jacket. It's clearly an off-the-rack suit, didn't fit him—like, he's one of those body shapes that doesn't fit real well in a suit. He opened the door and he poked his head in, and he looked around. He saw me sitting there. And he goes, "Hey man, I'm really sorry. I'm really sorry." And I'm thinking, "Oh, he's asking directions, what's going on."

KS: Yeah?

DM: He goes, "I'm really sorry, I'm just—I'm here for—I—I know this is dumb, but, I'm here from Verizon and I want to talk to you about our FIOS service. I mean, do you guys have Internet here, or—are you all set up with that?" And he's clearly *so* embarrassed, and he just wants us to say "you know what, we're all set. Here, you want some water? You look like you're about to pass out."

KS: Yeah...

DM: So I said, "We're all taken care of, we've got it all wired in." And he says, "Yeah, you sound like you're all set. You're probably all just...you know what, though?" And you see him kind of mulling it over, the gears turning. And he reaches in his little briefcase and he pulls out a flyer and he goes "if you ever just need FIOS service it's the number one service blah-blah-blah—" and he goes into this spiel.

And I go, "You know what, we're set." He's like "all right. It's cool. It's cool. Ahh. I'm sorry. I'm—thanks. Um. All right. Yeah. All right, man, cool." And he left.

So you know that he's obligated just to do that spiel at some point, you know? And he's desperate to not look like a douche, and so he's trying to preface it. And I think the preface made it worse, because he seems like a guy who knows better.

KS: Yeah.

DM: And that's less forgivable than a guy who's just, "All right, whatever. They told me to say it."

KS: Right. We've all been there. But what I don't like is when you can't connect with them on even that level. Like, if I went to that Maui Jims guy and I said, "I know you don't care about Maui Jims. It's just you and me. I don't want Maui Jims, so don't try to pitch me on 'em. But I will take these other ones. I know that you're just working here." And he's not allowed to be like, "Okay. That's good, sure." He has to go, "No! I am passionate about sunglasses, and Maui Jims are the ultimate in eye care." You know? I cannot connect to this man as a human.

DM: @STEVENFC on Twitter is saying that "Kris, you *must* give them a try. I need polarized glasses; Maui is my family's preferred brand." Maybe they're just that much better!

KS: Naw, I don't believe him. Or maybe that guy works there. Maybe that's the guy.

DM: That's him! Steven! Oh, dude. Man.

KS: I'm sorry! Did you find a better job? Did you...

DM: You made quite the impression on Kris, for him to still remember! Speaking of sunglasses—this is not Maui Jims, but here in Venice I'm seeing probably... it's getting up into the thirty-, forty-percent ratio: Among all sunglasses that we see, among everybody walking around, the percentage of them that are the black plastic with the neon arms.

KS: Neon arms? Oh, yeah, yeah.

DM: Neon yellow, neon orange, neon pink. It's very T&C Surf.

KS: I think it's coming back.

DM: We're seeing this a lot.

KS: And you know what? I think they're cheap, too.

DM: Yeah. When I'm at the beach I see them at the little boardwalk vendors. They've got the carousel deal and there's a million of 'em on there.

KS: This didn't take off, this didn't last for more than a month and a half, but you remember Kanye West's—the shutter shades?

DM: That's something else! I see the shutter shades—

KS: Those are like five bucks.

DM: I see those on the boardwalk too. And I don't ever see anybody ever wearing them? Maybe one or two people, and you never know if they're wearing them ironically. But I didn't know about the Kanye thing, so I thought "why are the shutter shades coming back? That's a really strange trend to be returning."

KS: That was why. But the thing is that you lose—it's like a Riemannian sum.[5] You lose 50% of your vision, but it's too granular. You know what I'm saying? It's not a 50% shade evenly like a pair of sunglasses. Like, I literally cannot tell if Venetian blinds are up or down. Because I cannot see them. They're not effective sunglasses. So I guess you're gonna get eye cancer in stripes on your eyeball instead of uniformly. That's not helpful.

DM: Everybody that works in retail ideally should believe in the product. But this is not always the case. Sometimes you have people, especially at corporate-level marketing departments, who don't actually have a good product—but they have to sell it regardless, and they have to make that pitch that "this is the best

---

5 For the uninitiated: the integral of the Gauss curvature on a compact 2-dimensional Riemannian manifold is equal to $2\pi\chi(M)$ where $\chi(M)$ denotes the Euler characteristic of M. This theorem has a generalization to any compact even-dimensional Riemannian manifold.

product ever."

KS: Because a person like that—they don't really have a hands-on with the product, but they are surrounded with the literature with the product, you know, and with the brand image and all that that means.

DM: Because the whole marketing relies on this keystone notion that "our product is worth selling." That's something that, if your job is a marketer, then you cannot challenge that core assumption because it just comes apart like a house of cards.

In fact, when I was working doing trailers, there was one presentation that we had to do for Disney. It was an internal sales presentation, which—every advertising agency that works for a movie studio ends up spending about 30–35% of their time working on internal marketing materials for the studio to show itself, and convince itself how great it is.

KS: Yeah.

DM: For stockholder meetings, and for departmental meetings, and all of this, just, B.S. But this particular one was about the technology that was revealed with the movie *Chicken Little,* which was called "Disney Digital 3-D."

KS: Okay, yeah.

DM: It's evolved into something else now, I don't think they even call it the same thing. But it's basically watching an animated movie in 3-D, that's what it is. And so this was a sales presentation to theater owners, I believe. And the whole idea was, we had to convince them that this was something worth retrofitting the theaters for.

And Disney trades on their pedigree more than any other company has any right to. Disney hasn't had a real, home-grown breakout hit in their animated division for—I don't know, decades. Since *The Lion King.* Or since *Tarzan,* probably. Maybe *Lilo & Stitch* would qualify, but even still, that's ten years ago. Ah, I guess seven years ago. But whenever it was. They trade on that *Lion King* imagery, and the *Tarzan* imagery, and the *Little Mermaid* imagery—

KS: Sure, yeah.

DM: —And the *Aladdin* imagery. They're just like, "We *are* this company that has such a pedigree." So anyway. The moral of the story is, this particular presentation had to be about all of the *firsts.* All of the ways that Disney is a trailblazer. So you'll hear, "First feature film to use the multi-plane camera: 1927, *Snow White.*" *First* this and that.

KS: "A company of firsts that are all good. That are all equally good."

DM: And so the nut that was the hardest to crack was the movie *Mary Poppins.* Because this was a landmark film for animation, the way it integrated animation and live action in 1964.

KS: Yeah.

DM: But it was not the *first* to do anything. Because that particular technology existed, in smaller measures, in other movies before that.

KS: In *Alice,* right?

DM: I think it was *The Poseidon Adventure.* Or there was something—I think *10,000 Leagues Under the Sea,* which came out in 1962 or -3, had some animated stuff in there. And it won an Academy Award for its special effects.

So anyway, we had to come up with something that was the *first*—this was Disney's claim to fame for this movie. And here's what it ended up being: *"Mary Poppins* was the first movie to win an Academy Award for Special Visual Effects for significantly combining live action with animation."

All of those qualifiers in there had to be in place. Because if you take *one* of them out, some *other* movie had done *that.* There were other movies that won different Academy Awards, or won different awards for doing the same thing, so on and so forth. But they had to be the *first,* so we had to put all these qualifiers in there.

KS: ...Then what?

DM: Well, and then—it just kind of goes to show that that brand image is so much more important than the merits of the situation. Because the brand image is what creates the demand for the product.

KS: There's a guy at Maui Jim Corporate who's convinced—and it's like a form of racism. It's like yellow journalism. They're convinced that Ray-Bans are gonna hurt—they're gonna *hurt* you. "You don't wanna wear that! *Oakleys?* Those are *dangerous*—that's sharp plastic—that's gonna fall in your eye! Maui Jim's gonna save you, buddy. And it's gonna do it in a stylish manner. And it's gonna save you 40%. And it's called Maui Jim and it's written real big on the lens" and I don't want that.

DM: But don't you want everyone to see what brand of sunglasses you're wearing?

KS: Yes! Yes I do. That's why I wear the T-shirt.

DM: The Maui Jims T-shirt.

KS: Here's some Twittering for you—the live power of the Internet. @TWITBANDIT says, "Well, this show looked good on paper, anyway. Or are you guys being ironic about the 'worst show ever' thing?"

DM: Wait. Are we being ironic about the worst show ever thing—well, *yeah.* I think we *are* being ironic about the worst show ever thing.

KS: Yeah! See, we're being very self-aware. Yeah, because clearly we wanted to do a bad show to offend @TWITBANDIT. That was *my* goal.

DM: I want the T-shirt that says "I'm wearing Maui Jims" and then it has an arrow that points up toward the direction of your face.

KS: How about "I'm with Maui Jim"? And then the arrow going up.

DM: And then I want the secondary—the extrapolation of the T-shirt that says "I'm wearing Maui Jims *in an unconventional place".* And then the arrow points *elsewhere.* Not to your face—could be anywhere!

KS: That's a far better—that's a *way* better shirt.

DM: Do you need the first one, or no?

KS: No! You don't need it! 'Cause everybody knows—you can *see* it. On your *face*. What *I* want is a shirt that implies an arrow with directionality. Like, pointing at *you*. Is there a way to do that?

DM: Out at the viewer, you mean?

KS: Yeah, at somebody who's reading it.

DM: Saying "you're"—but it wouldn't say "you're wearing"—'cause you can't predict what somebody's wearing when they're talking to you. Or do you only—oh, I understand!

KS: You could only talk to people who—

DM: Yeah, you only point your torso at people wearing Maui Jims! I see. So it's a self-selecting method where you can limit your interactions to other people that share your tastes.

KS: Yeah! And if you are on-board enough, then anybody else who comes up to talk to you, like "Hey man," you're like "Nuh-nnhh. Nhh. Rrhh." You just wave 'em off with a series of grunts!

DM: You have to keep your shoulders pointed away from them, lest the shirt be proven wrong. Right?

KS: Yeah, you don't want to do that to Jim!

DM: Because here's the thing—if the shirt is proven wrong, it has no power.

KS: Right. And you've killed Jim. Maui and all.

DM: If it's wrong once, it could be wrong *every* time.

KS: Yeah. It's a bummer. That's a much better shirt.

DM: "You're wearing Maui Jims." With an arrow pointing at the viewer.

KS: And you know what? If you're not wearing them, and you happen to see it, you might be like, "Hmm. Maybe that's in my future. Maybe I gotta think about that."

DM: Yeah, maybe it's metaphorical.

KS: Like we are all Americans after 9/11. We are all wearing Maui Jims. That's the same parallel that the guy at Corporate would make, I think. It's a powerful image.

DM: Everyone's wearing Maui Jims, they just don't know it yet.

KS: Yeah. You're wearing them on the inside. Now you just gotta show us.

DM: On Twitter, @SAMMYDJ2L says, "Bad show idea is to construct jokes and explain the punchline to death." We talked about this briefly before, and I think the main key here is that he wants us not to merely explain the punchline of jokes, but to *construct* the jokes, which is a very difficult and more time-consuming process than simply explaining existing jokes.

KS: I don't know if it's worthwhile! You know? Is it better—I mean, you could imply a joke and then explain it away. That takes a lot more talent, to be able to invent a joke wholesale, just on the fly.

DM: Right, just out of whole cloth. And then you have to explain what you've just done. It's sort of like doing a magic trick where you do it, you perform it, and then you go back and you deconstruct it. You say "watch my hands. Now, while I'm waving over here, my other hand is going around the back." Is that what he's asking?

KS: But they had that show! They had that show! Remember?

DM: Was it a show? Was it on television?

KS: The hidden—the secret magician! Who was it? The masked magician?

DM: Oh, the guy with the box over his head, or whatever it was?

KS: Yeah yeah yeah. He was wearing, like, a painting of a facehugger mask. And he went on FOX and he showed everybody how to do the tricks.

DM: This is—hold on. I'm too confused by all the masked people. There's this guy, who's in some kind of a mask. There's some other guy with a box with a question mark on his head, he's some kind of a thing. There's some other guy that's got, like, a mirror on his face where you can't see—

KS: Are you talking about the Unknown Comic?

DM: Yeah! Is that who he is, with the box—or is it a paper bag on his head?

KS: He's got a paper bag with the eyeholes and a question mark. But *man,* that's old!

DM: Right. Okay, so we got Paper Bag, we got Box, we got some kind of mask...

KS: You got Destro. He's got a—well, that's just cool. And Cobra Commander. More likely.

DM: This is a pretty funny story. There was a guy at the STAPLE! comics show, where he had one of those spinning rims on his face.[6]

KS: On his face?

DM: It was one of those cheap, like, the fake plastic spinner rims? Like a hubcap?

KS: Oh, yeah, yeah.

DM: And he had it mounted in front of his face. And so his entire head is this spinning turbine. He was a supervillain. And I thought that was pretty cool. He came up to me, and he kinda glared at me, and he leaned in really close. And I'm like, "Oh, man, I'm scared of the supervillain!" And he leans in close—he goes, "Spin it."

I'm like, "Oh, okay, sorry." So then I spun it, got it going a while. And then he went off, and went to terrorize some more people.

KS: Wow. That is a super-ineffectual villain.

DM: I like the idea of a supervillain who is reliant on others. You know, he likes to involve—because clearly, he could have reached up and spun it. But he doesn't want to break the fourth wall in that way.

KS: But that's no good!

DM: He wants to go out and involve other people.

---

6 STAPLE! is a comics and art festival in Austin, Texas. People come in costumes to these things; it's par for the course.

KS: You spin it and then he goes "YOU DID THIS" and kills a kid.

DM: Yeah, he's like "Now, what you have wrought!" And some other guy, the guy next to me—he starts feeding his arm through the thing! And it's like a meat grinder! And the guy's laughing, he's looking to me, he's like "YOU STARTED THIS! YOU CANNOT END IT!" And the guy's like "Oh my God, my arm, that's my arm—"

KS: And you're just sitting there praying, like "Slow down! C'mon, friction! Something's gotta stop that thing! It's so cheap, it can't spin forever!"

DM: "I thought it was made of plastic! It was from Pep Boys for $7.95!" But the guy's like up to his elbow now, and he's like "Oh God, oh Jesus and Mary, I just don't know what to do!" And it's like, well...?

KS: It's very accusative: "Why'd you spin it? *Why'd you spin it?*"

DM: "Didn't you know what was gonna happen? Didn't you see? *Didn't you see?*" And the guy's just laughing, just "Ho! Ho! Ho!" Because—this is why he's laughing. The guy's meat, and his blood, and his gristle, is feeding his gaping maw and *powering* him. He's like the Sarlacc. He needs *protein* into his *body*.

KS: Is he eating the meat? Or it just sort of a metaphorical—like he's feeding on the fear?

DM: I think that spinner thing is *pulverizing* that guy's arm.

KS: So you're saying, you're not seeing all of the meaty chunks, but some of 'em are going in there.

DM: I didn't see anything coming out the other side. So my only hypothesis is that it was actually *atomized*. It was so powerful—

KS: Wow. Like a nebulizer, but for flesh.

DM: Yeah, he was turning this guy's body into molecules.

KS: Like a meat vapor.

DM: And then using them for nourishment! That's the only possible explanation I can see.

KS: That's STAPLE! for you, though. You get the crazies out there. This one year, I was there, I swear some guy was drunk. I swear to God.

DM: Boy, whoa-ho, what a weirdo!

KS: Pretty nutty!

DM: We've got @RANEX on Twitter saying, "What did one prenatal twin say to his brother? 'Scoot over, there's not enough womb.' "

KS: Whenever I form a joke like that, I feel like you gotta go super deep. Like, you have to then say, "What did the prenatal *with a lisp* say to his brother?" And now you've explained why it's *womb* and not *room*. You know? I feel you have to get that in there.

DM: You have to explain every nuance of it?

KS: Yeah.

DM: Because the guy's like, "Well, no, *womb* is not actually the correct—I mean, *room* is what it would be." So when you set up the lisp...it seems like you're telegraphing the joke when you do that. Or is that the point? You actually want it to be an *anecdote*. You don't want it to be a joke, you just want it to be like, "Hey, listen to—"

KS: Whose anecdote is "What do these unborn children say to each other?" You weren't there. You didn't do that.

DM: Apparently they were really crowded. Maybe it's a very important issue. We have to talk about, you know, *in-utero space allotments* and there's going to be a whole industry of these bizarre devices—like putting up a cubicle wall in your uterus so that every twin has their own room early on.

KS: I was gonna say, that is a good secondary punchline for that joke. You say, "What did one prenatal twin say to his brother? 'Scoot over, there's not enough womb.' And then what did both of them say? 'Hey, who's this guy? Get him out of here! Why is he listening in on our conversation? There's already not enough womb, and now there's a full-grown man listening to us!' "

DM: This is what I want to see: I want to see a rigorous scientific study that—you know how twins sometimes develop that twin-language? Because they spend time with each other, and there are things that they share between themselves?

KS: Yeah, they just kind of complete each others' thoughts.

DM: I want someone to take a randomized sample of two hundred in-utero gestating twins, erect cubicle-walls in the uterus, and see if they develop that twin-language. Because my suspicion is that it's something that they develop before they come out. It's like a plot—they figure it out. They're like, "Dude, when we get out there we're gonna take this over. Let's figure this out now, because we're gonna be distracted." It's like diving into battle. You have your conversation *in the plane* when you're putting on your parachutes. You don't actually do it while you're on the battlefield, it's too chaotic.

KS: So you're saying, interrupt that key time, and you've broken a fraternal bond forever.

DM: Look, *broken* is a tough word. I just wanna say "let's compare." Because what you're *totally ignoring here* is that in order for this to be a rigorous scientific study, there's going to be *another* two hundred pairs of twins *totally unaffected*. And we're going to make sure that *no one* erects a wall in there—doesn't matter what kinds of commercials the mother sees, doesn't matter what kinds of sponsorships the father brings home from work, doesn't matter what kinds of billboards they pass in that car, doesn't matter how much Baby Björn wants to get his Baby Fingers in that Baby Womb. We're going to make sure those twins get all the nurturing possible. So there's a benefit here as well.

Look, I agree. Some children are going to be separated from their twin, possibly for life. Others are going to be just *so coddled*. And we're going to see: *what's that language?* We've got to crack that code, because these babies are plotting, and we don't know what they're saying. I want to find out.

KS: Can you imagine the shock on their faces when those two twins are three years old, and they're sitting there playing and they're going "goo goo muhn gah bluh bluh," and you come in, you're like "Huh mih nuh *nah*." And they go "oh, God. This guy knows. This guy *knows*!"

It would be worth it. Forty years of research just to do that. To scare some three-year-olds.

DM: You know what @MRBILDANGO said? He said, "To separate the twins, just draw a line in the gland."

KS: That one's more of a reach.

DM: That's not going to separate them, because you have to actually physically erect a wall. Have I said *nothing* in the last twenty minutes?

KS: That was more of a reach, because—it's a rhyming word, but there's no lisp that's going to convert *S* into *G-L*. That's not a thing.

DM: Okay, what if there was?

KS: Well, then I guess that guy probably has it. Let me tell—this is not a funny story, but it is a true story. I learned it in psychobiology class in college. They took a patient who grew up normally all his life, but then, because of a head injury, the connector part of the two halves of the brain—the corpus callosum—was severed.

DM: Right, right. I think I've heard this story, but go on.

KS: They were testing different parts of his memory. And so they're showing stuff to just his one eye—they're showing it to the part of the brain that remembers, you know, family. But then they're showing it to the part of the brain that does *not* remember family but remembers facts and numbers and stuff, and they're like "who's this?" And it's his aunt. And he's like, "Ahhh...um, I don't remember." And then he does something with his hands. Then he's like, "Emily. It's my aunt, Emily."

And they're like, "What did you do with your hands?" And he's like, "Oh, I drew *E* on the back of my hand. And so I knew it was Emily." It was his other hand from the other side of his brain controlling that part. But it wasn't the speaking part. You know what I mean? The other half of the brain knew the answer but couldn't talk, and was going "Goddamn it, it's Emily, how do I tell you? Okay, I can use my hand. I'll write on the other hand, get the signal to the other half."

DM: This is a different story. The one I heard—

KS: What did you hear? Did you hear about the—the sexy twin?

DM: —was about a guy who pronounced *S* sounds as *G-L*. And so the problem was, he couldn't order—like, he went to the sign shop. And he's like, "Can I have a glign?" They're like "whaddaya talking about? Get outta here." He couldn't get nothin'.

KS: Yeah. He wanted a glandwich.

DM: So then he went to try and get a cheesesteak sandwich. He goes, "Can I get a cheeseglake glandwich." And they're like "get outta here, you weirdo!"

KS: "Get outta here, you creep! I don't know what that is!"

DM: Look, I'm not saying he had an easy time of it. He came in here and tried to sell me some Verizon service. He's like, "Do you guys need any Internet servigl?" I'm like, "Cervical?" I thought he was talking about my neck. So I was afraid for my life—is this guy gonna hit me in my neck? Is Verizon after my spine?

Maybe they're leeching into people's cerebrospinal fluid, and they're gonna start charging them to get it back.

You know, I had Verizon service—and this is a true story—I had Verizon service, long distance. You have to get phone service to get DSL. Right? Even though I don't use the land line.

KS: Yeah, you do!

DM: So I got the cheapest phone service possible, and they started *charging me* for *not using it!* They started charging me a "low activity fee" of like four dollars a month because I wasn't making any calls.

KS: What'd that have to do with the G-L man?

DM: Because it was the same guy! It was the Verizon guy.

KS: The Veriglon guy.

DM: He came in here trying to sell me Internet glervice.

KS: Well, you know what? I know that guy, and once you get to know him—true friend. True friend, good guy. Good guy. So...I defend your honor.

DM: He had a kind of a shabby-fitting gluit, though. He should go down to the glore and get himself a better...

KS: I think it's catching!

DM: Anyway. So...we got more of these kind of puns about being in the womb on the Twitter, and I'm gonna not read them.

KS: But *some* of 'em are *good!*

DM: Heh heh, hmm. @ALEXDONO says, "Just imagine for a moment if there were no hypothetical situations." Well, let's see. Let's think about this. Let's really give it some thought.

If there were no hypothetical situations...then it'd be hard to theorize. Right? What else would happen?

KS: Yeah. Well, that's an Isaac Asimov story. And yeah, I'm gonna completely miss the point of the tweet. But that was—wasn't it? I wanna say there was an Asimov story where they found aliens who didn't lie. And that meant they didn't have stories, they didn't have actors. Because those are lies. You're *not* this character, you did *not* commit a murder, that's fake. And then they had to deal with humans who *could* lie, and lie all the time for fun, and what're you gonna do? You know what, probably: murderous rampage. I'm pretty sure.

DM: We got some people talking about your corpus callosum being severed. *Split-brain aphasia* is what @BETENOIRE says, then we have @THEGREENAVENGER talking about a guy who had no corpus callosum: "His hands mirrored each other unless he controlled it consciously. Also, he was a jerk." I imagine if you had that problem it'd be hard not to be a jerk.

And everyone's telling *you* that it was *Galaxy Quest,* by the way.

KS: For what?

DM: For the—probably the lie thing? Maybe it's something else too. We've got three people all of a sudden saying...

KS: Oh. Well you know what? A good enough movie to get confused with Asimov, I'll tell you that.

DM: I do remember the corpus callosum guy, though, seriously. And I remember there were things like: if they showed one eye a spoon, and one a knife, and they put a wall between the eyes so it's one eye seeing one thing at a time—

KS: Yeah.

DM: Then if you asked him to *say* what he sees? I forget which side is which, but he says "spoon," because that's the speech center of the brain. That eye sees—

KS: Oh, that would tell you which side it is, yeah. That's a good experiment.

DM: And if you ask him to *write down* what he sees, he writes down "knife." Because the writing center—*that* eye sees the other thing.

KS: That would completely corroborate my tale.

DM: Yeah, it's probably the same thing.

KS: So, not a liar. I didn't make it up, is what I'm saying.

DM: The problem is, if you are not a liar, I'm going to assume that you *never* lie. Right? Because you are one of this race of people that cannot lie. Is that fair to say?

KS: Yeah. I think that's base-case. You gotta go from somewhere, so let's do that.

DM: Okay.

KS: Now what?

DM: Well, that's good. That's good to know moving forward.

KS: Just go ahead. Take that ball and run with it.

DM: There's nothing that has arisen in our interactions to make me think that that's untrue.

Okay, this what I want to do. I think we're going to wrap up shortly, but I want to give a challenge to everybody out there. This is something where you can respond on Twitter.

KS: Oh yeah, good idea.

DM: You can respond on the Twitter; you can also leave us a voicemail. We have a voicemail line that you can—

KS: Oh, let me read it! Let me read it.

DM: All right. Do it.

KS: You can call us and leave us a voicemail, which we may play on the air, at (206) 337-8560.[7] And that doesn't spell anything, does it?

DM: No, I tried to make it spell something, and it spelled SPLIT-BRAIN-APHASIA-

---

7   Don't call this number anymore. The all-new Tweetline is (864) 64–TWEET. You can't change history, though...this is what we said, back then. So naïve!

zero, but I didn't think that was good to remember.

KS: It's not memorable. Not a good mnemonic, as they say. So what's your challenge?

DM: My challenge is: I would like you to tell us your stories of Unanticipated Victories. And these can be...if you're going to Twitter, make sure they're short and memorable; if you're going to have a slightly longer story, feel free to give us a call and leave us a message, but please, you know, don't ramble on. And I would like to know—I'm not going to say more than that, because I would like people to take that at face value, and give us your stories of Unanticipated Victories.

KS: And that's going to be the second one. And we're going to be using hashtag #TMH2. Right?

DM: That's exactly right. #TMH1, this is the hashtag for episode one; as soon as this show is over, we are moving on to content for episode two. So you will be using hashtag #TMH2 for show number two.

KS: You know what? I feel good about this show, because it's got a lot of rules, and I can really hang my hat from that. It's not haphazard.

DM: You only like things with structure.

KS: I want *more* structure. I know we kind of got away from the sound effects, but I was using 'em. I'm gonna find more, to further categorize different spans of time as we discuss them. That's what I'm talking about.

[ACCORDION STING]

DM: So my question for you then, Kris: If you need structure in your life—as soon as this show's over, are you just a ball on the floor immediately?

KS: No, I've got an elaborate ruleset and a d6 that I follow. I just carry it with me.

DM: "What's for dinner? Let's roll."

KS: "I wish I had more space on here to write my favorite things!" I've only got room on the sides of the die for like "BLT", "Spam". Not a lot of space. It's a shame.

DM: Depending on the condiments, you're able to mix and match different things.

KS: "Salt", "pep". Yeah. It's not a good life! It's not a good life. Not a *healthy* life.

DM: But at least you're not ever wondering about what to do.

KS: Yeah, at least I feel secure.

DM: And that's the main problem that I've seen with, just, going through life. Those periods of idleness. It's like, "Well, what now?" I don't know! If I had a rulebook, I could figure it out. But clearly Kris has it figured out.

KS: Aahhhh. Should we go to the theme?

DM: I'll end with this: I'm a little bit concerned that your rulebook, as you've added to it over the years, is now so big that you cannot leave the house. Because you can't carry it with you.

KS: I can't physically take it with me.

DM: It's too heavy.

KS: And you can't put content on the Kindle, is that right? Because I *would* take it with me. But I don't know how to do that. And learning how to put it on there is not in my rulebook! There's no dice-roll for that.

DM: Right, you have to meticulously hand-write your procedure for learning how to put content on the Kindle—

KS: And now the book is bigger! And *now* what're you gonna do.

DM: And your list of things to add to the book, you're already so behind on—you're barely in the, you know, third-grade birthday-party stuff. You've got a good twenty-six years of backlog.

KS: I'll *never* catch up on this one. "Look, I'll go out with you guys later. I got a big night."

DM: "I got to figure out how to use the NES Advantage."

KS: My Power Glove, yeah.

POWER PLAYERS

FORGET WIRELESS!

THE PRO XL WITH HUGEWIRE® TECHNOLOGY MAKES SURE YOUR GAME-WINNING BUTTON-PRESSES GET TO THE CONSOLE

LAME
STANDARD-WIDTH
WIRE

PRO XL

MADE FROM SURPLUS TRANSATLANTIC CABLE
SPOOL INCLUDED

DM: When I was in second grade, I remember we were getting drinking-fountain water. And I was drinking water—and I was also doing charades with my friend, because I thought of something to say and I didn't want to wait until I had finished drinking the water. And so I started enacting charades as I kept the water in my mouth.

KS: Okay...

DM: This is a true story. And eventually, he guessed what I was saying, and it was "Power Glove." Because I was doing the button-press on my wrist, and the whole deal.

KS: Oh, yeah.

DM: And then at that point, I'd had enough of the water; I swallowed it, and then I said the rest of my important message. Which was: "Pretty cool, huh?"

KS: That's as much of an imperative as it requires. That's about all you could think about it.

DM: Well, 'cause we saw it in *Nintendo Power!* And it's like, "Ho-oly smoke, that kid's wearing *sunglasses!* It must be *amazing!*" And his hair is windblown, and his room is burned—

KS: Yeah, and there's light coming out of the TV! Presumably from the *power*.

DM: And there's scorch marks all over his clothes. Clearly he's some sort of a burn victim. *Ikari Warriors* has actually—

KS: And his parents are all burned up, and they're, like, blown away!

DM: Right, everything from—I guess *Gauntlet* was a SEGA...Genesis game, right? *Gauntlet?*

KS: You could play *Zelda II*...

DM: No, *Golden Axe* was the Genesis game.

KS: Yeah, yeah.

DM: Anyway. Clearly, like, *Ikari Warriors* had manifested itself in the form of bullets coming out of the TV screen and had riddled the wall behind him with chaos. I needed that in my house. His mom was all freaked out, with her head half in the doorway, with one hand kind of splayed and her eyes wide...

KS: I'd take those pull-outs from the *Nintendo Power*—you put that on the door to your room? No parents are getting in there! *Kids only,* mom!

DM: Welcome to the *fun zone!*

KS: Yeah, and there's, like, Mario, and he's holding a star and he's all cool, and there's the guy from *Iron Sword,* or whatever.

DM: It clearly made an impression. There's Kid Icarus, there's the guy from *Rygar*. They're on all these crazy adventures!

KS: There's Simon Belmont, my favorite! He's gonna whip those nasty vegetables away!

DM: Hey, remember pop culture? Let's talk more about it. I like talking about pop culture, because it's things that we lived through, back in a more innocent time. Now our lives are horribly meaningless—we can only find meaning in the innocent joy of trying to beat *The Lost Vikings* for eighteen hours straight.

KS: I know. I played a game that had a lot of repetitive qualities recently, and I was like, "Man!" You know, when I was younger, I would not have given up this fast. I would have been at this for the next ten hours. But now, I don't have the patience.

DM: ...Well, this has been Tweet Me Harder, the world's first, best, only and last talkback-enabled interactive audio podblast. I'm David Malki !

KS: I'm Kris Straub.

DM: Thanks for tuning in.

KS: Follow the show at *tweetmeharder.tumblr.com*.[8]

DM: You can also follow us on Twitter at @TWEETHARD. We hope you will send us voicemails and tweets about Unanticipated Victories in your life or others, and we hope to take that material and somehow forge it into an even better show than today's. Not that this wasn't great.

KS: Yeah, it was pretty good. I liked it.

DM: Let's not sell ourselves short.

KS: Felt great.

DM: Ehh, it was all right.

KS: It was okay. Lot of nerves, though. Lot of jitters. Why?

DM: Lot of people giving us abuse. Well, a few people giving us abuse, a lot of people giving us great stuff to work with. And as we figure this show out, I'm sure there's nowhere to go but up, down, possibly sideways. Diagonal, if we get on some kind of ramp.

KS: That sounds like Dave Matthews lyrics.

---

8   Now you can just go to tweetmeharder.com. I mean, come on.

Houses Made of Bones

DM: Hello, welcome to Tweet Me Harder! This is the world's first, best, only, and last talkback-enabled interactive audio podblast.

KS: Hey, I'm Kris Straub.

DM: Hi, I'm David Malki ! Thanks for tuning in everybody, this is Tweet Me Harder Episode #2. Hopefully you understand the concept of the show: You can tweet us at any time and use the hashtag #TMH2. That will send us your tweets, and send anyone else who's listening your tweets as well.

KS: I like it.

DM: So far so good, right? We're off to a good start.

KS: Yeah. So last week, at the end of the show, you offered everybody a topic to Twitter. To tweet about.

DM: I did! We asked everyone to send us their stories about Unanticipated Victory. And the thing is, victory, as we know, in general, is pretty sweet. I think you'll probably agree.

KS: It's okay.

DM: It's better than the alternative. I mean, not always, I supposze, but in terms of just tooling around in your life *not* being victorious, or having victory? I think probably the latter is typically preferable?

KS: Well, the thing is that I think you really had to qualify with *unexpected* or *unanticipated* victory, because the word "victory" is so strong.

DM: Sure.

KS: And especially when you use it in the form "victorious," suddenly I'm like "oh God, what aspects of my life am I victorious in?" There's no way!

DM: And victory is defined, in a way, as being a challenge over adversity. This is something where you win, so, the unexpected or the unanticipated nature of this particular type of victory is *especially* sweet—because you were *expecting* to lose, or at the very least you were not expecting to have anything special happen. Right?

KS: That's true. I guess you're right. I guess I'm imagining a real struggle, but it might just be like, "Eh! All right, I did it."

DM: Well, unanticipated victory is arguably the best type of victory, because it represents such a swing from the expected outcome—which is by definition *not* victory—to victory. So I'd like to play a call that we received. We have our comment line, which is area code 206-337-8560. You can call anytime and we can play your messages—we're not going to play them for this show, obviously, but if you called right now we'd have it in time for the next show. But some people called in and give us their stories of unanticipated victory. Like this one:

> One time, I put a quarter in the gumball machine and TWO
> gumballs came out of it.

[*BOTH HOSTS LAUGH HEARTILY*]

KS: That's solid!

DM: I think that's unanticipated victory in its purest form!

KS: Yeah, that's like you've given the prototype, like the perfect way to sum it up.

DM: Right, you can put whatever terms you want into those blanks. "I put a blank into the blank machine and TWO blanks came out." And it works every time.

KS: Yeah.

DM: Doesn't matter if it's gumballs, doesn't matter if it's Bratz.

KS: What if it's dead guys?

DM: Here's what I want to know, though. Let's think about this: this is victory clearly for the person who got more for their money, right?

KS: Oh, yeah.

DM: But someone has to fill that gumball machine.

KS: Oh yeah...

DM: Someone had to buy those gumballs.

KS: But the thing is, we're talking about an exchange rate here. That gumball did not cost 25 cents. That gumball cost, like, a tenth of a cent. The guy who lost? I don't think he would call that a loss, you know? If we do another show with an unexpected failure, he's not going to be like, "I lost a gumball! I poured exactly 364! And I'm sittin' here like a chump."

DM: You're absolutely right. But here's the thing: *you* don't get to make that decision. You don't get to say "oh it doesn't hurt anyone, it's a victimless crime" 'cause this is how people justify theft! They go, "Oh, I'm not hurting anybody, oh that guy owns a business, he's not going to miss it."

KS: So you're saying this victory—it could have a consequence!

DM: Well I'm saying there's another side to it. I'm saying that for every extra gumball that somebody gets, that *is* another gumball that some other guy didn't sell. Because he's not making his money just on the sale. Like, his expense is not just gumballs, it's gas to fill up the gumball machine, it's gas in his car... .

KS: And you gotta compute the weight of that gumball, that goes into it. I understand. How much more gas did he spend because he's got that, you know, a quarter ounce of an additional ball?

DM: Or more to the point, does he have to come back more frequently, or more often, or sooner now to spend more time to refill the machine because it's emptier than it would have been? You're assuming that this is a fluke event. What if the gumball machine is broken? What if it's giving out two gumballs every time? Then his profits are literally halved.

KS: Let me ask you a scary question.

DM: All right.

KS: Have you ever seen anybody fill a gumball machine?

DM: It's funny that you say that. My brother actually owned a vending machine route for a number of years.

KS: Wow!

DM: And there were not gumball machines in particular because, as I said, it's so low-profit, but his job was driving around in a truck filling up soda machines and candy machines and I went with him, often. I was kinda young and helping out the brother, and we'd go to the Wal-Mart, and we'd go to the AutoZone or whatever it was. And he'd have snack machines in there, and we'd open 'em up and fill 'em up.

KS: Yeah, yeah. Did you get In The Zone?

DM: Man, we were in the Autozone.

KS: *(singing)* Auutoozone![9]

DM: And you know what the funniest part is? He tells me—now he eventually sold the route, after a while, and it's sorta one of these things that people who are entrepreneurs are like, "Yeah, easy money! Buy a vending machine route." And eight years later, they're trying to sell it to somebody by claiming, "Oh yeah, easy money, go ahead and take this off my hands." Because it's not like—you know, it is what it is.

KS: It's not fun.

DM: But the work is—speaking of unanticipated, the work that goes into it involves maintenance on the machines; it involves actively soliciting new accounts to place in the machines...

KS: Oh my God.

DM: And there's a lot of driving around. A lot of just...

KS: How do you pitch that?

DM: Uh, you have to find the person who's in charge of making those decisions at the company, whom often don't want to talk to you because they hear from solicitors all the time. If it's a corporate account like Wal-Mart...

KS: "I couldn't help but notice that you had a 1.4 square foot of floor, at the front of your store, that was not being used."

9 AD SLOGANS HA HA HA

DM: "I made a list of things that could go there: Upright sleeping cubicle? I don't see one of *those* vendors around here, right?"

KS: Right. And then like: "Has this ever happened to you?" This guy trying to put a bed there in front of his business? "This ain't workin'!"

DM: So anyway, it was the kind of thing where—my brother even told me the story. He used to be like, I dunno, a pizza delivery guy or something. He delivered some pizza to a really big corporation. Or maybe he was sweeping the floors or it was something really menial. And then at lunch he sees fifty vending machines along the wall of this massive company—some defense company, I believe, was where he worked—and he's like, "the guy who takes the money out of those machines, *he's* the guy makin' a million dollars!"

KS: *(laughs)* "Everybody's got a better idea than I do!"

DM: Cut to ten years later, he's lost 30 pounds, he's gaunt from the stress of driving around all day long trying to keep all these vending machines filled...and you know, it's the kind of thing where if someone loses their money in the machine, they have to leave a note, like, "lost one dollar." And every time he comes in it's like, "All right, well, who do I owe a dollar to this time?"

KS: Yeah, that sucks.

DM: So...

KS: I was going say, I was going to go to the Twitter and say @TOMRK1089 says...

DM: That's the one *I* was gonna read!

KS: Whaat! "So is there any action without negative consequence?" I don't know.

DM: That's a pretty good question, because in the case of the gumball situation it's obvious. Someone gains an extra gumball, and then someone else loses a gumball without intending to. There's definitely a dichotomy there.

KS: Malki, I am *sick* to *death* of your moral relativism. That is a win-win! The loss of that gumball was not sufficient to strike down that man!

DM: Wait, it's a win-win? So are you saying that this guy is like, "I'm so glad someone took this extra gumball off my hands!"

KS: *(laughs)* No, I'm saying that...

DM: "I had this extra gumball and I didn't know what to do with it!"

KS: Uh, maybe it's a win-blank. Because I suspect he didn't notice that it was gone. I mean, over time, I'm sure that he would say—if this thing was consistently spitting out two gumballs for every quarter, I think he'd notice. He'd definitely notice. But if it was a once-in-a-while fluke...

DM: But we don't know: *(a)* the conditions of this situation. We don't know if he has noticed, and our caller doesn't mention whether that's the case or not. And then number two—are you saying that in order for an act to be morally negative, then it has to be observed? Are you saying that morality cannot exist in a vacuum?[10]

---

10 Why does David start the list with (a), then follow it up with "number two"? Simple. Mid-paragraph, he applied a numeric cipher to the alphabet, to aid our deaf friends.

KS: Uhhh, yeah. For the purpose of this show, I'll fight that fight. I'll take that side. But you know what? You have a special insight because your brother did that. Now, if he's filling those machines with Cokes, I think you notice that. That's like 75 cents, that's like a buck. Right?

Somehow, a gumball, which I imagine is just poured out of a sack into that machine—there's just no way! Unless he has a perfectly-portioned bag that said on the side of it, "100 gumballs"...

DM: I'm not arguing that it's likely that he noticed. What I'm saying is, even if he *doesn't* notice, is it still a morally negative act? If you steal a candy bar from the store and you're sneaky enough that the shopkeeper doesn't see you, does that make it *not wrong*?

KS: Well I'm not—the thing is, I'm not talking about whether or not they notice. I do believe that you can do wrong and not have anybody see it. What I'm talking about is the *quantity* of the wrong. Somebody got an extra gumball.

DM: You were the one calling *me* out for moral relativism! The quantity of the gumballs...

KS: Yes, but this is relativism as favors *me*.

DM: *(laughs)*

KS: So... it's good. Would you deprive this guy his victory? You asked him for his victory!

DM: *(laughs)* You're right. You're right.

[THE ACCORDION MISTAKENLY PLAYS TWICE]

DM: Double time!

KS: We need to cleanse the palate.

DM: So good, it's got two accordion stings. Okay, next call:

> When I first moved to Los Angeles, I was living in a really shitty bachelor apartment, and after about seven months, I wanted to move out early. So I eventually figured out I had to ask the landlord to break my lease. They said it was no problem, and when I came back to pick up my security deposit, the check was $5,000 larger than it needed to be because apparently—although unknown to me—they were buying people out of their leases! And they were just assuming that I was taking them up on the deal. So they basically reimbursed me for the entire seven months that I'd been staying in the apartment.

DM: Okay, this is what we call The Gumball Conundrum writ large.

KS: This is where you want to go with that stuff. That's the Socratic method.

DM: The gumball situation assumes that the person gets a gumball without—he pays for one gumball and he gets two gumballs. In this case, the person wanted fairness—this is @POSIDUCK, by the way, the person who sent us this particular call—this person wants to go out even. He doesn't want to screw anybody, he just wants to end this on amicable terms, and he gets way more than he asked for. And it's the fault of the landlord. It's the cashier who gives you too much change. It's that situation.

KS: Right.

DM: Now in this case, @POSIDUCK doesn't like this apartment, so he's not going to act in a way that favors the landlord to correct their error. Is it wrong for him to then keep that money?

KS: You know what? There was something about my previous argument that now is hollow. Because once you convert from sugary, y'know, something you're only gonna enjoy for like five minutes... you know when you eat a gumball, you're not going to like it for that long. Usually I'm disappointed. But when you turn it into $5,000, I don't know if I can make the same claim anymore. I think that's technically a heist.

DM: Hold on a second, I want you to explain this to me. We were talking about victories and all of a sudden, systematically, we have shot down these people's victories as being immoral. "No! You don't *deserve* that gumball! *Or* that $5,000, because that $5,000 that you're keeping is punitive."

KS: This is Tweet Me Harder. We gotta take a hard look... we're gonna focus in, see what the deal really is.

DM: I really want one of those *Law & Order,* like, "*dun dunnnn.*"

KS: Yeah, that's the next one we need. Like when we catch somebody.

DM: Exactly. Did you ever watch *Fight Back with David Horowitz*? It was one of those consumer advocacy shows?

KS: Oh yeah! I loved that show!

DM: Yeah, I did, too!

KS: That was L.A. only, right?

DM: I don't know. I only ever saw it in California.

KS: I think he was a local guy. Oh, no, I think he had a syndicated show.

DM: Well, he's definitely a syndicated, like, columnist/author now, because I see his name all over the place. But he used to have this show called *Fight Back...*

KS: Do you remember the theme song?

DM: I remember *"Fight back!"*

KS: *(singing)* *"Fight back! Don't let no one push you around..."* That was the theme. And I haven't thought about it in literally 15 years. And when you said that, I remembered it![11]

DM: Yeah, I remember the really hard hits, "Fight back!" Umm... so what he would do was, he was a consumer advocate and he would take advertisers' claims or corporations' claims and he would try to find out the merits of them. So, for example, there'd be a commercial that would show a demonstration of a product—like the Samsonite commercial with the gorillas throwing around the suitcase. And they would enact it in controlled conditions, and they would try to find out if that claim was true or not.

---

11   *Fight Back!* ran from 1976 to 1992. The theme song to the old show can be heard at fightback.com. It's just as great as Kris remembers.

KS: Right.

DM: So that's what we're doing! We're taking your victories and we're saying, "No! Hold on!"

KS: We're testing them out: "This is not technically a victory. We have pressed it against a rigorous definition of victory, and your tale was found wanting. I didn't like it."

[ACCORDION STING]

DM: On the Twitter we now have a story of victory from @BABELGLYPH. She says—I assume it's a she—"My first roommate in college begged me to be her roomie; I said yes. One quarter in she ditches me for a single." And then I think the story continues... the rooming lottery for the next year comes around, and she's at the end of the list and @BABELGLYPH is just above her. There's only one room available, and she gets the last one. So this is a just-deserts situation.

KS: Oh, yeah.

DM: That's nice. This is similar to the gumball situation—through no active work on the part of @BABELGLYPH, still, the world has worked out in her favor. She's not actively trying to screw anybody.

KS: And I would say the difference here is that it's almost like recompense, you know what I mean? You were wronged, and then you got some sweet justice from the universe. Nobody's losing the gumball—she got screwed over and now she's getting to screw over the screwer.

DM: Exactly. I think the key here that draws a moral line between this and the gumball situation? Nobody's lost a gumball. You really put the fine point on that.

KS: *(laughs)* That's all I care about. That's only fair.

DM: Well, yeah. You want all the people who got gumballs to have paid for their gumballs, and you want all the people who want gumballs to have gumballs. And you want all the people who bought gumballs to be reimbursed for their gumballs, and thus the gumball equilibrium is maintained.

KS: The Great Gumball Continuum is sustained. Yeah. No, that's good.

DM: We have @HUGPARTY on Twitter who says, "I had a similar situation; I got two weeks' worth of pay at over double my salary and my boss let me keep it all." This is a situation where we need more information.

KS: Yeah—@HUGPARTY, go ahead.

DM: @HUGPARTY, yeah, fill in—take as many tweets as you need, but we need the rest of the story.

KS: That almost seems like an act of kindness. On the part of the boss.

DM: It does depend on how beholden the boss is to the corporation. If this is some massive corporation and the boss says, "Eh, just take it," or if this is a mom-and-pop operation and the boss is like, *(in accent)* "I would be destitute, but go ahead, I made a mistake, I deserve to pay for it."

KS: Oh, the poor Indian guy.

DM: Is that Indian? Why are you being racist? No, that was, that was...

KS: Sorry, Indian-American.

DM: That's much better. So, @HUGPARTY, tell us the rest of the information. What're the circumstances, why did you get the... these are the questions I want you to answer. Why did you get paid more than you needed to? What was the boss's reaction? Like, when you told him or her, or how did he or she find out? And why did they let you keep it? That's what we want to know.

KS: The boss's reaction was "Whooopeee!" Because he remembers being that age and how good that would have felt!

DM: "Oh, go ahead! You know what, you deserve it. Your life is hard."

KS: "You're a good kid."

DM: Oh, man. So, the response to the sort of victory-as-morality—like, the logical extension of that, from @CRAZYCSTUDIOS on Twitter, is "So can victory be moral?" Now, these victories we were describing: we were arguing for the immorality of them. But victory can certainly be moral, as in the example we just heard about the rooms, right? This is just deserts.

KS: Yeah. I guess... well, yeah. I mean, I guess it could be argued that you're being— that it's not nice of you to go, like, "Aah! Gotcha back!" You know, even though I think it's kind of a deal where that other person should be sleeping on a bus somewhere. 'Cause that's not fair. That's a lie. You should get caught. How deep do these go?

DM: You could certainly say that that person who left @BABELGLYPH high and dry the first time around and then got shafted the second time around—you could make an argument there that, you know, you could hear her side of the story: "Oh, I was having a really hard time, there were some things with my family, and I didn't—I wasn't able to stay in this apartment for reasons out of my control and I don't really deserve to be punished!" I don't know the situation. Are we willing to give her the benefit of the doubt?

KS: What if the other person who got shafted, the second go-around, was like—she got her own victory. She says, "This is awesome. I was hoping not to get that room because it had been tested and it was full of that black moss and radon! And I didn't want to live there!"

DM: So what happens is we have a Twitter—we don't really, but what if we had the Twitter that says, "My victory is, I put my name in for the dorm lottery, and I thought I was gonna be stuck with this room full of radon—because I learned later that it has radon in it—and my victory is, this crazy chick right ahead of me got the room before me and I didn't have to get it."

KS: Yeah, that's what you call a close call. You're just gonna wipe your brow and go "wheeww!"

DM: Or is that victory—oh... Does this suggest that victories are dependent on your perspective? Depending on your goal, right? Whether you've succeeded or failed. Your victory is dependent on what you're trying to do, and different people try to do different things.

KS: Absolutely! This weekend, I've finally cut myself the right way.

DM: *(laughs)*

KS: I did it! Huzzah! Right? It's a little victory. A little celebration.

[ACCORDION STING]

DM: All right, we have another call.

> *So, anywho, I just wanted to say you guys are doing a great show. I know you're only on your second episode but I can already tell you're going to go the distance.*

DM: We're going to go the distance, Kris!

KS: I like that!

DM: *This* is *our* victory!

KS: This is a little victory for us.

DM: We didn't expect that.

KS: That is... that is pretty sweet.

DM: All right, so we have more clarification from @HUGPARTY.

KS: Oh yeah.

DM: "I worked for a lawyer—just one lawyer, not a big firm—and it was a clerical error. She found out when I told her."

KS: Ahhhh.

DM: And she goes on to say—uh, @HUGPARTY, I'm going to pretend you're a girl, so I hope you're a girl.

KS: It's a girl.

DM: She says the lawyer said to keep it as a thank-you. @HUGPARTY was temping while her friend was studying abroad. So it was a clerical error, and keep it. Now, the question is: is this lawyer—this came out of the lawyer's pocket, because it was not a firm and it was probably some kind of payroll service or something; who knows. But this is a lawyer. She's probably paying @HUGPARTY, y'know, $8.50 an hour to do...

KS: Back-breaking legal maneuvers.

DM: Right, so it's sort of a preemptive out-of-court settlement against, you know, malpractice.[12] Or against wrongful termination.

KS: That's how they had to file it.

DM: And then @HUGPARTY goes on to say that the paralegal said *she* wouldn't have said anything. So @HUGPARTY's coworker says she would have just kept it, if it had been her.

KS: Oh, well, see, now I think it's a real victory, because you're rewarded for your truthfulness!

---

12 David does not know anything about law.

DM: Right.

KS: Right?

DM: Right. This is absolutely a victory free and clear, in my opinion, because had @HUGPARTY been asked to return the money, I'm sure she would have. Because she volunteered the information. And so the response was, y'know, "it's fine." So this is absolutely a morally clear victory. With no doubt.

KS: That's a solid one.

DM: Yeah. This has no moral downside. The person who was "wronged" said it's fine. They're not pressing charges. They're not pressing *moral* charges, such as it is.

KS: Is it wrong that I can't find anything in my own life like that? For the purposes of our discussion? I can't find any victories where it was, like, I was rewarded for a good thing that I did that nobody saw. That didn't happen. I only made out when there was an error in my favor, and I left.

DM: Uh, yeah, I'm having a hard time thinking of that too.

KS: *(laughs)* I have no good things in my life, is what it is.

DM: Well, what about the time when—oh, wait. That didn't happen to you, that happened to me.

KS: *(laughs)* Yeah. But we look similar, so you thought for a second...

DM: Yeah—I think it was the mirror, but I thought you were in the room.

KS: You were like, "Am I? Am I Kris? Is he having a victory? No, no! I feel good."

DM: Yeah, because that would require—I remember being confused at the time, because I didn't think you were very, in general, very victorious. So...

KS: You're right. You were like, "he's going to feel so good when—nope, that's me. That's me. He's probably still having a real crappy time somewhere."

DM: So if you have none of these morally clear victories in your life, do you have any *morally ambiguous* victories? Where you were victorious at someone else's expense?

KS: Um, lemme think, lemme think. No, I feel like my victories are like, uh, "not allowed to leave work until 5. Left at 4:40, nobody saw. Nobody saw."

DM: But are you salaried, or hourly?

KS: Um, I don't know. What's the one where it counts? What's the one where it matters that you didn't stay eight hours?

DM: Well, hold on, if you're salaried, then you get paid the same no matter how much you work.

KS: Okay, I wasn't salaried.

DM: If you're hourly, you get paid every hour that you were there.

KS: What's the one where I'm taking money from the company?

DM: Well, that's what I mean. It depends on whether or not you said you were there until five, or you didn't say you were there until five.

KS: What's the one where my actions just really caused a problem for somebody in payroll and they could not figure out the source and probably lost their job? And part of that was because they're not very good at payroll, so it's not all me!

DM: Again, this is a situation where you're like, "well, they deserved me stealing from them. If only they hadn't left the gumballs out in a big bowl, I wouldn't have taken 30 of them even though I only dropped a dime and a paperclip in the slot."

KS: And you know how long you can use a paperclip? You can use it over and over again. You know how many papers that's good for? You keep that, you hang on to that, that's good for the rest of your life.

DM: As long as you dropped something in there...

KS: You give a man a fish, am I right?

DM: Put a paperclip on a string, he'll eat gumballs for life.

KS: Yeah, well I would say that's not fair. It's *his* fault that he's got a machine that can't differentiate between a quarter and a coconut.

DM: I'm thinking of the March of Dimes cardboard thing where it's just a whole box with an opening full of candy and you're supposed to put something in the slot. And it's like, well, "suggested 25 cents" and it's on the honor system so you put a paperclip in. At least you're putting something in the slot.

KS: Yeah, March of Dimes, I got a victory. Those dimes marched right in my pocket.

DM: Look, how much would they spend to buy a paperclip for the office? At least a quarter, right?

KS: Oh, man.

DM: Paperclips are at least a quarter apiece.

KS: I don't think so. Where are you getting them?

DM: There's a guy comes by with a bag. I buy 'em from him. Wait, how do *you* get them?

KS: He's a small businessman. It's good to support the town economy.

DM: Well, here's the thing! I don't know where the paperclips you buy, where they're made—mine are made right here in town. He has a wire-bending machine.

KS: *(laughs)* I get mine overseas. Child labor.

DM: You have Laotian paperclips.

KS: Yeah. They're beautiful though.

DM: No, mine—there's this guy named Leo and he comes around with hand-crafted paperclips. I think he extrudes wire from old aluminum cans—he has an extruder that looks like a big spinning wheel—and then he puts it in a vise and he bends it around. He used to use a mold but now he just does it by hand. The guy's 84 years old...

KS: *What?*

DM: ... And he bends his own paperclips that cost twenty-five cents apiece.

KS: What is this super, this human-interest incredible story that you're telling?

DM: I'm just talking about...I like supporting local business, I like encouraging handcrafts.

KS: You're helping this old man buy medicine and I, like, got an intern fired.

DM: I think there should be a whole farmers' market for office-supply products.

KS: *(laughs)* Like hand-pressed paper? "It's *near* letter-sized. It's close. And it's much better quality."

DM: "It's got that ragged edge. It's hand-made paper! Does not fit in your printer."

KS: It's like, "cut to fit."

DM: "Unless you have our handmade printer," and you point over, and it's just a guy with an ink pad.

KS: He comes to your house—"Tell me what it needs to say." Sampling inks...

DM: @Daniel6 says: "Bank error in your favor. Collect $200."

KS: Hmm, I don't know what we can learn from what Monopoly's trying to teach us about that.

DM: Monopoly—you know Monopoly was actually created as a tool to teach *against* the hoarding of money?

KS: But the goal was to get the most money!

DM: Right, but don't you realize that every time you play Monopoly you end up angry? And shouting at everybody?

KS: What if it just taught people to be angry?

DM: The goal is to make the hoarding of money a disagreeable experience.

KS: Look, I... I mean, that makes sense to me, I get where they're going, but they made that game way too fun and colorful to make that hit home. You've got a fun little man, you've got colorful paper money that you like to count and hold and look at. It's a lot of fun.

DM: You're supposed to be repulsed by his moustache.

KS: Yeah, the game should have just been this gray, sad world.

DM: It should have had more browns. Baltic Avenue should have had a lot more mold.

KS: Yeah, it just should have looked like the gameboard came out of *Silent Hill*. It should have been a miserable—it's a punishment for kids. It's not a game.

DM: "You're going to play Monopoly." "Noooooo!"

KS: "You're not sharing your toys? We're playing Monopoly tonight."

DM: "No Daddy, please, anything but that."

KS: "You *know* your mother hates playing Monopoly. You *know* she's tired after work. But now we have to play it. 'cause that's what you did."

DM: "This is an abusive relationship, Charles."

KS: "You shut up and you spin!"

DM: "Charles, I want to go to counseling."

KS: "We are playing Monopoly. You are monopolizing my emotions!"

DM: *(laughs)* I think Boardwalk and Park Place should have that really offensive gilt, like, not G-U-I-L-T but G-I-L-T...

KS: Gilt, yeah, with gold.

DM: Yes. If you've ever been to Orange County and you've seen the headquarters of the Trinity Broadcasting Corporation, the religious TV station...

KS: Oh yeah! It's ridiculous.

DM: It's all so ostentatious.

KS: Yeah. God loves it, though, so...

DM: I think it should be like that. Where it's like, "look how fancy it is! Is *this* what you wanted? All of this *luxury?*" It's like, "No, I *don't* want to bathe in liquid gold, I *don't!*"

KS: Yeah, you go in and the bed, the mattress is made of Pure Gold!

DM: "Isn't that what you want?"

KS: It's the softest precious metal, so that's gonna work out for you. The most comfy bed!

DM: "We'll hammer it, to fit your body!"

KS: *(fake crying)*

DM: "Why would you ever want to get up? Your sheets are made of platinum!"

KS: "Noooooo..." And then two weeks later it's like, "eh, it's not so bad!"

DM: It's like the Midas touch thing. "You know what, actually? At least I know what to expect."

KS: Yeah, this is the devil I know at this point. I get it.

DM: Yeah, it doesn't matter. The cool thing is, King Midas, once he got used to eating gold, he didn't have to worry about "oh my banana's spoiled," it's just, all right, pick up a rock. It's all the same.

KS: Why wouldn't... let me ask you something. Now we're really going off-topic.

DM: No, this is the topic.

KS: That's fine. With King Midas, was it any part of his body? I mean if you gave him a kiss, *you'd* turn into gold? 'Cause that sucks. But if it's just his hands, he could just wear gold... golden gloves, if you will, and he'd be fine.

DM: I think it's probably any part of his body. I think that's what makes it—at least in, I'm sure there's different retellings of the story, but that's what makes it a curse, is that he can't touch anything with any part of his body. Otherwise he'd just be like one of those monkeys that learns to paint with his feet.

KS: Yeah, that makes sense.

DM: He would just do that.

KS: Well, okay, is his curse context-sensitive? Because he could go outside and touch the Earth, and then everything just becomes gold immediately.

DM: I don't buy the "the Earth" thing because "the Earth" is not an object. The Earth is made of stones and rocks and...

KS: But then if that's true, he'd only turn the outermost layer of your skin to gold. I mean it'd be painful, but you wouldn't die.

DM: Well your outermost layer... is still you.

KS: In fact, he'd be doing you a favor. You'd take that gold... yeah but it's cells, dude. If he's walking barefoot in the garden, and he's only turning a little bit of that dirt that's just under his feet into gold, then if he grabs my arm then I am losing a little skin but I am getting a gold bracelet.

DM: *(laughs)*

KS: And that is a good—I *thank* you, King Midas! A generous king!

DM: I think that only works up to the point where he oversaturates the gold market, and gold loses its value.

KS: Yeah, the town is just—the economy is just a wreck. They can't export it.

DM: Exactly. Everyone's like, "more gold? No."

KS: "I got gold brooms."

DM: Hey, you know what becomes really valuable?

KS: No.

DM: *Silver*.

KS: Oh yeah!

DM: Becomes more rare than gold, all of a sudden.

KS: That's true.

DM: It just moves up the ladder. It's like, "finally! Knocked off gold off the top of the list. Silver is coming up baby, make way!"

KS: He's in bed with those guys!

DM: "Here comes silver!"

KS: "I got the curse on purpose so I could help out my friends, the silver lobbyists."

DM: They're like, " 'Ey, 'ey, Midas, why don't you get the gold curse? And then we'll get you the antidote. I know a guy who knows the antidote."

KS: "Okay, which gypsy do I need to piss off?"

DM: "Not the one on the left, that's the ruby gypsy, we don't got no cure for rubies." "Don't be silly, there's no cure for rubies, I mean, don't be an idiot."

KS: It's late at night, he goes up to the old crone, "Uh, excuse me?" She goes, "Rubies!!" "Nope, all right, go over there, here she is."

DM: "Excuse me, I'm looking for, uh, I'm looking for gold?" "Oh yeah, just turn down the corner, take a left, and then into the hovel."

KS: Good stuff. Here's a tweet, from @TPARADOX, which I thought was interesting: "I think you're thinking of a Philip K. Dick story"—we're back on Monopoly— "where a Monopoly knockoff teaches kids to give all their money to Mars." What? That's not a story. From Dick, I could imagine it.

DM: I like we're unilaterally denying that it exists. "No, you're wrong. Mistaken. Doesn't happen. "

KS: No, you—that's not it. That must be a joke I don't get.

DM: I think—here's the thing about Philip K. Dick stories.

KS: That's an old Monopoly joke I don't get.

DM: There are 48,000 really obscure Philip K. Dick stories.

KS: Oh.

DM: It's like, "you remember the Philip K. Dick story where everybody walked around wearing a giant ostrich head, and it turns out they were all in a warehouse underneath the ocean?"

KS: *(laughs)* "And we didn't learn anything. But I had to take it apart for English class. I had to diagram sentences."

DM: "It was sort of—it was more of a premise than a story. And it was in a short story collection, and it ended before anything could happen. But I do remember everyone was miserable."

KS: "I do remember it was not Philip K. Dick but a guy on the subway was telling me this and I left before he stopped talking. But he was urinating the entire time."

DM: "So I assumed it must have been really good."

KS: "Clearly, they give him that much pleasure that he should lose control of his bladder. It's a great story. It's the mark of a good story."

DM: Well, yeah, I think that is the mark, right? That's—what's it called? What's the term where it's like, "Yeah the story was good, but it was only a half-pisser."

KS: *(laughs)* It was a pisser, yeah! Why would you do that? And half-pisser mean you just piss down one pant leg? Just one leg!

DM: Or only half as much? Or half as intense? Because with that sort of thing, you know, it's either you're pissin' or you're not. And it's just a matter of volume. And power.

KS: Right.

DM: And frequency.

KS: I don't know about you, but once I get going, that's going to full stream at some point. I mean, it's not just going to trickle out. I don't care how long the book is.

DM: Let's change the subject. @RANDOMTECHGUY on Twitter says: "The IRS is holding onto my 2008 refund because they claim I didn't file in 2006. They're making me re-file." This sounds bad so far.

KS: Yeah.

DM: He says, "I got a $700 refund in 2006. And now they want me to re-file and they want to give me the refund again."

KS: Wow.

DM: That's pretty good.

KS: That is good. That's good if you don't get in trouble, because I had a friend who had a similar circumstance where they were paying their—what is it called when they pay their taxes quarterly? Is it just quarterly taxes?

DM: Estimated taxes.

KS: Estimated taxes! Yeah, there you go. And she paid her estimated taxes, they filed with their accountant, the IRS gave them double back the refund that they thought, and they figured out that it was because they forgot to take into account that they were paying estimated taxes all year. And they ended up arguing with a woman from the IRS who was saying, "No, that is *your* money! You keep that money!" And she was getting belligerent, and they were like, "No, this is not our money and we don't want to get in trouble in five months when you figure out the error." And she had an attitude like *"We* are the *IRS,* we don't have problems like this." So it took her a couple days and a couple phone calls and she said that mid-call, the woman figured it out. And she was getting very angry and very frustrated with her, and then the woman was like, "hold on a second."

She goes away for ten minutes, and then she comes back and says, "Let's find out how to take care of this. I'm sorry for the difficulty but... this money is not yours and you *cannot* keep it." And she was like, "What are you... I wasn't going to keep it. *I wasn't going to keep it.*"

DM: Yeah, that's the thing with the IRS. You always have to figure that they're going to figure it out, like you said, eight months from now, you know? And then you've gotta pay penalties...

KS: You're going to be, y'know, "At least I got that three grand." And they're gonna take it. There's a tweet here that I thought was pure as well. Look at this one: @LYMANALPHA says here's his victory: "When I got my $350 cymbal for my drum set signed by Mike Portnoy of Dream Theater." Clearly a dream of his, to get that signed, a fan...

DM: I guess so? I want a little more background on this, like, why is this so unanticipated? Obviously I realize this is an unusual circumstance, but he didn't say...

KS: That's true.

DM: Did he go to a concert with the cymbal in his hand? Or did it show up in his mailbox? I'd like to know a little more about the background...

KS: "Portnoy's my uncle!"

DM: "Excuse me, Mr. Portnoy? Uh, yeah, I have a complaint."

KS: "Yeah, what is it?"

DM: "Uh, my complaint is that you did not laugh at the pun on your name."[13]

KS: Oh my God. "What do you want from me? I'm in Dream Theater!"

DM: I don't know what that is.

KS: I think they sing songs about Valkyries and stuff.

DM: Oh, hang on...

KS: I think it's like super orchestral rock.

DM: Is it like Rush where it's all nerd stuff?

KS: I think it's a little nerd stuff, yeah.

DM: Oh, he does say later—or earlier, he has it less precisely put—"the time I was able to get a top-of-the-line cymbal for my drum set, while having it autographed by one of my favorite drummers."

KS: Was he selling them?

DM: So he says... "I *was able to* get." So I still want to know the background on how this works.

KS: That actually seems broader. It seems like now I'm seeing this guy with a van full

---

13 "Portnoy's Complaint" was one of Jefferson Airplane's first big hits, as well as the name of an algorithm optimization technique.

of cymbals.

DM: Well, he says he was "able to get a top-of-the-line cymbal," and he was able to get it signed. So it seems like it was tough for him to get the cymbal to begin with?

KS: Tough to get the cymbal. Tough 'cause expensive, or tough because rare? Expensive because rare? Or maybe... I don't know.

DM: Well, he said it was a top-of-the-line cymbal, so he was able to... yeah, I don't know. I don't know anything about drums, so...

KS: Wait, none of my...

DM: Cymbals are the thing you hit with your foot, right?

KS: Nooo, it's the friggin', it's the metal thing.

DM: Oh it's the metal. That's the... that uh, the stick! That you use to hit the...

KS: It's like a sideways gong.

DM: Oh, the metal one is the stick, right?

KS: What? What stick?

DM: The stick you use to hit the round ones.

KS: Noo, that's the—you just use the thing. You just use the...any stick, any stick can hit the cymbal.

DM: Wait, I thought there was a word for that. Like... drum-stick.

KS: No, I think you can hit the... yeah. Drumstick.

DM: What? No.

KS: If you're playing the drums, you don't have to switch sticks to hit the cymbal! And then you gotta go back to your old sticks!

DM: Wait, what kind of sticks do you use to hit the, the... other drums?

KS: You hit the... just a drumstick! Right? Just made of wood. Natural and pure, made from the earth.

DM: Drum. Stick. It seems like there'd be a lot more creative name than that.

KS: You know what? I don't like the way that it's been co-opted.

DM: What's the one that has the—oh what? For the chicken lobby?

KS: Chicken, ice cream... friggin' ice cream, that's the worst one! Chicken drumstick, ok, it's so antiquated I can believe it. That thing—that ice cream cone has no business being called the drumstick!

DM: *(laughs)* So antiquated. You're like, "Well, hold on. They were stupid 100 years ago. So we'll forgive them."

KS: Well, Grandpa liked it, so we'll call it a drumstick for him. It's a leg. It's a chicken leg. And it flares at the end with meat; I'm sorry, it doesn't look like a stick.

DM: Wait, are drumsticks flared?

KS: No.

DM: So why is the chicken leg a "drumstick"?

KS: I don't know! I mean, even when you take all the meat off, and it's just a bone, I think it's just a "bone." I don't think you call *that* a drumstick.

DM: Wait, do you call it a "bonestick"?

KS: No! You don't even call it a "drum bone," which makes a lot more sense and which would kind of unify this whole thing.

DM: What about a bone stick?

KS: That's kinda cool, though. "Bonestick" sounds like a brand of T-shirt from the early eighties.

DM: Or is that a verb? "Hey, check it out, I'm gonna bonestick 'er."

KS: "Oh yeah?" —I don't know who his friend is who would go, "Oh yeaaah?"

DM: *(laughs)*

KS: That's his math teacher.

DM: But you can hit other... you don't have to have "drum sticks" to hit drums with. You can use—there's a metal one, right? What's the one that looks like a brush?

KS: I think it's just a "brush."

DM: No! Are you telling me that drummers are this retarded? That they don't have special names for everything?

KS: Yeah, I think it's basically like—whatever shape it is, they just go for it.

DM: What's the name of that...

KS: You're lucky the drum is not called a "circle." It's got its own word.

DM: Well, it looks like an oil drum, right?

KS: Oh yeah, I guess it does. It looks like something you could put things in, like a drum, a round drum... oh my God, you're right! Drumming is awful! That cymbal's worthless now! You got it signed by a drummer? It's, like, *damaged* it.

I have a story about getting signatures. Scott and I wrote that animated series,[14] you know, and one of the voice actors was a cool guy and a collector of various things. And for whatever reason he knew that I like ELO, and I like Jeff Lynne, and so at the end of the thing, he says "Did you get my... I got you a present, did you get it?" And for the longest time I couldn't get it, it was held up at UPS or whatever. Finally, I get it—and he had bought me a copy of, I think it was *Eldorado,* on LP that was signed by Jeff Lynne! Which was something that I'd been trying to find my entire life, and I'm always getting outbid on eBay, and I don't care what the rules say, *there are snipers! That is real!* It's not mediated. It's cutthroat. I hate eBay.

Anyway, I've read so much about forged signatures by him that I can't enjoy it. I just assume that it's fake. It might very well be real. It might be great.

DM: So this is an unanticipated failure.

---

14   Seasons 19–23 of *Smurfs: The New Batch*

KS: Yeah, this is an unanticipated—this is like, I had victory in my hands, and then my own folly ruined it! And had its own victory.

DM: Well, @LYMANALPHA offers a clarification. He says, "It was at George's Music in Orange Park, Florida, and I did not expect either. Portnoy in Florida? I also heard Mike's very pompous too." So I don't understand still. Is this a signed thing that was at the store and you bought it, or you bought it and he was there and he signed it?[15]

RUINING THE ELO FAN ECONOMY:

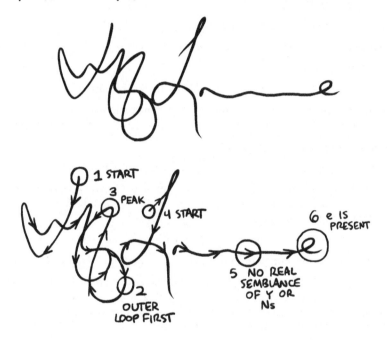

KS: No, I'm expecting that because, if it was signed, I don't think he would have said "Portnoy in Florida?" Because Mike Portnoy does not like Florida.

DM: Oh, is that a known...

KS: Oh, also! I think it's because Dream Theater, aren't they friggin' Norwegian? Like, they're not an American band. They're like from Sweden. So maybe that was a rare thing to see him at a store in Florida.

DM: Ok, so we're working under the assumption that he was at the store and he signed it there. And he bought the cymbal and then had him sign it. So if this is incorrect, @LYMANALPHA, give us a clarification. If anyone else wants...

KS: That sounds like a victory to me.

---

15 This is a situation where it would have been better to just talk to Lyman on the phone or something.

DM: Anyone else that wants to weigh in, of course you can tweet using hashtag #TMH2. We have some more tweets. @JINXVILLE says, "They call chicken legs drumsticks because there was shortage of actual wood drumsticks in the Depression." Are you telling me that they used chicken bones in the Depression?

KS: To drum? Or to build with? 'Cause I...

DM: Maybe to build with! They had to confiscate all the wooden drumsticks and use them as building materials.

KS: See, exactly! Here we have a tweet, that because of its length, is kind of ambiguous, because they have a shortage of wood drumsticks because they were using them in buildings.

DM: Right, they're using them to hold up windows.

KS: Yeah, so now they have to build homes out of bones.

DM: Right.

KS: Which you don't see in any of those old comedies because it's pretty dark.

DM: Well, you know, all those Twenties and Thirties really lavish musical numbers, they were to distract people from the crippling poverty all around them.

KS: From having to live near bones!

DM: Right! They didn't address the bone-cabins phenomenon.

KS: That's why the only buildings in America made out of wood were the theatres! It's like, "Get away from those bones for a while, for an afternoon, stop thinking that you're living inside of a dead thing."

DM: Right, it's bones—and they're sealed up with congealed chicken fat.

KS: Yeah. Then in the sun, your house would just melt, and the flies were ridiculous.

DM: Every night, "Well, we've finished our home. We can go back to sleep in our bones." And then in the morning you have to get up before your house melts around you. And then the rest of the day: "Well, it's back to work rebuilding our home. At least labor is keeping us honest."

KS: That's why—they had to get up early anyway, to look for work or be depressed. To create the Depression.

DM: Right. You know what, that's probably a good point. We would probably have fewer Depressions if we just raised the price of depression. So people couldn't afford it!

KS: Yeah. Kind of reverse that effect.

DM: 'Cause here's the problem—too much free depression running around, so there's a glut on the market. That's what causes Depressions.

KS: Yeah.

DM: When there's too much depression it's too easy to be depressed, then it's like, well, now everyone's depressed. And then you have a Depression. But! What if you were able to raise the price of depression? Or make it more rare in some way, like maybe just restrict access to antidepressant medications. And you give everyone good honest labor! Like building bone houses every day. And then no one can be depressed! They wouldn't have time to be depressed!

KS: That's why the WPA was formed. That's why they enacted that, so that you could just build some bone homes. There are still bones in our highways, you know. That's a big part of our infrastructure. Nobody talks about it.

DM: @LYMANALPHA weighs in with a clarification and says, "he was there, and I got it signed." So this is—we understand now how it's working. "DT is American, and they play prog metal. Portnoy is one of the biggest and best drummers ever." So, "biggest"... I don't know, how big is this guy? 300, 400 pounds?

KS: I dunno, he could have been really big. Maybe it was a surprise...

DM: Maybe he was a 7-foot-6 kind of thing.

KS: It could have been a surprise to see him at George's Music, because it's like a hobbit music store.

DM: Right, 'cause George is a well-known hobbit.

KS: It's got a low door. George is a small man.

DM: It's got a circular doorway with the knob in the center.

KS: It's in the hill. Knob in the center, which is not the best mechanical advantage because when you're short you need that leverage...

DM: Well, we have to assume that the knob works like a regular knob works. It turns a latch that goes into the doorframe. But what if there's a difference? What if it's a radial latch where when the door is closed, it actually sends bolts—or it just widens the doorframe so that it sticks in the jamb, and when you turn it, it contracts the edge a little bit so that it can open.

KS: That sounds like such a hassle.

DM: Yeah, but they're hobbits. They gotta fill their time.

KS: That is friggin' impossible. Why don't they just put the knob near the hinges? Then you really gotta push it.

DM: Because this way, you can open it either direction. You just have to remember to put it back when you're done. It's like saloon doors. The hinges only go one way, but there are multiple hinges at offsets, so it really goes any direction.

KS: That's a good sight gag. A cowboy's going up to a saloon and he's like "sorry, we're closed for the night." And he's got a padlock on the saloon doors.

DM: That's pretty good.

KS: 'Cause you could still crawl under and steal the alcohol.

DM: I thought you were gonna say, there's a pull sign on there, and he's pushing on it.

KS: And the guy behind him is like, "Ya idiot!"

DM: When I was a kid working at my parents' shop, we had doors like that—they were "push" doors, and people would pull on them and they wouldn't open. And so they'd cup their hand up on the glass and look in, like, "Is it open? It's 2:14 in the afternoon!" And then sometimes they would see that there was another door around the side of the building, and so they would leave the totally unlocked door and walk around the side of the building, which was a pull door. And then they'd come in that way. "All right, now I've got it figured out" was their expression.

KS: "I can only pull. I got two handicaps: I only can pull, and I can only turn left in a car. It takes me longer, but..."

DM: "Because only the one turn signal works!"

KS: "Yeah, and I'm a good citizen."

HOBBIT DOOR

HOBBIT BANK
VAULT DOOR

DM: I do like remembering that sometimes, after the store was locked up, my parents would still let customers come around the back if they had a question. So what they would do is, they would gesture to the person on the other side. They'd see them through the window and they'd gesture, "Come around the back."

And I didn't realize that that was a discretionary move. Like, you know, "we're closed, we're not going to invite everybody, but this guy looks like he's rushing up, he just missed us by a few minutes, we never leave right on time anyway." So when I was a kid and I'd see people running up to the door, or, like, they'd come up to the door and it'd be locked—they'd look in and see me as a little kid just pointin' like mad to the side. And then I'd run around to the side of the building and then point *further* back, to the other door to the very back of the building...

and then they'd be like "Where is this child leading me? To die?"

KS: "To a mystery! I like this!"

DM: And then at the back, I'd run back there and I'd open the door and I'd be running to make sure that I'd be there when they arrived. And then I'd open the door and there they'd be! And I was like "Well! That's all I can do. I'm just a kid." I'm not gonna help them, I'm not gonna find what they need.

KS: "Got change for a fifty?"

DM: ...I'm not gonna, you know, help them as a shopkeeper.

KS: That's got to be very rewarding as a child, though, to know that you helped.

DM: "I did it! He came back because I did it!"

KS: Yeah! And then he just robs the place.

DM: He goes "thank you very much. Give me all your money."

KS: Yeah, the whole time you're forgetting the part where he's got a mask on and a gun in his hand. You're like, "Around the back! C'mon! What's *with* this guy?"

DM: He's got the giant sack with the dollar sign on it. He's like, "Excuse me, my bag is empty. Can you help me out?"

KS: "I'm having a very bad problem with my robbery. It's not working out for me. There's no money inside of here that's not mine."

DM: "I need to get my bag filled. Can you give me an estimate? What would it take to make my robbery work again?"

KS: "...I think all of the money in our register!"

DM: So, we have @EDGYSWORDBEARER on the Twitter saying, "If drums were circles, how would you distinguish them from cymbals? Not all cymbals look like hats." Well it's very simple. The drum is the circle. The cymbal is a disk? Right?

KS: Well, yeah, exactly.

DM: The stick? I've already determined the stick is a "stick." The brush is a "brush." The pen—the drum pen is a "pen." Is there a drum...? He said that there's drum hats, right? So some are "hats." Drum hats? Drum paper?

KS: Yeah. Drum hats.

DM: Is there "drum paper"? That's what goes on the top?

KS: Yeah, some of them are really thin. They look like you could write on them.

DM: Right, so that's drum paper.

KS: Yeah.

DM: So what else do we got? We got drum sticks, drum paper, drum pens, drum hats... drum ties? Is there drum ties? That you could wear around your neck? For like a mobile kit?

KS: Um, I like that idea. Just get a deflated drum.

DM: What about those *Karate Kid 2* drums? How do those fit into it?

KS: I don't know, but you can carry those with you. That's for sure.

DM: You can hang that from your neck. That's a drum tie, right?

KS: I have a great distinguisher for @EDGYSWORDBEARER. He's saying, "If drums were circles, how would you distinguish them from cymbals?" Well, obviously, it's a case of the guy doing the drumming. I mean, the drummers are the ones who made up the names. When you're sitting in a drum kit, you look down, you see the drums: circles. They're circles. You look up, you see the cymbals? You don't see the circle. You see the side of it. It looks like a hat.

DM: That's true.

KS: Right? If you look from up top, you would say "it's circles, circles everywhere. I don't know which one to hit first." That's why they sat down. That's why they started sitting down.

DM: It's a frame of reference.

KS: Yeah.

DM: And so what about the one that you kick? What's that one?

KS: Foot? The foot drumming? "Foot circle," probably. Yeah.

DM: Probably "foot circle." What about the one that kinda sounds metally? That's got those wires under it?

KS: That's "metal helper."

DM: Metal helper. Right.

KS: Helps you... yeah.

DM: Because—that way if you need sort of a metal thing, then that helps you.

KS: It's not really a primary part of the kit. You don't really play that. You play that when you want to add a little zest. It helps the song out.

DM: It's like spice. Drum spice.

KS: Yeah, it's a little spice.

DM: All right. Okay. So we've got drum paper. We talked about that. We talked about drum ties. Drum belt? Is there anything you can wear around your... any sort of drum... like, I don't know much about music, but is there a sort of drum that can kinda keep your pants up?

KS: There's a whole continuum of clothing, probably, that helps drummers. Like a lifting belt, you know? That you wear when you work in a warehouse.

DM: I wonder, at what point did drum suspenders give way to drum belt?

KS: I don't know. But at some point it went out of fashion. There's only so much you can do with a suspender.

DM: Right. You don't see those very often. Because here's the thing: suspenders—with a drum suspender you want two things. You want: (a) keep your pants up, (b) create a jazzy sound. And the thing about drum belts is they keep your pants up, sure, but they do it in a—like, the physics of it are different. They do it in a cinching motion, not in a holding tight, lifting motion.

KS: Right, it's not a gravity... yeah, exactly.

DM: And so you have to re-engineer the drum part of it itself, because the physics of it are different. You can't get the same sound from it.

KS: Yeah, it's probably why you don't see them as much. Or pants, for that matter.

DM: Oh, there are no drum hats. @LYMANALPHA says, "High hats are another type of cymbal. Drums are cylinders." So, something called a snare drum? I don't think that's right. Snare drum sounds like a...

KS: Oh, that's like a trap.

DM: ...Like a trap, so if you're drumming for bears in the woods, you'd need a snare drum to keep your campsite safe.

KS: That makes a lot of... You know what? I gotta hand it to drummers. We started out this conversation thinking that they're kinda dumb.

DM: Yeah, I certainly had no confidence in their intelligence at all.

KS: But they've got their bases covered.

DM: Is that a drum term? Or is that a... oh, that's a baseball term. "Base."

KS: Yeah, I'm mixing my metaphor. What I should have said is, "They have all their drums... beat..."

DM: Circles, right.

KS: Sounds, right.

DM: Is that where we get the term "drum circle?" "Well, you certainly have all your drums circled." And then all these people get together—everyone who has no jobs, because they've got all their drums circled. Then they just play music.

KS: I want to say that's why. That actually was a big thing in a neighborhood I used to live in, in Dallas.

DM: Was it?

KS: Yeah, it was kind of a hippie neighborhood.

DM: Oh, yeah, 'cause hippies—ah, this makes a lot of sense now—'cause hippies are the ones who feel like they have everything solved, right? Like they have no...

KS: Right, and they don't have any jobs. So now we're starting to see the whole depression, bones thing roll in.

DM: Right, exactly. So they hang around: everyone who has all their drums circled gets together with their chicken bones, because they don't need them for their house because they have already, um...

KS: They're vegan.

DM: Yes. That's the missing piece of the puzzle.

KS: And finally. And finally!

DM: It all comes together.

KS: And @JUSTABEAR says, "Would a washboard be suspenders or a shirt?" Well, it's for washing your clothes so it doesn't matter. It's not really germane to the conversation.

DM: Yeah, I mean, I have seen... well, you have a distinction between drummers and percussionists. Right? Drummers don't like to be called percussionists in the same way that pilots don't like to be called airplane drivers.

KS: Okay.

DM: Or is it the other way around?

KS: I don't know. I think "drummer" is cool, though.

DM: "Drummer" sounds like an awesome word. "Percussionist" sounds like seventh grade—you're in seventh-grade band.

KS: Yeah. It sounds like you're a dork. That's what it sounds like.

DM: You have to wear white sneakers and you have to wear the band jacket.

KS: Yeah, you don't want to be a percussionist.

DM: Okay, so "percussion" is the act of hitting something. So is a boxer technically a percussionist? That's why a drummer doesn't want to be lumped in with—okay, I get it. It's a square/rectangle kind of thing. A square is a rectangle, but not all rectangles are squares.

KS: That's why they call it a sweet science, 'cause it sounds real good. Yeah.

DM: I get it. So a drummer is a percussionist, but a percussionist could also be like a boxer, or a construction worker. They hit stuff with hammers, right?

KS: I accidentally percuss things during the day too. So, technically...

DM: We're all percussionists at different times in our lives.

KS: Yeah.

DM: What about: can you be a metaphorical percussionist? Can you really hit something? Like, "man, I really hit that one."

KS: Like hit a high note? Hit a home run?

DM: Yeah. Baseball players are percussionists.

KS: These guys are all...

DM: *Good* baseball players are percussionists. Bad baseball players are, by definition, *not* percussionists. Like, if you are not a percussionist, you are also not a good baseball player. The better percussionist you are, the better baseball player you are. Unless you are a pitcher in the American League, in which case it doesn't matter.

KS: Blackjack dealers? Percussionists. Because you have them hit you.

DM: Yeah, they're hitting people all day long.

KS: Yeah. They're really good at it too. And they get paid high. I think...

DM: Hey! And blackjack dealers on a riverboat—you'll see them wear a straw hat. Maybe this is where we get the term "high hat."

KS: I thought you were gonna say, "And blackjacks: you hit people with them to take their money."

DM: What *is* that thing? I've heard this in Hardy Boys books my whole life. What is a blackjack?

KS: All I know is that it looks like a beaver's tail. And I think it's a little sack filled with ball bearings.

DM: Well, that's what I didn't know—if it was something flexible or if it was something rigid. Like a shoehorn. It always looks like a shoehorn in the pictures.

KS: No, it's a little baggie. It does look like a shoehorn, but I think it's a little baggie full of metal balls. Which seems like not the most stealthy weapon. You're walking around the room rattling around these balls.

DM: "Boy, someone's coming." *Rattle rattle rattle.* "No, it's just change in me pocket. Pay no mind."

KS: "It's just my tiny spherical keys, that I don't want to hit people with."

DM: I wonder if in Canada that sort of weapon is more effective. Because everyone is carrying change in their pockets anyway.

KS: Just 'cause of all the metal money?

DM: Yeah, because in Canada, single and two-dollar currency is only in coins. There's no bills until you get to five dollars. And so people have little coin-purses. People carry coins in their pockets all the time, and so it's more common to hear change jingling around. So a ball bearing filled-blackjack is not going to be as conspicuous.

KS: Oh, yeah.

DM: I wonder if America doesn't want to go on the coin-dollar standard 'cause when Canada did it, they just cut off bills and said, "All right, everything's coins from now on." America's been trying to introduce these coins gradually, but maybe it's for our safety. They don't wanna—they wanna do coins 'cause of international pressure, but also 'cause of the mint lobby. But, I really think that if we had more coins—in a country as big as America, if everyone had coins jingling in their pockets, you'd see a rise in blackjack attacks.

KS: Yeah, and not only that, but if you were a blackjacker and you got on a roll, there's no limit. I mean, you basically—the way we are now, we've got so few coins, you start from zero, you're not gonna blackjack anybody.[16]

DM: Right.

KS: But imagine, you've already accumulated, like, four pouches' worth of these

---

16 This is a good example of how we somehow start talking about different things. David's talking about how a society with more coins in the pockets will allow blackjack-ers to strike with impunity (using ball-bearing-filled blackjacks), because people will become accustomed to the rattling sounds. But Kris has bridged over to blackjackers accumulating blackjack ammunition by robbing people of their coins and using them to stuff additional blackjacks. From this point forward, Kris is always talking about black-jacks filled with coins. David never catches onto the transition.

coins, you're gonna do an easier blackjack the next time!

DM: Right.

KS: It's just going to get easier.

DM: It's sort of like when you're playing a video and you get better and better weapons.[17] The only way that the game keeps it fair is you have to fight harder and harder monsters. But in real life, a human being is a human being. A blackjack to the skull is basically a blackjack to the skull.

KS: Yeah.

DM: And so what happens is you have this great imbalance of power between blackjackers and their victims.

KS: But you know what? It comes back around, though, because once the blackjack gets too big, because you're so rich with coins, now you really gotta have the arm strength to nail those guys. You know?

DM: And they get stronger and stronger.

KS: And then you're working out, and then you're like a buff—you're like a huge healthy, wealthy man.

DM: Hold on a second. @MRBILDANGO is saying, "A blackjack is a little hard flexible rubber thingie that you whack someone on the head with."

KS: Hmmm...

DM: "Hard flexible rubber."

KS: I don't know. I don't know why you would hit someone with that.

DM: Maybe @MRBILDANGO has only been exposed to training blackjacks?

KS: Oh. Yeah.

DM: And then when you graduate to the full-on metal ones, then... you know. But I think he must have only gotten to Level 1 or Level 2 or something, because he's only got the rubber ones. He's only had experience with those. We'll forgive that.

KS: That's okay. Play a little longer and you'll get there.

DM: And you know why it's all right that he hasn't had experience with the real thing? Because we live in America, a land that has outlawed coin money and thus the incidental blackjack attacks. I wonder how many other things the government has saved us from, without even, without—and no one gives them any credit.

KS: Thanks, Government!

DM: Unless there's a giant rash, you know, of some problem—and it won't be blackjack attacks, because we have that solved, 'cause of the money thing. You know? It's like every time there's a 9/11 it's like, "Well, Government didn't save us." But how many other things *have* they saved us from?

KS: Well, *my* head's not bashed in. So...thanks, America... What do you say? Tweet Me Harder!

---

17   Video game, obviously. Or, not!

DM: I know what *I* say.

KS: What?

[ACCORDION STING]

DM: I think that's the end of the show! We have two different people, @CRAZYCSTUDIOS and @EDGYSWORDBEARER, talking about blackjack: winning blackjack in a casino as an example of Unanticipated Victory. I disagree slightly, because I believe that if you go into something gambling, you may kinda hope you'll win, but rarely do you *expect to lose.* You feel like, "Ah, you know what? It'd be really nice if I won." Even if you kinda know you're gonna lose...

KS: Yeah. If you expected to lose, then you wouldn't play. I wouldn't even go in.

DM: There are people that say, "Oh, I'll just blow this twenty bucks" or whatever. They kinda figure they're gonna lose, but they're not actually *expecting* to lose. In which case, if they were, they'd just throw the money in the trash. Because it's better in the trash than going to further the, um, the casino. You know what I mean?

KS: Well, there's so much other stuff to do in Vegas besides sit in front of a machine or a guy you don't know. Right? Or is there not?

DM: ...Wearing some kind of hat. Right.

KS: Yeah, probably with a hat on. But, I mean, whenever I've gone to Vegas I don't want to gamble. I figure that money's gone.

DM: Yeah, although I will say: I went to Vegas recently with my friend Todd. We were driving home from Utah. We stopped in Vegas just to have some dinner at a buffet. And it was like, "All right, I'm just gonna gamble like once." Like, I put $1 in the slot machine; I put one bill on a roulette thing. And I sort of have a tradition—almost, I've only done it a few times, but—with roulette especially: you play one spin, you put it on red or black, and then win or lose, you walk away. So you've either doubled your money or lost it, and either way, you are done.

KS: Yeah.

DM: Which I think is kind of a fun thing to do. And I won! And then I did a slot machine thing. And I came out of it a couple dollars ahead. And Todd was like, "I'm gonna do it, too." And Todd lost every time. So after doing this several times on different games, I walked out of there like $38 ahead, and Todd was down like $16.

KS: Pffft.

DM: Which is unusual, certainly. And that may be some unanticipated victory. But, it was foreshadowed when we were at a gas station in Vegas on the way up on our trip. It was like, I don't know, two in the morning or something. And in Nevada, of course, they have slot machines everywhere: in gas stations, truck stops. And I put some coins in, and it was that same sort of thing: "I'm gonna play one round and then walk away." And I won, like, a dollar. And so we had to try and get the attendant—it was one of these things where there are several machines in the truck stop, and you have to get a ticket and give it to the attendant to get your cash. And this attendant did *not* like being disturbed at two in the morning by this guy to give him his $1.

KS: It's his friggin' job!

DM: I know, that's what we were arguing! "It's your job. What else are you going to do?"

KS: If you don't give—if you play favorites like that, you don't want to get up and get a dollar, the whole system falls apart.

DM: Exactly. And I think it goes the same way with gumballs or with $5,000 refunds. If you have a standard, you have to stick to it. Otherwise your morality means nothing. It's dependent on your whim.

KS: You know what? Now I get it. This show was to prove that point to me. I'm sorry I ever took the opposite side, 'cause I think you're right.

DM: It's a metaphor.

KS: Every gumball counts!

DM: Every gumball counts.

3

Hammerin' Hornets

DM: Is it... You're gonna hafta tell me if the music is going 'cause I can't hear a thing.

KS: Yeah, we're going right now.

DM: Awesome. Welcome to Tweet Me Harder, I'm David Malki !

KS: I'm Kris Straub.

DM: Welcome to the show. This is, as you know by now, the world's first, best, only, and last talkback-enabled—what is it?—talkback-enabled interactive audio podblast.

KS: There you are.

DM: You can tweet us at any time. This is show number three, so please use hashtag #TMH3, T-M-H-3. This show is about hubristic missteps.

KS: What is—now what's the word? I know what missteps are. What's "hubristic?"

DM: Hubristic?

KS: For the people at home.

DM: Showing hubris. Hubris is pride. Too much pride. You think everything is going to turn out okay, and you were overconfident and you got just deserts handed to you. Now, it sounds a little bit *bitter* when I put it that way, but hubris is generally considered to be unqualified pride.

KS: There you go.

DM: Is that a good description?

KS: Yeah, I think that's the key. It's not just... You felt pride that you shouldn't have, so: downfall. You know what I mean? Like, that's a very Biblical thing.

DM: Heh. Yeah, it definitely has precedent in all the mythology of every culture ever known to man or beast.

KS: I don't know how much mythology beasts have, but...

DM: Just because you can't read it doesn't mean it's not there. That is very anthropocentric of you.

KS: I'm sorry. I'm sorry, *rabbits*.

DM: *(laughs)* They're listening. They're out there. You know what they're saying in response?

KS: "What's wrong with our creation myths?"

DM: I was gonna say rabbits don't really make much of a noise.

KS: Oh, well *now* who's racist?

DM: Heh. I know, I just prefer to keep the rabbits down.

Everyone has been tweeting to us and sending us some calls. We asked everyone to share with us tales of their hubristic missteps, and I think we have quite a few to share with you today.

KS: Man. I haven't looked since we, uh—the last time we tweeted was about an hour ago.

DM: We've got plenty. Do you wanna hop right into it, or do we wanna... We've had some people telling us that we should play more with the Twitter, so I'll tell you what: if at any point, you want to contribute a brief counterpoint to anything we say, in just a few words, this is your charge to do it, and we guarantee you we will—well, I'm not gonna guarantee anything but...

KS: We will try to get it in there.[18]

DM: ... And then we are going to mock your point of view. *Or,* come around to your point of view, if it's particularly well-reasoned. But keep it under three words or so.

KS: I will probably secretly come around to their point of view, but make fun of them, you know, verbally. Out loud.

DM: Have you heard about this? There is a new book out that talks about extremism— I was reading a review of it—and some of the studies have shown that when you have people with divergent opinions discussing things, they don't tend to agree on a moderate opinion, they tend to polarize.

KS: Oh.

DM: I think anytime you've seen any argument on the Internet, or even offline, I can understand why that would be the case. You get people more entrenched in their positions, and even if you show them evidence, each side just picks the evidence that supports their position. And you get everyone further apart than they were to begin with, because they get defensive.

KS: I just figured that's 'cause everybody's douchebags. Essentially.

DM: At the core.

KS: Deep down. Now what were you saying about hubris?

DM: I think it's a good point that you've raised, that you might secretly realize the logic of someone else's position, but you want to save face, right? You want to keep arguing.

KS: Well, this is something that happens—it doesn't happen so much to me, but I know it's happened to Scott in the past,[19] and I can understand the logic of

---

18 We do not ever get any of it in there.
19 Olympic figure–skater Scott Hamilton.

it—like, you tell a joke, or for the sake of a bit, you're acting, like you're going to practical-joke somebody.

DM: Right.

KS: And not only is the practical joke not going over well, but they don't even know that it's a practical joke. And for you to reveal it will only show that you are bad at assembling a practical joke.

DM: *(laughs)*

KS: So the way to save the most face is to continue with your ridiculous opinion that was supposed to be too out there to even be real.

DM: Sure, and you're trying to find evidence to justify it now, and you're making these ever-more specious arguments.

KS: Right, "I really *do* think that carrots are Nazis! I don't *care!*" And then you gotta go with it. It's sad.

DM: Yeah, It definitely is a saving-face thing. I'm trying to think of a situation where the way to save your pride would be to admit you're wrong. And unfortunately those sentiments are often mutually exclusive.

KS: No, you can't—you gotta be right. You *gotta* be right. But you know what? I'm sayin' let's jump in, and maybe we should hear a voicemail to start with.

DM: All right, here we go:

> My aunt once took an entire day off from work to scatter enriched soil on her lawn to help it grow—only to find out the next day that her 90-year-old dad went ahead and removed it all, and threw it away in the backyard, thinking that he was doing her a favor by cleaning up her messy lawn. So, yup, that's sweet.

DM: I don't know where the hubris is, there. To be perfectly honest.

KS: "I will make these plants grow! Oh, God, I should have known better. I should've known better."

DM: I can—okay, well, let's dig deeper into this. If the whole idea that this is a hubristic misstep, then the hubris must've been on the part of the aunt, right?

KS: Yeah.

DM: To think that her 90-year-old father wouldn't misinterpret the situation.

KS: Wouldn't pick dirt up off of a lawn. See, but no: my interpretation is that the hubris comes from her playing God. "This lawn will live! I will make it grow—and be healthy!"

DM: So the 90-year-old father is Fate intervening and saying, "No, only God can give life to these things."

KS: That's right. And then after she came home, all the dirt was gone and next to her bed was a Bible. And he's like, "You need to read this. You need to get right."

DM: *(laughs)* "I'm really worried about you, Maureen. You've been doing a lot of strange things recently: spreading soil on the lawn, watering things. Don't you know, rain comes from God?"

KS: He's like, "You got it upside down. There is soil under the grass already. Why would you put it on top?"

DM: "You're inverting the natural order, Maureen."

KS: "This is perverse!"

> *Hi, guys. The mistake—mistakes, actually—that I have to detail aren't my own, but instead my grandmother's, and the three of them all happened within less than two weeks of each other. Her first mistake was attempting to remodel her kitchen, and the way she decided to do it was just smashing the hammer through the wall. And it turned out that she had a hornet's nest inside the wall...*

DM: Okay, I'm going to pause it here. This already paints a pretty great picture.

KS: What I've learned is that old people make mistakes.

DM: Trying to remodel the kitchen. With a hammer. So we understand, now it's just, "Well, I have to knock down the old wall, let's just swing into it as hard as I can."

KS: I won't learn. There is no point.

DM: Yeah, so this is definitely, from step 1: Hubris. "I know how to do this. It just takes a hammer. Let's just *(hammer-swinging sound, 'whaappshh')*. I can make it happen." And then, instantly: Hornet's nest. Already, this is enough.

KS: In the wall?

DM: Oh, yeah.

KS: That's cruel. It's not even like a pipe burst.

DM: *(laughs)* Yeah, exactly. Sort of like, you're digging in your lawn and you're like, "I hope I don't hit a sewer pipe!" and you accidentally hit a cache of wild dogs.

KS: *(laughs)* Exactly.

DM: One jumps out at you and starts tearing at your face...

KS: "Why didn't I know better?!" Ah, come on, life!

DM: "I think I can lay the foundation for the deck. I'm just going to dig a six-inch trench so I can lay concrete." Next thing you know... snakes!

KS: *Hepatitis?* Come *on!*

DM: Prostate cancer!

KS: I don't need this.

DM: All right. Let's continue the story.

KS: All right.

> *... so the hornets all escaped and started attacking her and her dogs. And she reached blindly under the kitchen counter to try and get some bug spray and it turned out, for some reason, the only thing she had was purple spray paint, which she continued to spray all over*

herself, and her dogs, and the kitchen walls.

So my uncle came home to her passed out on the floor covered with spray paint and bees and the dogs covered in the same. And they're all Pomeranians so they need to be shaved, and so she took them out back later in the week—just in her yard, to hang out—and one of them was on the ground and she went to pick it up and a snake bit her. She called her daughter, in Washington state—as apposed to anywhere in New England--and asked what kind of snake she thought it was. She said, "probably just a garter snake or something." Turned out it was a copperhead.

She went to sleep and ended up waking up with her arm probably three times the normal size and having to go to the hospital. And so, when she came back, she still refused to wear any glasses to see, you know, if it was spray paint or bug spray, and she decided to let all of her dogs and cats in one day and she ended up letting a skunk in with all of them, which freaked out when it got in the house and ended up stinking up her entire house for all of her recovery.

DM: This is like the opposite of a Dr. Doolittle situation.

KS: I was gonna say, I've seen Mr. Magoo. Like, now it's not funny. This sucks. A lot.

DM: Just animals attacking you at every turn.

KS: That's true! Every one of the elements of this story is that animals hurt you.

DM: We have insects. Then we have reptiles. Then finally, the greatest class of animal: the mammals.

KS: Even the mammal betrayed her.

DM: Moving up the food chain. It's like, "All right, we're gonna give you another chance." Nope? Bring out the bigger guns: snake time. Nope? You've still got problems: here come the skunks.

KS: And then a man bites her.

DM: Yeah, finally, she is stepped on by an elephant, and then a man argues with her for a while. Because Man has the greatest weapon of all: his rhetoric.

KS: Exactly. And then in her attic there was a hive of aliens.

DM: Right, exactly. There is some sort of gelatinous alien goo that slowly drips down through the cracks in her ceiling and falls into her mouth as she sleeps.

KS: And you know what? It's smarter than us. So you get the whole progression.

DM: And then God tells her, "Only I can make it rain."

KS: *(laughs)* "Why didn't you ask me to remodel for you? That wall is load-bearing!"

DM: "I wouldn't have done it, but I at least would have appreciated the effort. I like being thought of now and then."

KS: "You know what, I listen to the prayers. I don't do them all, but..." Yeah, that's awful! That's a terrible story.

DM: So we have a Twitter here, "She was really cruel to the hospital staff and ended up getting gangrene on her snakebite."

KS: Who's tweeting that?

DM: I think this is the real person. This is @EMVASSEUR. I'm pretty sure this might be the actual, real person that knows this story.

KS: I think it is.

DM: So she *did* eventually end up pissing off Man, in the form of the hospital staff. And you know what they did? They cycled. 'Cause with gangrene—gangrene is like a necrosis, right? Is there any sort of bacteria involved with gangrene? Because they were just gonna start at the bottom of the food chain and just go up again.

KS: *(laughs)* You know what, I think—

DM: They went around the horn...

KS: —Somebody can correct me, but I think necrosis is the death of cells, so it's the absence of a threat. It's the body itself deciding to lay down and quit in the face of this.

DM: It's the classic conflicts, right? Man versus animal. Man versus man. Man versus self?

KS: Yeah.

DM: Eventually it gets to the top of that hierarchy, and then the body is now just rebelling against the actual person controlling the body. It's the soldiers rebelling against the general.

KS: "I'm not getting stung by your inaction again. We're gonna die. I'm gonna kill us."

DM: "I've had it up to here! You've got no idea what I'm going through down here!" The toes are just like, "Dude, screw this. Screw it."

KS: *(laughs)*

DM: Oh man, no. Emily said the arms swelled up.

KS: Swole?

DM: Swelled up.

KS: They were swelling.

DM: And the snakebite is on the arms, so if the arms were getting gangrene at this point it's like the arms are—you use your arms, right? It's not like a toe we're talking about, it's not an earlobe. It's the things that make you dexterous.

KS: Yeah, you gotta piss off some huge faction of the body to have your arms betray you.

DM: They're like, "Listen. We have to strike preemptively at this point."

KS: *(laughs)* "We can't... it's better to just be in a graveyard. I don't think that this is a good thing. We're not having a good life."

DM: *(laughs)* Oh, man.

KS: "I got stung!"

DM: Okay, so this is what I really wanna know: This really sounds like an Amelia Bedelia kinda situation.

KS: Oh, I never read that, sadly.

DM: Amelia Bedelia is the kid's character—a character from a kid's book—and she took everything literally. This was a book that relied a lot on homonyms.

KS: Hmmm.

DM: So it's like, "All right, Amelia, I want you to put some stakes in the ground to put up the tent." And then she'd go to the butcher shop and get some steaks. Like, it's that kind of situation.

KS: Yeah.

DM: And so there's the humorous wackiness of the situations she gets herself into. So this is sort of like that, writ large and tragic and the in-real-life version where it's like "oh my goodness, everything has horrible consequences that result in death."

KS: Every once in a while you'll see a scan of that obituary where the guy got hit with a bowling ball at the alley. It's like, it's funny in a million cartoons, but now nobody's laughing.

DM: *(laughs)* Right, exactly. @cephalopod_gal on the Twitter says, "Gangrene can be caused by infections or lack of blood flow." So in this case it was probably the swelling that caused lack of blood flow that caused the tissue to die, is my guess...

KS: I'm saying it was the body. It was the body.

DM: Definitely the body rebelling against itself. And trying to mutiny, probably, or...

KS: There was nothing in that snakebite. That thing was clean.

DM: If the body can't mutiny it's just going to jump off the cliff. It's like, "rather die than serve this master."

KS: It's probably better for her to learn the lesson, you know? And not assume, "Well, wait a minute, I'll bet my gangrene was caused by infection from an outside source. There was nothing wrong with what I was doing."

DM: *(laughs)* "I'll keep on going doing what I was doing." So Emily, what I want to know, follow up question: What is the rest of her life like? Is this a common occurrence? Is it like, "Oh, Aunt Maureen, up to wackiness again!" Or is this like, "Oh my goodness, this couldn't have happened to a nicer person: a bunch of hornets, and then the snakebite, and then spray-painted her dogs, and then she got gangrene at the same time. And also, skunks."

KS: *(laughs)* As if it wasn't bad enough.

DM: Right, yeah. I kind of want to know the continuing adventures of Aunt Whatever-Her-Name-Is, because this sounds like a story rich in entertainment value.

KS: Yeah, you know on the way to the hospital the back of the ambulance opens and the gurney flies out on the highway.

DM: *(laughs)* Yeah...

KS: "Whooooaaaaa..."

DM: Oh, man. Yeah, she flies off and then gets stuck to someone's windshield and is hanging on to the driver's window and the passenger's window with the two outstretched arms, and the driver is swerving back and forth...

KS: And she flips into the back of his truck and on the side of it, painted large, it says, "Bat Salesman."

DM: *(laughs)*

KS: "All kinds of bats!"

DM: *(laughs)* You just hear the squeaking and the *(weird squeak noise)* and all the flapping and then it's like "BANG, BANG, BANG, BANG." And then the door opens and all the bats sort of carry her out and she's flying above the freeway...

KS: "Whooooaaaaahhh..."

DM: ...And then she gets dropped inside a huge semi-truck and you hear the "BAAAAH"—and you just hear "CRASH" as she goes through the roof of the trailer. Then on the other side of the trailer you see "GLASS."

KS: *(laughs)* "Broken Glass Hauling."

DM: I know, you'd think they'd have safety precautions.

KS: It's a cottage industry.

DM: @Tᴘᴀʀᴀᴅᴏx says, "One time a road was closed, but I knew the work was past a side road, so I passed the signs. They had it blocked. I had to turn around into the muddy field. I got stuck and had to call Triple-A at 3 A.M. in my mom's van."

KS: *(laughs)* I like... I mean I'm imagining that the "mom's van" part of the story was, uh, mom wasn't pleased, as opposed to the Triple-A guys going, "What is this, your mom's? You got a Windstar, huh?"

DM: *(laughs)*

KS: "We're just razzing ya."

DM: At three A.M. the Triple-A guy really loved just joking with you about how crappy your car is. That's the first thing on his mind.

KS: *(laughs)* "There's no way that this piece of junk could navigate that road!"

DM: "There's no way that this gets more than twenty-five miles to the gallon."

KS: Sorry about your mom's van, @TPARADOX.

DM: Okay, so what I want to know, @TPARADOX, if you're listening, follow up, give us more details. We want to know where were you going at three A.M. And then let's know a little bit more about the story.

KS: Here's another one. @MIDDLERUN says, "I took a year off before university to earn money, and spent most of the year unemployed and the rest in a minimum wage job I hated." Oh.

DM: That sucks.

KS: That does suck. The question is, though: is it hubris because if he had gotten that degree, he'd be having a great job? Or, I don't know. Maybe the market just sucked.

DM: Maybe he thought, "Well, I don't need to go to college right now. I'm qualified enough, I can just fend for myself on my own. I don't need, you know, whatever the next step is. I can kinda figure out my own thing."

KS: "I've got just *enough* college."

DM: *(laughs)* "I've seen classes on television." I wanna know just how much the hubris plays into this. So, @MIDDLERUN, if you could tweet us back and let us know: were you unemployed because you could not find a job, or because you just slacked around? And I can totally see—when I first read this, my picture of the situation was that his hubris was "I'll be able to go get a job." And then he was just unmotivated and didn't realize that, you know...

KS: *(laughs)*

DM: He just sat on the couch all the time and was like, "Well, I guess maybe I should look in the classifieds. Or I could just watch Adult Swim."

KS: "Or I could just wait to be discovered. "

DM: "I'll spend a lot of time in coffee shops tossing my hair."

KS: "Where's the local Schwab's? What?! They don't have them anymore?!"

DM: All right, so a little more detail if you are listening, @MIDDLERUN. I wanna know: were you unemployed by choice, or despite your best efforts?

KS: @EMVASSEUR writes us back. She says, "This is her usual life, just two weeks of it. She has a tendency to key cars and stuff, so this is karma." All right.

DM: Yeah, I'll buy that. Absolutely.

KS: You know what? I feel better.

DM: Absolutely. I think she deserved it. Why don't you give us her number. We'll call her and just, you know. Talk to her. We'll annoy her.

KS: *(laughs)* She says, "I don't care. I'd do it again!"

DM: @STEWPED says, "Going to art school thinking they would actually teach me how to draw. Fifty grand wasted. Could've learned on my own from books."

KS: Hmmmm.

DM: This is a tricky situation, because I think this really depends 100% on the circumstances. This is not always a mistake. In fact, I think the hubris would have been going, thinking you know everything, then realizing too late your lack of qualifications. I don't know if there is a lot of hubris in wasting money on art school, because that seems like a fairly reasonable thing to expect would work out fairly well.

KS: Yeah it's not like some fly-by-night scheme where they're like, "I'll do it the easy way." You know?

DM: Right. Now, granted, we don't know what the art school is. Maybe it was that—what is that? The Minnesota whatever, where you have to draw the pirate and the turtle?[20]

KS: *(laughs)* The one in the '70s comic books?

DM: I remember I sent them a thing when I was eleven years old and they were like, "Write us back in five years, kid. We'd love to have you."[21]

KS: Jeez.

DM: But it's like a correspondence course kinda thing. And as for art school—I've heard the same complaint about film school, people that say, "Why would I spend a hundred grand on film school when I could just take a hundred grand and make a movie?" And it's a valid thing to say, but I mean, I learned a lot in film school. Especially in a field where you don't need the credential, like in the arts—no one asks for your degree. It's not like medical school, where you have to pass a test and everything to be qualified in the field. So a lot of people think, "Yeah, I'll just skip it." And that's fine, you know, whatever they want to do.

But I definitely appreciated going to film school, because it bonded me with a lot of like-minded individuals. We went through a lot, and we kind of grew up together. And now, years later, we're still friends and we're friends of a different sort than the people I've just met in the world as adults.

KS: But you all got a disease from handling the same film at school.

DM: Right, so we have to reconvene every six months and we have to keep reinfecting each other. This is the crazy part. We want them to find a cure, but the problem is the disease has some weird half-life where it gets really really faint in your system

---

20 Art Instruction Schools, the correspondence school Charles Schulz attended in the forties and later taught at, and which has really no other claim to fame.
21 David didn't realize at the time that it was a school you had to pay to attend. He thought it was a contest you could win, so he drew the *heck* out of that turtle.

and goes into regression and it is impossible to detect. You'd think this would be a good thing! However...

KS: I was gonna say...

DM: Every now and then, it'll flare up. You'll be bedridden for months tossing and turning; you're vomiting out of every hole; you've got all kinds of toe problems; three kinds of gout in all of your extremities; gangrene I'm pretty sure is one of 'em. You don't want this to happen. Let me tell you, it's not good. So you definitely want them to find a cure.

So we have to convene—it's like a Stephen King kind of thing, where every six months we have to meet in a diner and sort of rub up against each other to increase our level of infection.

KS: I was gonna say that each of you worked in different departments of the film school, and each of you, you know, you're touching the celluloid, you're getting the stuff developed, and it gave you this disease. Five different strains of it, but you've discovered that if you have the other four people's strains in your body, then it keeps yours at bay.

DM: Right, and we create Voltron.

KS: Yeah, exactly. You become some sort of a disease-bearing, bloated, Voltron-man.

DM: And everything, all of the symptoms of one disease, are the opposite of the other. So when I have the chills, I want the guy with the fever to come over and give me his disease. So they just cancel each other out.

KS: So you're fine.

DM: Yeah, We're fine.

KS: Good, I like this disease.

DM: Okay, @TPARADOX clarifies...

KS: You can meet a lot of good people that way.

DM: ...Yeah, you make lifelong friends. Well, the life is not long, but it's really rich.

KS: You had your friends there.

DM: @TPARADOX clarifies the muddy-van story. He says, "I was returning home from a grocery run my mother sent me on." At three in the morning? Really?

KS: Wow.

DM: What's so important at three in the morning?

KS: Cigarettes.

DM: All right, she was expecting you to not come back, you realize. She sent you out for cigarettes hoping you wouldn't come back.

KS: "Take the construction road."

DM: @THEGREENAVENGER says, "I just assume that the worst is going to happen, so when it does, I wasn't guilty of hubris."

KS: I guess. But does it have to be unexpected? I mean, let's say that you decided to build a machine.

DM: Now hold on...

KS: I don't need to create a metaphor here. We are already there.

DM: No more of these machine stories.

KS: No, no, it doesn't matter. You're gonna build a machine to knock down a wall in your kitchen, all right?

DM: Okay, yeah, absolutely.

KS: And you're so smart, you built this machine, there is no *way* it can go wrong. And you bust the wall down—and inside of the wall is a machine that makes hornets.

DM: *(laughs)*

KS: Okay, so if you assume "this isn't going to end well," is that any less hubristic? You know what I mean? I think it's as bad—I think it's just as bad.

DM: Yeah, because why would you do it, if you see where it's going and you're like, "There is no turning back now. This is going to end badly but I've got no choice but to press forward." That's not much less hubristic.

KS: If you kept going, you thought it was gonna turn out okay. That still counts. That's hubris.

DM: *(laughs)* You wanna play another call?

KS: No one is above the law. Oh yeah, go ahead.

DM: All right, here we go:

> *Hey Tweet Me Harder, this is Erika Moen, and I just two days ago had a hubristic misstep. First thing—there's three parts to it, and I hope I don't run out of space or my time runs out, anyway—the first thing is, I get up before my husband does, and I don't like to turn on the light because I want him to sleep and not be disturbed by me getting up and getting dressed and stuff, so I always get dressed in the dark. Uh, so I put on my clothes, put on my shirt, my shorts, socks shoes, head out, bike down to my office, and I'm in the elevator, going up and I look in the mirror. And I realize that I haven't actually put on my shorts, I've put on my husband's boxers. And they are really blatantly boxers. In the dark, you know, similar enough, but in real life I'm definitely wearing the husband's underwear.*
>
> *So, I guess I'm kinda stuck in that for the rest of the day. And that's part one. And then, lunch time rolls around, and I have this bag of vegetables. I've never bought one of these before, but you buy a bag of veggies and you put them in the microwave in the bag and they kinda, like, get steamed from all the heat.*
>
> *So I put those in and I go outside to get some Parmesan cheese, and I'm thinking I'll go down to the pizza cart and I'll get one of those little packets, you know, I'll totally pay for it. And I get down there and there is this huge line, and instead of little packets I see that*

they actually have just a shaker of cheese. It's right up at the front, in front of everybody. So I was like, "Well, fuck. It's not like I'll get a packet anyway. Might as well just bypass the line and go get some Parmesan cheese to put on the vegetables that I am microwaving upstairs in the office. So I take out one of their little paper napkins, and right in front of everybody in line, right in front of the lady serving the pizza, I start shaking out this Parmesan cheese into my napkin, like a hobo, wearing my husband's underwear on the outside. Everybody's looking at me; I get kind of self-conscious; I, uh, decide maybe I'll go back inside.

And I get up the elevator and there is this really strong cabbage-fart smell really thick in the air, permeating the air, and the closer I walk down to the office--mind you, this is around a corridor, I have to walk around two corridors to get to the office—and the closer I get the more intense this old-shoe cabbage-fart smell gets. I go back into the studio—and this is a studio, there's a lot of people we all share space with, and they're all like, "Erika, are these your steamed vegetables?"

And I guess I had waited too long to actually use these veggies or something, because as soon as I open the bag the smell erupts. They had already smelled kinda rank anyway, but I opened that bag and it was just heinous, and it filled up the whole floor of the building and it was all my fault, and I had my little paper napkin full of my hijacked Parmesan cheese, wearing my husband's underwear and that was my biggest set of three mistakes that I made, all in one day.

DM: All right. (*clears throat*)

KS: Oh my God.

DM: I'll actually forgive you. I don't think the Parmesan cheese is too much of a problem. I think that's actually understandable. Obviously, you look a little weird in the whole boxer-short situation, Erika, I don't envy you there...

KS: But that wasn't even the end of it. She gets to a place where they were like, "What did you do?" And she looked inside the napkin and in the napkin are her husband's shorts, and she is wearing the cheese. That's all she's got on, is cheese. How did *that* happen?

DM: And so, she's wearing the cheese, and so the only thing left to do is open up the bag of vegetables, step inside it, close it after her, and just try and go to sleep.

KS: (*laughs*) And just sleep peacefully. Sleep it off inside a bag of vegetables.

DM: Just hope nobody notices.

KS: What a sweet image. But, you were saying?

DM: Erika, this really sounds like a horrible situation, and I don't envy the embarrassment you must've felt. Um... I don't see the hubris, though, to be perfectly honest. This seems very well-meaning from every angle that I can see it. You don't want to wake the husband, so you don't turn on the light; you wanna have vegetables so you just have vegetables, you know, you don't realize—you don't want to waste old food so you're just, "All right, I'll have some vegetables."

I'd like to see, though, Kris, if you can mine some hubris from this story.

KS: I think the greatest downfall of this entire story is the absence of light in this living space: She didn't look at the vegetables; she didn't look at the clothing. There's all kinds of problems that could've been solved by *looking* at things, and maybe the hubris is the, uh, "I don't need to look. I got the whole thing down. I know what clothes look like. I'll put it on my body. Whatever."

DM: "It's fine. Everything's fine. I don't need to check the expiration date. It's probably all right."

KS: Yeah, that's rough.

DM: Thank you for calling in. Your life sounds horrible.

KS: *(laughs)* Let's not talk again.

DM: *(laughs)* So @tparadox follows up on the Twitter. He has an update to the van story. "She sends me out when she thinks about it, and usually she thinks about it at night." He goes on to say, "I enjoy night driving anyway." So this guy is looking for excuses to just cruise the open road, in the middle of the night. I understand.

KS: Maybe he's addicted to these types of mistakes, is the problem. That was his only—

DM: He's looking for opportunities to get himself into trouble, subconsciously, because he wants the thrill of being in danger.

KS: He owns *hubristicmistakes.com* and he has been waiting for a chance to tell these stories.

DM: And his hubris is thinking that we're not gonna track him down and sue him for plagiarism. I'm very litigious.

KS: *(laughs)*

DM: That's my hubris, in thinking that I can bring a case for something like that.

KS: "There is no way that this guy made it up on his own. Like a week before that, I used this phrase."

DM: "We put it on the Internet, it's on Twitter..."

KS: "The record is there. It's like a poor, poor man's poor man's copyright."

DM: All right, we have @MIDDLERUN tuning in on the Twitter with more details about looking for a job. He says he looked for work—I'm assuming it's a he—but in a small town, jobs are hard to find. So thought that he could find a job. Was unable to. Probably didn't look terribly hard, although I'm sure he asked around vaguely.

KS: Or whatever.

DM: ...Goes on to say that in Australia, if you earn under $18,000 before uni, you qualify for "youth allowance," so you get free money.[22] He earned $9,000. So I guess this is a system—I've heard about this before—where you have to prove that you are not an imbecile. And then they're like, "All right, well, you did some good work and here's some money to help you go through university." @MIDDLERUN failed to prove that he was not an imbecile, so we are sorry that your life is horrible.

KS: What a pressure-cooker. Although, I mean, I guess that takes the pressure off the school, because let's say you get a job so you can get paid at university, and you end up making fifty grand that year: You're not gonna go to school. You're gonna go do that, and then they don't have to pay for you.

DM: You think so? You think they're trying to give you an incentive to go join the working world, so that they then do not have to pay you?

KS: Yeah, that's one student they don't have to worry about giving money to.

DM: I think we need more clarification on the rules, because I feel like it doesn't work that way. I don't think that the Australian government is trying to scam its citizens. But *our* government is trying to do that all the time,[23] so...

KS: I think Australians are sly, crafty people that like to steal, and make money the easy and quick way, and be lazy.

DM: Yes. This is true.

---

22 "Uni" is, of course, the Australian colloquial abbreviation for "unitard," meaning the compulsory age when all citizens must begin wearing a unitard under their clothing. So everyone's ready in case of an emergency. Really, it's a pretty good system.
23 "Our" meaning, of course, the Belgian government.

KS: This is my take.

DM: ...After all, they are all descended from criminals.[24] Is that racist?

KS: I would like to mention that I've been there, so... I have a little more knowledge than, perhaps, some. Also, I was 12.

DM: @Pvponline says, "All the money I spent for dog training on an 8-year-old dog that we never trained right when he was a puppy, and expected them to fix." So, this is the hubris in thinking it wouldn't be that hard to train this dog, I guess?

KS: I guess.

DM: "Old dog, new tricks," It's a whole *saying,* Scott.[25] It's in the *language.*

KS: It's an *old* saying, too. It's not new.

DM: Well, actually, let me ask you this: Some of those old sayings—there's a lot of truth to them, as we've seen, as Scott can testify with his wallet—but what about the ones that are proven wrong? How are people supposed to know which old wives' tales to believe and which have the kernel of truth, which is why they've sustained for so long? Who's the authority?

KS: I don't know. I'm trying to think of some dumb ones.

DM: There's all that stuff, like "don't swim a half-hour after eating." And, all right, you get a cramp. I understand. I guess. But it's not that big a deal, I don't think, really, unless maybe my hubris is thinking it's not a big deal, of course, and then I'm gonna go—I'll go swimming right now. After dinner, I'm gonna go to the Y, check it out. Put the lie to it.

KS: And then you just get hit by a train in the ocean.

DM: A train, in the Y swimming pool. My hubris was, I thought the train tracks didn't run through the Y.

KS: But they really do!

DM: @Stewped, on the Twitter, gives us some more information about art school. He says, "After four years there, you realize that all the students that drew really well all taught themselves, and they confirmed it."

KS: You know what, though, that's not unheard of, because when I went to school—I went for computer science. And, I mean, I learned stuff, but I learned how to *think,* more likely. I didn't really learn computers. I already knew that going in. You know?

DM: Right.

KS: And at the time I was really upset because I thought, "I'm not gonna use all this theory." And I didn't. But I think it was part of learning *how* to think about things, you know?

DM: So what I wanna know, @stewped: did you get *anything* out of art school at all? Or is it just the student debt? Clearly your position is that the student debt is not

---

24   Oldest racist-Australian joke in the book. This was delivered ironically, if you can't tell. Jeez we hope our cred is intact after you read this!

25   The aforementioned Smurf-show collaborator.

worth what you did get out of it, but what I wanna know is what you *did,* even in a small way. What you got out of it. So please let us know.

KS: Oh my God. All right, here's a tweet: @cozo1 says, "I dropped out of high school two days before graduation to prove a point. Missed out on ten grand in scholarships and grants."

DM: Yes! More details, please: What was the point? Tell me what the point was, please. Now here's the thing...

KS: "School is a bunch of BS. I'm gonna rock and roll!"

DM: ...If I'm gonna wager on what the point was, this is my suggestion: it's "I learned all the stuff, but I don't need your stinking degree. Your *certificate.* It's just a piece of paper. I'm an intelligent individual." Let me know if I'm right, 'cause I've heard this argument before.

KS: Yeah, I mean—I think that, unfortunately, the only important part *is* the piece of paper. That's the only thing that matters.

DM: When we graduated at my high school, they gave us the diploma. And then they gave us a *miniature* diploma, wallet-sized, laminated, presumably to carry around with you, should you ever need to present your diploma.

KS: But you can get those at gift shops. You can get those at Niagara Falls and stuff. That's just *there.*

DM: But mine had my name on it.

KS: No! You know.

DM: It was exactly a miniature high school diploma, from my high school, with the signature and everything.

KS: What kills me is that it's not like college. It's a high school diploma.

DM: Yeah, I know. Now here's the thing: in the town where I grew up, I'm wondering if a high school diploma was sort of, like, "Yeah, you're gonna need to prove it to me, because I know where you're from. You're gonna have to produce some sort of physical documentation that you actually graduated high school."

KS: Or graduated from *our* high school. It's like being a Freemason: you're loyal to the town.

> Hey, *Tweet Me Harder* guys, this is Dave. I got a story.
> Hubristic missteps. Back in, like, high school, my mom and
> my sister had a huge blow-up, and it ended up with my mom
> kicking my sister out, basically, and my sister split, right?
>
> Couple minutes later, my mom looks at me and she's like, "Go get
> your sister. Talk to her. Talk some sense into her. Bring her back."
> And I'm like, "All right, I'm gonna do this, Mom. I'm gonna save
> the day." And I bolt out of the house. And my mom had told me
> where she saw her heading, and so I bolt out of the house, jump
> the wall, I'm running down Beach Boulevard—this is in California,
> by the way—and I'm running down the street like I'm on fire.

*And I can see her! She's, like, maybe 75 yards down and I'm
just running like I'm on fire. And I pass this huge crowd of
people. They're looking at me like I'm crazy. And I get like,
I don't know, ten yards away from my sister and I realize
that it's not her. So I stop, take a couple puffs off my inhaler,
and I waddle, waddle back to my house in defeat.*

KS: In my formulation, that story was like, "10 yards away, I look, it's not my sister, and I'm fully nude, and uh…"

DM: "I'd expected she would be happy to see me. That was my hubris. That she would be excited to see me fully nude running down the street after her. You see, we had some history. It was nothing weird! We like to compare and contrast."

KS: "I find it's the purest, most natural expression of caring, is to appear nude. Because at what other point are you more vulnerable? And in this way, hope to draw her back to her family."

DM: "To express that you trust her."

KS: "To express the trust as being given to her. And it didn't happen that way. I was beaten. It was very painful, but I didn't learn my lesson. And that's the hubris part."

DM: "Then I saw someone else that looked similar to her on the other side of the street, so I went sprinting after her. She got into a bus. I ran at 45 miles per hour, for 18 minutes. I broke the land speed record. Turns out it was a dog with a strange haircut."

KS: *(laughs)*

DM: Isn't that how those stories always end? It's like: you see them on the park bench, but it's just one of those dogs with long silky hair?

KS: I don't know.

DM: Or is that just a *New Yorker* cartoon from 1974?

KS: I think that's the one, yeah. I think that's the only time it's been used. It's a very formative—it's a peek at your development where you're like, "That must be a thing. Oh, it was just this guy."

DM: @Cozo1 contributes some more information about dropping out of high school. "I was going to fail AP English, despite passing the exam and gaining the college credit the class was for. This was after a miserable couple of years in this school district, and they wanted me to take summer school for an AP class." So he took the AP exam, which is obviously not for class credit. He got the college credit, but he was going to fail the English class, which was obviously was graded separately, based on assignments.

It sounds like @cozo1 has had problems with school. And we've all had problems in high school at different times. Myself? I had an unfortunate hairstyle in high school. Kris, I hear that you were hated by everyone.

KS: Basically.

DM: This is just my supposition, from knowing you now.

KS: *(laughs)* Yes, it's lessened, but now it's just a mild dislike.

DM: Now everyone has just some mild feelings of revulsion.

KS: Anybody I talk to, at some point, they're gonna go *(shuddering noise)*—just a shuddering.

DM: "Did you feel a chill?" Or, "Did someone drop a scorpion down my shirt?"

KS: "I just felt nauseated for a second, but I think it's gone now."

DM: All the bacteria in someone's body sort of roils as you walk by. They feel the energy sweeping through their body, and all the little guts of it just kinda swim around...

KS: "I just felt sick for a second."

DM: Everybody's just sort of *(gurgling noise)*, "I got a little bile backup in my esophagus. I don't know what that was."

KS: "I don't know what that is. Hey, you wanna hang out later?" "Um... no, I got stuff to do."

DM: "I gotta, uh... I gotta wash my, uh, the inside of my mouth out from all the, all the acid taste."

KS: "I gotta do something that *doesn't* involve my entire body protesting."

DM: "I gotta go remodel my kitchen with a hammer."

KS: *(laughs)* That's gonna be the callback forever now.

DM: This is @sentry_. He has a 48-part novel.

KS: Oh my God. How am I missing this one?

DM: It's not on the hashtag, it's just on the Twitter.

KS: Oh.

DM: The prologue starts with a reminiscence of his early days. I think this requires a dramatic reading.

KS: Okay. Well, you wanna mount it off?

DM: "To this day, I still remember the occasion when I was young and in a daycare center, and made an absolute ass of myself. Every morning, we were given a bowl of dry cereal, and a glass of milk. I absolutely hated to drink milk, but was able to tolerate it in my cereal..."

KS: It's good so far.

DM: "For some reason, we were not allowed to combine the two, but I always sneakily managed to do so, anyway. One morning, the birds were chirping. I was strolling along the meadow lane. I was so worried about being caught that I tossed the milk into the bowl as quickly as possible, only to discover that this morning they'd given us *apple juice!* It's one of the few embarrassing memories I still recall. Not profound or life-changing to be sure, but the earliest instance of hubris, thinking myself so clever, and presumptuous."

KS: You know what? Is it his avatar that's doing this?

DM: It's not helping!

KS: He's looking off into the distance like, "Let me tell you a tale. A seminal tale of why I am the way I am and why I am so great."

DM: "Behind these sunglasses lurk the eyes of a poet."

KS: "Tonight you will learn, and you will be a part of my legacy."

DM: "Come! Let me tell you all the tales of my life, starting with the first, from preschool. Tomorrow, tale number two, from Day Two of preschool, and we will continue so on and so forth, keeping an equal ratio between the day the tale occurred and the day the tale is told."

KS: "It would appear that the blanket I was using at naptime—as I settled in, the tag was near my face and not on the other side. I had flipped the blanket 'round."

DM: "I didn't know! I was only a child! But you see, I felt I was too clever for the school system: 'I'll merely invert my body! That way, I will have my head far from that scratchy tag.' But oh! In my hubris…"

KS: "Ooooh…"

DM: "My head was so near the feet of the other sleeping children, I paid the price that day, sir! I paid the price, in odor!"

KS: "Are you gonna order, or what?" He's at a restaurant.

DM: "Uh, yeah, I'll have the—how about a large fry?"

KS: "We're all out."

DM: "Ooooooooohh, this tale shall be told…"

KS: "Another story!"

DM: "… Twenty-five years from *this* day, by the time I catch up to where we are now. I will make careful notes. Your name please, for the record."

KS: Oh, here is another Twitter: "A personal fear of mine," @GRANULAC writes, "Fell off my treadmill at the gym, in front of dozens of mean, fit New Yorkers, while trying to smoothly shuffle my iPod." Yes, I don't like it.

DM: "Smoothly… everyone is watching you, seeing how gracefully you shuffle the iPod."

KS: They're pointing at their ears, like, "Take your headphones off." And when you take your headphones off, they go, "Don't like the song?" "Nah, I just thought I'd go forward, past this one." "Eh, why is it on your iPod if you don't like it, heh?"

DM: *(laughs)*

KS: And then some guy in the back: "Yeah!"

DM: "That's a good point! Why is it on your iPod? That's valuable space you could be taking up with something good!"

KS: "Uh… look, you guys, I don't want any trouble." "Look, all I'm trying to do is teach you about iPod optimization, all right? You're wasting a lot of valuable drive space on that. It's only 8 gigs, it's not the biggest thing in the world, you know what I'm saying?"

90

DM: "Look, you think you can fit your whole collection on there, you're sorely mistaken. Unless you got a small collection. I'm not saying there's something wrong with that, but maybe you don't like that much music. Maybe you only like a few different types of music. Is that okay? I mean, I'm fine with that."

KS: "Why should you not like all kinds of music?" "Yeah!"

DM: "Hey, I heard this guy's got bad taste!"

KS: So, I don't ever fidget with my iPod on a treadmill, because of terror.

DM: @Sentry_ chimes back in here. He wants to clarify. He's like, "Listen, my life hasn't had that many embarrassing moments."

KS: Of course it hasn't! You've had a wonderful life; that's why you had to dig deep.

DM: "So many triumphs! So many victories!"

KS: "I couldn't have been more than three or four, when I distinctly recall thinking that I was regularly getting away..." I expect another one. We'll wait. We will wait.

DM: We're just having fun. We're just having a good time wit' youse.

KS: We're just having a good time! I don't know what you're talking about all the time. Oh okay, here we go. The rest of the ellipsis: "...I distinctly recall then thinking that I was regularly getting away with some kind of excessive feat."

DM: Oh, man.

KS: Ahhh, @sentry_.

DM: So, Meredith, I want you to follow up on the treadmill story.[26] How mean were these New Yorkers? Like, were they mean just 'cause they were like, "Hey, we're big guys, we're bulky." Or were they actually mean, in that they laughed at you when you fell off?

KS: When she falls off, some guy goes, "Ahhh, my workout!" Like, he can't finish now. "Ah, dammit!"

DM: I can see, like, the treadmill sort of sweeps her backward and her feet go flying in the air, and her arms go flying, and the iPod comes up but it's attached to her ears still so it's yanked on the cable, and the iPod comes back down and hits her on the top of the head. Meanwhile, her face hits the treadmill and goes rolling off the back—

KS: And the guy behind her is like, "What is this, amateur night? Dammit, my rhythm! What about my lats?"

DM: If we've learned nothing else, you people are a bunch of hubristic jerks!

KS: You can't get anything done!

DM: You know what, is that mean? Is it mean to call everyone jerks? You guys are just human. You know what? I think it's only fair to end the show with examples of hubris from our own lives. Isn't that fair?

KS: Oh, man. Yeah, I mean that's totally fair.

---

26 How'd we know @granulac's name was Meredith, you ask? Well, who doesn't?

DM: All right, go ahead and start.

KS: *(laughs)* Why are you trying to generate one? I'm gonna...

DM: I'm trying to think of one.

KS: I gotta dig deep. I wasn't ready for this. I should have been. I knew what the topic was. I think most of my mistakes were not like, "I'm too good for this. I'll show 'em," and then I blew it. Mine were like, "I hope I can make it through okay!" And then I don't.

DM: Right, because of your critical lack of confidence.

KS: Yeah! Is that hubris? Is that reverse? Like, "I'm *not* good enough to solve this." And sure enough, it didn't work.

DM: Meredith writes back to say, "It took 15 seconds of stares before a single guy helped me up." So, yeah. She's on the floor. The treadmill is moving, you know, violently, and messing up her hair. It's still kind of churning her hair like an eggbeater. The iPod has fallen off its plug and is ten feet away underneath some other treadmill that some guy is just banging down on, over and over and over, so she can't reach her arm under it. Uh—her legs are both broken, kneecaps are shattered, blood oozing all over the concrete. She's got her hoodie twisted around herself so her arms are totally inaccessible. The cable had been threaded through her hoodie and out her sleeve, but now it's wrapped around her neck. She's choking. Her skin is turning purple.

KS: And the people behind her are like, "I'm in the zone. I'm in the zone. Don't break it, don't break it. I'm almost there. I got my third wind."

DM: "I understand what they mean about the runner's high."

KS: "I will check on her in 4 minutes and 30 seconds. That's all I got left."

DM: @Sentry_ writes back. He says: "Let me ask you. You're not at all fascinated when you're able to trace one of your current personality traits to an early memory?" I actually think that is true. That is fascinating.

KS: I'm super fascinated.

DM: Some of the things—I'm fascinated by everything you say, @sentry_—some of the things that I hear, or I find myself doing in life, are things that I realize I have been doing my whole life without realizing.

KS: Oh man, that is the most paralyzing kind of discovery, I think.

DM: Why is that?

KS: 'Cause I'm hypersensitive about that, like, making a realization like "You know what, I think I'm kind of a jerk when I say that to people. I better stop." And then a little bit later I'll dig deep and I'll go, "You know what, I've been saying that for the last twenty years." You know? "No wonder these particular people didn't like me, in that situation I remember didn't go very well." Yeah.

DM: It can have a negative consequence in that way, where you realize, "Yeah, I've been a jerk in this way my whole life." And there have been moments when I have had that realization as well. But I think it has positive effects too, because it makes me feel like I'm doing the right thing. If I'm doing this, it's not happenstance that I've stumbled into this particular thing. Whatever it is. Because it's something that my whole life has been leading to. It's, when you add up, you know, *a* plus *b* plus *c* throughout my entire life, it can only add up to this.

KS: Yeah.

DM: This is the result of that equation. So it makes me feel like, you know, things are moving forward purposefully.

KS: Yeah, I mean, sure. I guess.

DM: I can't speak for you, obviously.

KS: No, I don't...

DM: As we've already talked about: microbacteria in other people's bowels recoil at your presence.

KS: They just rotate in the colon 180 degrees. The cell walls shift and then...

DM: The person is just wrenched around.

KS: It is an unnerving experience, this sensation. You don't want that to happen.

DM: @MILESGROVER writes on the Tooter: "Isn't it hubris not to think of a good story for your own show?" Yeah, we didn't think that we were gonna have to come in here and bare our souls.

KS: You know what it is: I thought I could generate it. I thought that, given enough time...

DM: You thought that you were clever enough and you could just go on the fly.

KS: ...I could figure it out. That is a good description of my failing. 'Cause you know what? *Many* is the time I've done a live show and thought—you know, *now* my expectations are very low. So I go in there and there is no more hubris anymore. But at the time I was like, "I'm a funny guy. I can get this done. Put a microphone in front of me, it's gonna be the best." And then you got twenty people listening and they are miserable. Just wondering, "Why? Why did I bother?"

DM: Like everyone listening now, right?

KS: Yeah. But they toughed it out for almost an hour now, so we must've been doing something right.

DM: @STEWPED, by the way, clarifies his story about art school. He says, "I'm angry now. I can't think of any techniques I learned. At least nothing I'm using currently." So that is... I still don't know... I think that's more *tragic* than anything. You know? Our heart goes out to you.

KS: Yeah. I don't know that there is anything to take away from that.

DM: Yeah, life is miserable. Everyone should feel bad.

KS: Feel bad for him, 'cause that's pretty rotten. I'm ashamed on his behalf.

DM: Yeah, you know what? I was in a situation recently where—I don't know, maybe this is my hubris. My hubris is, I feel like, "Everything can be fine! Everything is great in life!" I've known people that have kind of fallen apart after an unexpected tragedy...

KS: Yeah.

DM: And you look at them afterwards, and it's, you know, it's a difficult thing to— man, this is gonna be a funny show—it's a difficult thing to endure, and you realize, "Ah, it's never gonna happen to me. It's fine. I'm never gonna have to deal with anything that difficult." And that's all of our hubris, right? We all feel like we're invincible.

KS: Yeah, I mean, I guess if you wanna be a bring-down. Absolutely, that's what the deal is.

DM: I have a boxcutter over here somewhere. I'm just gonna cut my wrists right now.

KS: Just hurt yourself. Why not?

DM: Hold on a second, let me find it. *(scuffling around)* Ow! How do people *do* this?!

KS: It's really coarse—it is not a sharp blade.

DM: Jeez.

KS: It's for cardboard.

DM: Yeah, I was cutting boxes all day.

KS: Let's close the show out with, let's see here, @SENTRY_ writes us back. He says, "I don't think hubris is a very regular quality in this day and age. People can be a lot more cautious and..." And that's all the time we have, everybody.

DM: *(laughs)* No, he goes on to say, "People can be cautious and apologetic nowadays.

94

Embarrassing stories happen frequently, but I don't see hubris all that often." I think it may be generational. I think we have a group of people that are, on the whole, more cautious in this generation, just because—I don't know. It's a mix of being more considerate, perhaps, and aware of other people's feelings. And also not wanting to make waves. People are afraid of offending other people.

KS: Yeah, but I feel like that's exactly why it's hard for me to find a hubristic mistake on my part, because that would require... At least early on. Maybe now that I have some confidence, I could find one, but all of my saddest, most embarrassing stories are from my youth. And they are all like, "I hope she likes me." And then I didn't have the courage to ask her out, and that's it. That is where it stops. There is no "I thought I was the best, then I found out I was not the best."

DM: Actually, that brings up an interesting point. This is a tangent that I'm gonna go on for just a moment if you'll indulge me. "I think she likes me." This is a thing I wanna unpack a little bit, because...

KS: *What if she doesn't?*

DM: ...I'm starting to get a little bit tired of stories—and I talk about movies in particular, but it could be any kind of story, or any sort of narrative, where the romantic plot involves a person trying to win over someone that they think is cute—could be either gender: it works both ways in different types of movies. And then does whatever it takes to win them over, and there is no attention paid to the qualities of that person. They are just this sort of romantic object to be fixated upon.

KS: Yeah.

DM: And this is the kind of story that on the one hand, I think is retarded. And on the other hand, I think it's dangerous, because it sort of puts a weird mentality in people's minds in some way, where that's all it takes. "Well, look how beautiful she is. She is my perfect angel. If I leave love poems on her BlackBerry, she will know it's me, and I will win her over with my romance."

KS: "With my romance." I don't like those because not only is it not realistic, but the women in there, I don't like. It's like, "She's a workaday woman. And she's adorable. And look at her, she's singing and she's not even realizing she's singing while she's at the gym, and it's so cute." And, you know, in real life you'd go, "Goddammit, lady, stop. What is wrong with you?"

DM: Well, I'm talking in particular about *Paul Blart: Mall Cop*.

KS: Oh yeah. Well, you know.

DM: This was a movie I saw on an airplane, by the way. Now here's the thing...

KS: Don't analyze that! There's no... *why?*

DM: People work hard to make movies.

KS: No they don't!

DM: No one sets out to make a bad movie.

KS: Oh, all right. I guess.

DM: But, why did that woman in that movie—what was her quality that made her a desirable romantic interest?

KS: You'll forgive me if I haven't seen this particular piece of cinema.

DM: I know you have.

KS: No I haven't! I wasn't on that flight.

DM: Come on, I thought you went and saw it with someone.

KS: No, I didn't. *Paul Blart: Mall Cop?*

DM: I don't know, dude!

All right, let's end the show with this: @cozo1 says, "I have a friend who thought he could eat a heaping spoonful of cinnamon and ended up coughing and vomiting for 10 minutes." *(slow clapping)*

KS: Nobody every wins with that. And he tried to wash it down with a gallon of milk.

DM: A gallon of milk, and a whole nest full of hornets.

The Hogwashers

4

KS: Hello and welcome to Tweet Me Harder, the world's first, best, only and last talkback-enabled interactive audio podblast. I'm Kris Straub.

DM: I'm David Malki !

KS: You're listening to the fourth episode of the show. As you listen, you can participate from your Twitter account using the tag #TMH4. And, you can also subscribe on iTunes by going to *tinyurl.com/tweethard.* Or click the RSS feed at our site, *tweetmeharder.tumblr.com.* David, how ya doing?

DM: I'm doing great. I'm really excited for this show—I thank all of you for tuning in and, I—boy, man, what a great day. Monday. Start of the week. Haven't done a show this early quite yet, and I'm excited to see how it's gonna go. Is everyone tuned in? Or have they all got a case of the Mondays?

KS: Ah, yeah. *I* got a case of the Mondays.

DM: Are they going to go into their little box with their blue blanket? And they kinda pull it over them but they, you know... they sleep in a box?

KS: *(laughs)*

DM: I never got that Garfield bed thing. What's that box he's sleeping in?

KS: Yeah. He wraps himself like he was a loaf of bread.

DM: Right. Is that a lasagna pan he's sleeping in? I'm not really sure. Now, here's the thing: I understand cats like sleeping in boxes.

KS: Yeah.

DM: But, this is something that has been referred to as his *bed.* What? I mean, the cat beds I've seen are, like, pillows, and soft...

KS: Is it healthy for Jon to maintain his addiction to lasagna by making him sleep in a pan?

DM: "You can have it every moment of the day!"

KS: Like sleeping inside of a crack pipe. That's not healthy.

DM: *(laughs)* Yeah. Jon is an enabler here. This cat—I mean I understand that part of the Garfield mythos is, the cat likes to eat. Like, that's a bedrock principle of Garfield. I understand that wholeheartedly.

KS: Yeah.

DM: But lasagna is such a weird thing for a cat to eat. It's got a lot of tomato sauce.

KS: Has anybody ever tried to give a cat lasagna? Because I imagine—just diarrhea immediately.

DM: Now, the mythos is that Garfield was born in an Italian restaurant.

KS: Oh. *Wow.*

DM: He's got that tomato stuff in his bones. This implies two things. One: Anyone born in an Italian restaurant is susceptible to Italian food. Whereas I would think it would be the opposite. I would think—like, I worked in my parents' auto shop for a long time, and I don't really like being in auto shops very much.

KS: And you don't want to eat, uh, auto parts?

DM: Yeah, I don't want to eat oil filters. And number two: this suggests that you can make a cat like something by simply making sure he is *born in that place.*

KS: So I could make him born in *shut-the-hell-up* and then he'd just be a really good pet.

DM: Right. Yeah, you could get him to be born in a convent where they have a vow of silence, and then the cat would never speak. I don't think—I mean this is specious reasoning, but this is what it implies. That's the logical extension of it, isn't it?

KS: So you're say that Jon created Garfield. *Made* him like lasagna. When Garfield was a kitten, he used to, like, kick Garfield's tiny foot at Odie. Just a picture of a dog.

DM: Because Odie was Lyman's dog. Odie was a late arrival to the scene. So maybe he just made Garfield exert that primacy?

KS: *(laughs)*

DM: He's like, "I want you to be the master of everything. And I'm going to be your patsy." You know, "I'm going to be very passively guiding you towards this behavior." Because he has to make Garfield think it's his own idea.

KS: Right. But it's almost like this entire universe, you're saying, has been generated to uphold these tenets of Garfield. You know, when Lyman wasn't needed anymore, he went away.

DM: That's right. He delivered his dog, served his purpose, and now he has vanished.

KS: Right. And all the other animals that we don't really—I mean, I don't even know if they are in the strip anymore.

DM: So what you're suggesting—let me get this clear—what you're suggesting is that if you keep walking down the street you'll see, just, the road fade into a grayness. This is *The Neverending Story*'s Nothing.

KS: Right.

DM: The world only exists insofar as it serves the purpose of Garfield and his sphere of influence.

KS: Right. Now, you might be able to find the road to the airport, because doesn't— Jon visits his mom on the farm.

DM: Right, and there's a whole extended universe from the cartoon series which does not really appear in the strips. Binky The Clown, the TV studio—but those streets look awful familiar. Every time you saw that animation, it's the same city sidewalk.

KS: It's almost like it was a loop. The same block over and over again.

DM: Exactly! Because Garfield can only conceptualize four houses at a time.

KS: He's certainly got a cat's brain. He can't imagine the variety of architecture that you might find in human dwelling. In a city. So, yeah. I'm saying that it's an exercise in solipsism. The whole strip.

DM: We have a Twitter from @ERTCHIN saying "doesn't that also suggest that the vast majority of Americans should love hospital food?"

KS: Why, because they spend a lot of time in—

DM: Because they were born in hospitals.

KS: Oh, I see. But they don't give you that food as an infant.

DM: Yeah, but did the Italian chef give Garfield the lasagna? I guess maybe so. I don't remember the story particularly well.

KS: (*attempt at an Italian accent*) "This cat, he-esa gonna die, I need to feed it a-lasagna."

DM: (*making his own attempt*) "I don't have anything to feed him. All I have is-sa this lasagna that the customer rejected because it was too full-a salt. I give it to the cat."

[BOTH HOSTS LAUGH]

KS: "This will help him live."

DM: Why? What would lead to the chef giving the cat lasagna? That doesn't even seem intuitive at all!

KS: Maybe the chef was trying to make him *into* lasagna, and he didn't bake correctly and he lived. He survived.

DM: So Garfield was supposed to be the *ingredient* for the lasagna, is what you are saying.

KS: Yeah. It's kind of a womb metaphor.

DM: Is this why the chef is always trying to raise his own litter of cats?

KS: —He was trying to find his way back.

DM: Yeah, you're right—because otherwise that's a health hazard. You don't want animals in your restaurant.

KS: That's not okay.

DM: (*Italian accent again*) "The price of a hamburger is-a so high, I will raise these animals in the back and when they get big enough"—*and* that's why, see, Garfield was one of several generations of cats that had been bred—

KS: As *lasagna cats.*

DM: Here's the thing—how old is Garfield? 1976? He's thirty-three years old. So frickin' fat, right?

KS: Yeah.

DM: These cats are genetically selected and bred to be like the cows that get slaughtered for food, where they just eat and eat and eat their whole life and get fat and fat and fat—and then they're slaughtered.

KS: It's true!

DM: And that's what Garfield does. That's all he knows. Just eating, eating, eating, but the ax never falls.

KS: So you're saying, Garfield never got to fulfill his purpose.

DM: Yes. Exactly!

KS: And that's why he's so miserable.

DM: That's why he hates Mondays. He doesn't have a job! What? He's going to go to work? No!

KS: I think part of Garfield is that he knows he was supposed to die.

DM: Right. Because here's the thing: Sunday is a big day for big family dinners. And every Monday is another day that he's still alive. He was *not* put into lasagna this week, and so he's trying to figure out, where is my purpose—And he doesn't know. It's all subconscious at this point. It's all sublimated. And so it's "I'm alive another week. My purpose is unfulfilled."

KS: He starts to get real down on Sunday nights and it just progresses on into Monday. And you know what, he probably stayed up all night just racked with guilt and bad feelings. He doesn't even understand where they come from. He can't eat away the pain. That's not going anywhere. So he just stays in bed all Monday.

DM: Exactly. And then his only friend is Odie, who's trying to sympathize—because he's just a dog, dogs just like everything—but the dog will never understand. A dog doesn't have a complex concept-holding brain like a cat does.

KS: Well, yeah.

DM: And so Garfield knows he can never explain this to Odie.

KS: He'll never make that connection.

DM: Right. So he just hits him in frustration, like, "Ah, you will never share my pain. So I'm gonna make you feel a different kind of pain."

KS: Why did Jon want to wade into all that? Is there a point?

DM: This is what begs the question: is Jon the mastermind here? Or Is Jon just the patsy? "Oh, I'm gonna take a cat," without realizing the severe psychological problems?

KS: I don't think Jon knows that Garfield was a meat-cat. I think that's a surprise.

DM: The "surprise" implies that he's going to find out someday.

KS: Well, I mean, I don't know what he would do at this point. I mean, he's Garfield's owner and he loves him. He's not gonna—it's like adoption.

DM: He's probably *not* gonna kill his cat and put him into *any* sort of food. Lasagna or not. Or even just Hamburger Helper.

KS: The sad thing was, if Garfield was given the opportunity to be cooked in a meal—an Italian meal—that he would fight it, you know? He wouldn't realize that that's actually what his heart was crying out for.

DM: This is a profound metaphor. For the one thing that would make him whole, he doesn't recognize because it seems like it would be so harmful.

KS: Yeah, but I mean, it would, literally, be harmful though. But that instant, you know, before he loses consciousness because of the heat, in the oven, would be the greatest moment of his life.

DM: Do you think he would ever become cognizant of it? Or is it just a longing that can only be satisfied post-mortem? You know, it's like his ultimate purpose—

KS: I don't know...

DM: Is it something that he will actually recognize when it happens? He just knows he's unfulfilled in the meantime.

KS: No, no, no. His fulfillment is only brought about by his destruction, and so I don't think he would be able ever consciously acknowledge it. You know?

DM: So the best thing he could hope for is just to come up to neutral. Just come up to *not*-despondent.

KS: Yeah. And I would say that that was aptly portrayed by Lorenzo Music, and then later by Bill Murray in the movies. Talk about rising to the level of just average emotion.

DM: *(laughs)* Very deadpan.

KS: Yeah. Of course he can't feel joy.

DM: Did you know that Lorenzo Music's performance in the *Garfield* cartoon was an imitation of Bill Murray?

KS: That's so weird.

DM: Yeah, he was imitating Bill Murray because he was also a voice actor in *The Real Ghostbusters,* if I understand that correctly.

KS: Yeah, no he was—he absolutely was Peter Venkman. Yeah.

DM: And of course also in... *Gummi Bears.*

KS: Oh yeah that's right. So this guy's made a career out of, just, aping Bill Murray.

DM: Well, Bill Murray wasn't a Gummi Bear, was he? Or *was* he?

KS: No, he wasn't, but Lorenzo Music was the fat bear!

DM: You know what I'm picturing? I'm picturing Bill Murray, like, in the live-action *Gummi Bears* movie, directed by Harold Ramis.

KS: *(laughs)* Look, it's a trifecta! *Ghostbusters, Garfield,* and now, the last role...

DM: *Gummi Bears.*

KS: *Gummi Bears.*

[*ACCORDION STING*]

DM: Even though this week is very early, something has yet happened.

KS: Right.

DM: And that is, I have been loaned a car. This is a... I don't even remember what it is. A Mercury Mariner! Have you ever heard of a Mercury Mariner?

KS: No. And I think I know why.

DM: No, I haven't either.

KS: I don't like that name.

DM: A Mercury Mariner is basically a... I think it's a Ford Explorer. You know how cars—

KS: They're on the same chassis.

DM: Same exact car, different name plate. And you know, a lot of GM cars are the same. Like, Chevy and Pontiac are the same car, Isuzu and Mitsubishi are the same car. Or, excuse me—Plymouth and Mitsubishi are the same car. All this kind of stuff.

KS: Yeah.

DM: So I think a Mercury Mariner is a Ford Explorer.[27]

KS: Okay.

DM: But that's what you can picture. This is a hybrid. And someone has loaned me this car for the week. This is some sort of social media networking, uh, outreach program.

KS: For cars.

---

27 We later learned that the Mercury Mariner is actually a clone of the Ford Expedition, which is an Explorer all bloated up on protein shakes.

DM: For—yeah. Retained by the Ford Company.

KS: Huh.

DM: And they said, "Hey, you like to Twitter and blog and stuff. Do you want to drive a new car for a while?"

KS: *(laughs)* That sounds like a sitcom.

DM: I don't really want to call it a quid pro quo, because I don't think I am expected—

KS: They're not getting anything out of this at all, is what you are saying.

DM: I think I would be within my rights to give them nothing.

KS: They kinda did it to themselves. They were hoodwinked by you via them, is what you are saying.

DM: Right. Exactly. I didn't even actively try and fool them, it was somebody—you know what I think it is? This is what I legitimately think is going on. Because this is not the Ford Company; this is some company either hired by, or that have sort of farmed themselves out, to Ford.

KS: They're researching advertising venues.

DM: Yeah, it's like, "Let's get our tendrils out there in social media." Like there's someone in some boardroom that's using the word MySpace inappropriately, and it's like "All right, we've got to get on all the Twitters and all the Faceboxes and—"

KS: *(New York accent)* "The kids are on the MySpace. Don't you want your business to get myspaced? All right, come on, I'll show you how."

DM: Exactly. And it could literally be some, you know, hip social-media company guy walking into a Ford boardroom and saying, "You're on the verge of bankruptcy and I can solve your problems—and it's MySpace!" And so there are these guys that are like, "All right. Yeah. That sounds pretty good."

KS: Like "I don't wanna get fired. I wanna seem like I'm thinking about this."

DM: I'm not sure what the vectors are. Like who is hoodwinking who into believing that there is any sort of actual value to this whole endeavor.

KS: It sounds like both parties in this deal believe the other party has way more power than they actually do.

DM: Yes. Exactly. That is exactly was happens.

KS: It's just a huge bluff.

DM: And everyone has somehow been convinced, either through some systemic informational failure, which is what I suspect, that I am a valuable person to be involved in this operation. So they have loaned me this... I think it's—I've got this info sheet. I wanna say it's a 2009. Might be even a 2010. Uh, Mercury Mariner. "2009 Mariner Hybrid 4-wheel drive."[28]

KS: Okay.

---

28 Later on the social-media company working for Ford wrote and asked, "Did you ever blog about or mention the car?" David sent them the link to this episode. Perhaps they appreciated his candor! However, he has not been offered any further cars to test-drive.

DM: "Ice Blue clear-coat."

KS: Yeah!

DM: It's a bright color.

KS: They had extras lying around.

DM: Yeah, well, I don't think anybody is buying them. To be perfectly honest. So I have this car. And so I've driven this car, now, for I think—maybe six miles in the course of my errands today.

KS: All right.

DM: And from my perspective this is a pretty good trade, because my alternatives are: *(a)* walking or *(b)* my twenty-seven-year-old Mercedes.

KS: Uh-huh.

DM: And my twenty-seven-year-old Mercedes is…I mean, it's a good car. It's a solid car.

KS: It's a car that your father got when Mercedes called him and said, "Hey, if you make a bunch of phone calls—if you send a bunch of telegrams—"

DM: Back in 1982. Right. Exactly. "Let's sit down over a phosphate." And here's the thing about the 1982 Mercedes-Benz. If you are going to drive a car from 1982, Mercedes is probably about your best bet. And let me explain why. Do you remember what the cars looked like from, like, the early and mid '80s?

KS: They're real boxy.

DM: Yeah. If the cars from the '90s—like, the analog is that they are a used piece of soap. The cars from the early 80's look like they are building materials. Like they are two-by-fours and cinder blocks.

KS: Yeah.

DM: Like if you ever had the Happy Meal from back in the '80s when it came in a box. You know? It's like you could imagine that's the shape of a car.

KS: That was the concept at the meeting. One of the first ones.

DM: Yeah. "Kids love Happy Meals. Now, I wanna see this operation extended to car format."

KS: "It's called synergy. Can you imagine seeing this thing at a drive-thru?"

DM: So there's definitely a sort of unattractiveness that pervaded all domestic cars in the entire decade of the '80s and even the '70s—the '70s were a little more stylish. The '80s was an unattractive-car decade.

KS: It's funny that you mention that, because, yeah, in the '60s they had all these round forms and in the '50s you got cars that look like, you know, sci-fi rockets.

DM: Right.

KS: And then we get into the '80s it's like "No curves! Forget it."

DM: *(laughs)* Yeah, I wonder what that thinking was.

KS: "I'm going to stack things on this vehicle."

DM: Exactly. Is it so you can balance your groceries on it without sliding off? Because you can't do that with a 1999 Taurus.

KS: No.

DM: They'll slide right off.

KS: Yeah, you're losing all the eggs.

DM: In fact, we have a tweet here from @ERTCHIN that says, "When I think Mariner, I definitely think about driving on dry land." So yeah, excellent name. Excellent name.

KS: I think about a soccer mom wearing boat shoes and just, pretending. And hoping.

DM: "I'm gonna go for it"—SPLASH. Cut to: The insurance company calls her up, it's like, "Explain it to me again..."

KS: "The adventure? All right..."

DM: So I've been driving the Mariner and let me say, it's a good car—I mean again, when the alternative is the twenty-seven-year-old Mercedes, very few cars are not a step up in terms of, like, friendly driving experience.

KS: Yeah.

DM: I cannot say that the Mercury Mariner is the best new car on the market, because if you let me drive like a Toyota or a Honda or an Isuzu or even, you know, some sort of Chevy Malibu or something—it's *all* going to be a step up. Regardless of what it is. So. A couple of things that are really interesting, though, about this particular car: I've been driving this car, again, six miles total. Maybe 5.8, but I had to find parking, so maybe six miles.

KS: Okay.

DM: And, it's got one of those things where, you know when you back up it has a sensor? And so it beeps. And it beeps with increasing frequency the closer you get to whatever obstruction is behind you.

KS: That's nice.

DM: So you know how far you are.

KS: Okay.

DM: So I'm like, "this is kinda cool." So I'm driving this thing; first time I'm backing up. It's going, "beep beep beepbeepbeep" and I go, "What? No backup camera?"

KS: *(laughs)* You're so spoiled.

DM: I'm totally entitled at this point. It's like, there's a decal on the window, "Sirius Satellite Radio." I'm like, "Awesome. Let's check out this Sirius Satellite Radio." And here's the thing about this car, this car has, like, multi FM/AM tuners; it's got the CD players; it's got this—like a built-in iTunes hard drive kind of deal— where you can load your CDs onto your car's internal jukebox.

KS: Jeez.

DM: This has an aux input for whatever external device. It has a USB input for your iPod so it'll actually display the thing on the iPod, you know, the track name and everything. This is a high-tech car. And I'm looking at the Sirius Satellite

Radio— "Ugh, subscription is not active." I'm like, "Oh come on. This is B.S." Where the alternative on the twenty-seven-year-old Mercedes is: I have a radio with a dial.

KS: You're like, "I'm blogging about this. Where's my Sirius?" You know what, though, as far as the rear-view camera? The pricey thing is the screen. That camera is not going to cost more than, you know, what is it? Fifty bucks? And that's retail. They get those for ten.

DM: Well, this already has a built-in screen that has a GPS map display—also has all your radio navigation B.S.—on the screen itself. So they're not lacking in LCD touchscreen technology. This is built into the dash of the car already.

KS: Yeah.

DM: Maybe the backup camera is some sort of patented device from some other company. They can't just slap it that into every car. I thought you just took whatever you wanted, because you know, once one guy comes up with a good idea everyone has to compete and make their same version of it slightly different.

KS: Yeah, I really think that's the case. I'd be surprised at the restraint—and possibly the laziness of Mercury—that they would not incorporate that idea into this car.

DM: Exactly. So, Mercury Mariner is down one strike for no backup camera. And also, we got @ALOHAAIRCARGO on the Twitter, who says, "The Mariner's more apt to look like those amphibious naval boats that drive on land that people convert for tours." Yeah. The Duck Tour! This car is The Duck Tour 2009.

KS: "I've got my Mariner. You know what? They took out the functionality where it can go in the water, but it's still a Mariner, baby."

DM: "Has not been tested, however. So I may go off the pier before the day is over. Just to try it out."

KS: Yeah. @SCIENCEDOG tweets, "Is the parking brake an anchor?" I like the idea of them going like, "Mariner, adventure, I like it. Let's make everything in the car look like a boat part!"

DM: This is what I want to see. I want to see—I wanna be looking, like, straight-on across the street as the Mercury Mariner tries to parallel-park, right? Pulls up alongside. Backs up. It's got, like, the "beep beep beep beep." Backs up very slowly. Fits into the parallel parking. Right?

Goes into Park and then you see underneath—KUGHHHH—anchor just drops onto the concrete.

KS: (laughs) Do we have—you know what? Do we have to have beeps sound like beeps? Can we make them like a seagull call? To kind of go with the theme.

DM: Yeah. Or can we have some sort of a sonar ping.

KS: Ah! Can the car have a periscope instead of a rearview mirror?

DM: @SCIENCEDOG also says, "Ford has a patent on the door unlocking/locking keypad. No other company can use it." So this Mariner does have the door unlocking keypad. In fact, I used to have a '98 Taurus; had the same thing. And that, I tell you, *that* is a handy little device. You don't need your keys. You can open your trunk from the keypad. It 100% eliminates the problem of locking your key in the car. Just—that problem is *gone*.

KS: What if you have anterograde memory loss?

DM: Um. Okay. The problem still exists.

KS: Let me ask you a question, since I've never played with those things. It's a keypad, right?

DM: Yes.

KS: It's got five buttons?

DM: It's got five buttons, yes.

KS: And the numbers are all doubled up on there?

DM: Right. It's just like—you know how there's three letters on each number, if you're doing phone dialing?

KS: Right.

DM: It's the same concept.

KS: Yeah. So in other words, if your code is 2-4-6, I could put in 1-3-5 and I could get into your car.

DM: It's the same code. Right.

KS: Somebody work that math out. I feel like that is not as secure as ten buttons.

DM: Right but it's still plenty secure—it's still *five-button* secure. Which is sufficiently secure, I think.

KS: Are there a lot of numbers in the code?

DM: There's five numbers.

KS: It's like, "it's a one-number code."

DM: Yeah. *(laughs)* You just hit a button until it works. Look, it's a five-number code, and if there's five possible digits, it's five to the fifth. That's plenty of combinations.

KS: Nah, that's five to the...That's five factorial, right?

DM: Five factorial? Is it? Five times...

KS: I think it might be.

DM: No, because you can repeat. So it's five times five times five times five times five.

KS: You know what? I could brute-force that overnight. I could get into your Mariner. How about I take home a *Mariner* tonight?

DM: Okay, you're going to get into the car, and then what are you going to take?

KS: I'm going to grab that sweet, ah... you know... Anchor?

DM: Anchor? *(laughs)* I wake up in the morning, you're still lugging the anchor down the sidewalk. You're carving a furrow in the street—

KS: Still just *thrilled* with my get. I'm just like, "Whee-OW!" Pumpin' my fists.

DM: @Hugparty says, "The door-unlocking keypad is great when you're visiting a jail, because you're not allowed to have anything with you." Yes. So if you were breaking out of jail, you have no keys in your pockets, you can just hit the keypad, hop right into the car and you're off to the races.

KS: "We took the liberty of changing your keypad code while you were in jail. It's the equivalent of keeping your key. We didn't want that security hole, basically."

DM: You're going to have to file to find out what your actual, new keypad combination is. Because you have to file all these forms, it's like you're knocking on the window, "Excuse me? Excuse me, trying to escape. Ummmm, locked out of my car. I'm sorry. I'm really sorry to bother you. I know it's three in the morning."

KS: It's kind of like you going to another government agency, but you don't have a valid driver's license, and they're not going to arrest you in the parking lot because "hey, I saw you pull in but you don't have a driver's license." They just wouldn't care. You're allowed to file those forms. Like, "Are you supposed to be in the jail right now?" "Yeah... technically." "All right, well..."

DM: It's like one of those things where, like, the illegal immigrant can go to the hospital and they are not supposed to report their immigration status. They're supposed to concentrate strictly on giving care. It's the responsibility of the immigrant, to actually, you know, put their real name on their form, versus Juan Morales, or whatever the alias is.

KS: Yeah. Which might also have been his name.

DM: Yeah. I'm assuming that's his name. Because he's an honest guy, hardworking fellow, pays his taxes. He's going to put his true name on the form. I dunno what you're insinuating.

KS: He's just here legally.

DM: (*laughs, then transitions to a rueful sigh*)

KS: So, but here's the question—

DM: (*in some strange accent*) "I used to be the President, now I am..." (*gives up on accent*) "...ugh, valet parking." Yes. What's the question?

KS: So you've got this car, right? And you're going to enjoy this car for a trip.

DM: Yes.

KS: Then when you go to give it back, are you going to be upset about that? Do you think you're going to miss it?

DM: I feel like if I had to give it back today, after driving six miles, I would already miss it.

KS: Mm-hmm.

DM: Am I going to buy a 2009 Mercury Mariner? No.

KS: That's the question. You just miss *newness*. But not this car.

DM: Exactly. I just miss *something*. Something that works.

KS: "I miss quality."

DM: And this just happens to be the one that they gave me. It doesn't have to be this per se.

KS: "I miss *function*."

DM: Yeah. That's exactly it, because—here's the thing about my Mercedes. In my garage, in my apartment building, there's one of these gates, you know—it opens up and it leads you down into the garage. We have the parking spot right next to the gate. So, once I had my door open, and I was digging in the car and someone else comes into the garage. The gate catches onto my door and pushes my door further open, beyond where it's supposed to be, and kind of breaks it. And I had to take the gate off the track to free my car door.

KS: Jeez.

DM: So now, when you open my car door, the bracket—some internal bracket—is bent. Such that it requires sort of jimmying open. It will open partway, and then you have to yank it a little bit, and it goes "Rrrrrrr-CUNK," and it goes kinda past the rough part and it opens the rest of the way. So it makes this bizarre noise every time you open it.

Compared to this: With the Mercury Mariner, it *didn't* do that. So that's one step in the right direction.

KS: The door in the Mariner literally just disappears because of nanobots that will deconstruct it, then reconstruct the door when you're done.

DM: Right. That would be a plus-one. But just straight even is, "Eh, door opens like a regular door. No problem."

KS: You don't have to worry about how it works.

DM: Right.

KS: The guys at Mercury figured that all out.

DM: The guys at Mercury, who are really just the guys at Ford...

KS: Or whatever.

DM: All right. But, enough small talk.

KS: Enough small talk.[29]

[ACCORDION STING]

DM: So, we do have a theme for the show.

KS: Yes. We did have a theme.

[ACCORDION STING AGAIN]

DM: There it is.

KS: Ha ha. I already did it.

---

29   Short-lived attempt at a catchphrase!

DM: Oh, did you really? Awesome. Last week we asked you for questions and the problems in your life that we could solve. Many listeners and tweeters have—is that? That sounds kind of weird. Tweeters? No.

KS: Tweetsmen.

DM: Tweetsmen, yes. Many tweetsmen and tweetswomen have—

KS: Tweetswomen.

DM: Have tweeted us their twoblems and we are going to twolve their twoblems.

KS: *(laughs, then sighs)*

DM: Aagghhh.

KS: It's adorable.

DM: Is it?

KS: No.

DM: No. Ah. So. Let's twolve some twoblems.

KS: *(laughs)* You changed the consonant pair.

DM: A little bit, it's a little bit different.

KS: So what do we have? We got any voicemails?

DM: Yeah, let's start with a voicemail.

> *My question is, I would like to get some advice on what to write in my resumé. I am trying to get a new job because, apparently, my job right now is "hating my job." I am looking for advice on what to put in a resumé, applying to the Science Museum of Minnesota at the accounting bureau.*

DM: Okay. So question number one to this person is: What are the requirements for the job you are seeking? It seems like that would be the logical place to start with what to put in your resume. Right? Does that make sense?

KS: Yeah. Like, I mean that is something I suffered with for a long time—was just putting every damn thing I did on the resume, when nobody cares.

DM: Right, it has to be relevant. And it has to be interesting. I was once in a position where I was talking to someone who was, at that exact moment that we were having a discussion, they were looking through resumés that had been submitted for a job opening. And one person had submitted an eight-page resume with experience going back to 1964. High school jobs. And it's like, "No. Just—what?!? No." And that's the extreme example, but the more sort of to-the-point example is, you know, you don't wanna leave out things that are significant, but your judge as to what is or is not significant should be: the people who are filling this job—what are they looking for?

KS: Well, let me ask you this. Is it a detriment to be applying to this museum in Minnesota, the accounting bureau, with interesting things on your resume? Maybe that's a negative. Because it doesn't sound interesting to me.

DM: *(laughs)* Okay, so if her previous job was hating her job, let's try and figure—let's spin that into, what are the things that she did at that position that could be relevant for this accounting position at the museum? So: "A strong emotional involvement with the position." I would put that.

KS: Yes. You'd say, in a way, she was vested.

DM: Right. Exactly. She had a personal connection to the work. Inspired a very intimate association with the position, with her co-workers.

KS: Yeah. I mean, it begs a little bit more detail, because I don't know if she hated her co-workers or just the job. But in any case, you could say that she did have that close emotional bond with the work itself.

DM: Right. Exactly. Now, @THEGREENAVENGER says, "Excellent computer skill, great experience, good organizational skills and attention to detail." This sounds like this is going to be a generic plug-and-play. In every resumé, just put that in. That's fine.

KS: I would never hire this person.

DM: Because that's boring. You want someone who can get emotionally invested in the work, right? You want someone who's going to come to work everyday and is going to either, like... Okay. Let's just put it plainly: You don't want someone that's going to have a gut-roiling revulsion to the job. But, you kind of do want someone who's going to leap into action and they love the work so much. So when you see strong emotional involvement with work, at least you're going to hope that's gonna be good kind of emotional involvement. Right?

KS: I'm going to go with you on that. I'm going with you on that but I'm going to take a little bit different tack. Okay? Top of the resumé, you got her name. Then next to that: clip-art sunglasses. And then, next to that, in quotes and italics: *"Shake things up."*

DM: *(laughs)*

KS: Right?

DM: Yes. Absolutely. 100%. I am a hundred percent on board with that.

KS: Think outside the box.

DM: All right, next question.

> *All right, so I have some advice I'd like to request. How would you go about, like...what's a good process for naming something? Whether it be a comic or an art project. Typically people advise getting names that are, you know, easy to remember or catchy, but like—How would the creator know that something they've chosen is, like, of a good quality? Is there a way, a possible test or should you just go with your gut. You two seem particularly good at this so I was thinking maybe you'd have something good about it, say.*

DM: Okay. So this guy has something he needs to name and he wants—he doesn't want us to name it, he wants a process that he can plug in to use whenever he *does* need to name it. He wants to be able to have a step-by-step, follow-the-recipe procedure.

KS: Yeah.

DM: Is this something that you think we can provide, or should we just name his thing?

KS: Um. Well. I think we can provide a recipe. And then we can go ahead and name it.

DM: All right.

KS: Yeah. My recipe is just take two smaller words, stick 'em next to each other.

DM: That's pretty good.

KS: And you've got a winner!

DM: I would say, step two: look for that thing on Google.

KS: Oh yeah. That's always next.

DM: Yeah, if there's anything like that, skip it. Next words. Make a new combination.

KS: Change the word a little bit.

DM: Right. Because every, I don't know... probably every dictionary word, for the most part with the exception of medical terms, are probably—that domain is already taken. But there's going to be an exponentially larger number of possible domain names from a combination of two shorter words.

KS: I guarantee you—this is off the dome—I guarantee you, *chefbulge.com* is ready for you to use for your business.

DM: "Chefbulge" is ready. What else we got? *Grapenasty.com*. Probably free.

KS: Yeah that's probably... and you know what? That really invokes a logo. Like, I can see it already.

DM: Yeah. It's a grape looking kinda nasty. Sunglasses.

KS: Probably flippin' off the viewer—with a gloved hand. I'm fine with that. There is nothing wrong with that.

DM: One of those Mickey Mouse gloves with the little seam and the three lines.

KS: With the three seams. Right. Exactly.

DM: Yeah. *Wheelbuckle.com*. Probably free.

KS: That's got a classy, old-world feel to it.

DM: Yeah, that's for your seventeenth-century cheesery.

KS: Yeah. There's nothing wrong with that. In fact, I would say just put an E-R-Y on the end of that. The Wheelbucklery.

DM: The Wheelbucklery... yeah.

KS: You might have a really classy kind of a cottage. It's sort of like the Cracker Barrel restaurants, you know?

DM: The Wheelbuckle Emporium.

KS: ...Yeah, that's gonna get driven right into the ground. But for the first couple years it's gonna be a great place to eat.

DM: Exactly. It's gonna be really good and then it's just gonna to be shuttered after eight months. But it's a good name. Wheelbuckle. I can see the logo.

KS: It is a good name.

DM: Okay, what else? *Treehonker.com,* probably free.

KS: That's... I'm sure that's available. I think that these are very—it's not hard to name. The problem is having—

DM: *Necklaceoftears.com?*

KS: Yeah. It's all gold.

DM: I swear, literally, a woman walked by outside my window wearing a big ol' necklace—it just came to my head. "Necklace of tears." Because she looked like she was having just a horrible day. Like, I wanted to comfort her, but her tears are probably acidic so I just skipped it.

KS: But you know what? This guy, if he names his service or product Necklace of Tears, you've got a demographic right there.

DM: Yeah, I see a black website. I see sort of purple-y, kinda drippy writing.

KS: Yeah, and the logo's way too big. On the website.

DM: She's in Times New Roman, white.

KS: In fact, the logo's really big and it might have a spiderweb behind it. And I think it has—somebody has autographed it? It's like it's a piece of art. And it might be blinking. I'm not sure.

DM: @Mmmatthew says, "Bathchowder." Yeah. You see? Absolutely.

KS: *Now* you're getting it.

DM: Now you're getting it. All right, so, step one, mash two words together. Step two, check it on Google. Step three, register the domain. If all those things happen totally unmolestedly, then your name is secure. Right? So let's name this guy's thing now. Now that we've put forth the recipe, I think it's time for us to definitively, and with a 100% guarantee that this is a successful name, put forth the name for whatever his project is. Whether is a comic, whether it's a book, or whether it's a restaurant or whether it's a new medical procedure—it's time to name it.

KS: Okay. The first thing that came to my mind, literally 40 seconds ago when you started that... was "hogtravesty."

DM: Good. The thing that came into my mind was "sternumwasher."

KS: Both useful in different ways. And you know what? Feel free to use either one, and let us know how it went.

DM: Or mix and match. You could go "hogwasher." Which might—that's not bad actually. That—I'm not 100% certain that that's going to be free. Hogwasher is a good description for someone. I would have that on my business card. I'm a hogwasher. The monocle and top hat, like, with a wink. Like (*goofy cartoon voice*) "Yeaaaahhh! I'm just joking because I'm going to give you a little bit of a hogwash. I'm an entertaaaaainer."

KS: And you know what? Another good sort of corollary tip is: If you happen to find that hogwasher.com is not available—which is a good name, it might be taken—drop that E. Like *tumblr.com*. Hogwashr. And now it's new-media.

DM: "Hogwashr." Yeah, now it's Web 3.7.

KS: So you're looking to the future. That monocle's got a laser sight coming out of it.

DM: @SCIENCEDOG says, "Your show needs commercial breaks so we can get food and use the bathroom." All right.

KS: Is that advice for us? Or maybe we should take that on as him asking us for advice.

DM: Okay. So how do we solve this problem?

KS: Well do you have any, like, empty bottles like around your computer? I know the type. You've probably got like an old Mountain Dew two-liter sittin' down there. You're not gonna finish that. It's flat. Just go to town.

DM: How long of a break does he want, if he wants to get food, and then digest the food, and then use the bathroom?

KS: That's like a five-hour break. That's an enormous break.

DM: Get real, @SCIENCEDOG! I thought you were a dog that knew science.

KS: *(laughs)* I thought you were a dog of science.

DM: All right, next question. We've solved that. @TWEETFAT says, "Advice? A bear is attacking me. What do I do? What do I do?" The answer is: Make yourself look big.

KS: Yeah.

DM: So here's a couple ways you can do that. You can write articles for e-zines. That'll increase the number of Google hits that your name gets.

KS: *(laughs)*

DM: You can make really nice business cards. Don't get VistaPrint cards. Get a nice card from a good printer. Use nice paper. Use a different kind of paper and/or a different printing process than other people's cards.

KS: So it stands out. In the Rolodex.

DM: Yeah. There's some sort of textured linen paper. Maybe use a thermographic logo. You definitely want it to be a slightly different presentation. So, that'll make you see important.

KS: And you know what? Kill a bear beforehand. Carry that around.

DM: Right.

KS: You know, don't get into the situation. The best medicine is the preventive kind.

DM: Right. Ounce of prevention.

KS: Yeah. You're a little behind, my friend. I don't know what to tell you, but that's more advice for everybody else.

DM: Yes. Kill a bear, carry it around. Get nice business cards. And submit your articles to e-zines, and you can just copy and paste other people's blog posts and put your name on them. That's totally legitimate on the Internet. Next question.

KS: Here's another one. I got @TSOKOLOFF saying, "I'm trying to organize a hiking trip, but my friends don't have hiking boots and I don't have any extra to lend. What can I do?"

DM: Well... where are you going hiking that you need boots? It seems like there is a lot of hiking that doesn't require boots.

KS: You could hike at the mall.

DM: Yeah.

KS: And buy some sweet boots while you're there.

DM: You could hike along a major thoroughfare. Then you could just use regular shoes.

KS: You could hitchhike. That's right in there.

DM: Ooooooh. Hitch-*hike*.

KS: You might not even need a car.

DM: Yeah, and you're going to fit in more with the hitchhiking culture if you don't wear shoes at all. Or, wrap your feet in rags.

KS: You know what? We make lemonade here at Tweet Me Harder. We are solving problems.

DM: You could also go to the park, and then you can have a nice little "hike" on the grass. You could take your shoes off and have a really enjoyable time.

KS: Here's another one. This sounds like a comment on the other. @CUBEWATERMELON asks, "What if the name of your comic is also the name of a type of donut *and* an Australian rugby team?" I wanted to mention that, because given the name is "cube watermelon" and the avatar is also a cubed watermelon, that that is the name of the comic. But apparently it's also the name of a donut and a rugby team in Australia.

DM: So here's my advice: Make your comic about a donut-eating Australian rugby team. This means you can tap into ready-made promotional opportunities.

KS: Yes. You know what? Early on they might even enjoy it...you approach them and say, "Hey, I do a comic strip. It's 'Cube Watermelon' and I couldn't help but notice that your rugby team is named the same thing—what a coincidence! Maybe we could work out something."

DM: Right. Or you could approach them and say, "I have made a comic about your rugby team. It is slightly veiled. So it's not a direct—"

KS: It's a little metaphorical.

DM: Yeah. "There's a lot of metaphor. Also... um, there's kind of a lot of donuts in it, but it's sort of a thing. You know? It's a spoof." Then you go to the donut company and you go, "I've made a comic about your donuts. And, um, there's some rugby in it, true, but some of the donut stuff is sort of symbolism—"

KS: Everybody's got to have a hobby? Am I right?

DM: "And, you know, it's about relationships and *Ethan Frome* taught us that donuts are very fraught with symbolism..." All right, next question. We've got @NATEMAN, who says "I can't decide what I want for lunch today, any advice?" Well, @NATEMAN, it's evening, so the answer is burritos.

KS: Whatever you have in the fridge.

DM: We have another tweet saying, "The leftover Chinese food in my fridge is two weeks old, is it still okay to eat? If not, what are alternative uses for it?" Well, it depends on the type of food. With Chinese food, you typically get eighteen of those little square boxes of white rice. Right? Steamed rice.

KS: That's right. And that's usually what's in there.

DM: Right. So, rice is one of those foods that—it only works as leftovers in very particular situations, because it's really dry. Like, if you try and microwave it or something, it gets really dry.

KS: You can put more water in there, though.

DM: Put a little water in there. Put a little Saran Wrap or something over it. Don't microwave it in the container, because, of course, the handles are metal. It's sometimes okay, but here's what I would suggest doing with the rice. What I would do first is melt some butter in the skillet.

KS: Yeah.

DM: Put your rice in there. Use kind of a lot of butter or margarine or whatever you like. Put the rice in there, roll it around in the melted butter and get it really coated. Get it kinda yellowy.

KS: Oooh.

DM: And that'll soften it up pretty significantly. And then, once it's sort of yellowy and really well coated, it's broken up from those chunks where—in the fridge it kinda gets in these square chunks and stuff.

KS: Yeah.

DM: Then get your whisked egg mixture. Add it to the rice. And then basically just make scrambled eggs. In and around the rice. And then you have sort of this rice-egg mixture. And then: this is going to be the blandest food ever. You'll have a really nice texture, but you can season it. I use a little sea salt. Or some sort of a flavored salt is going to really bring out the taste, and you can eat that with a fork or wrap it in burritos, have some nice breakfast burritos. That's my recommendation.

KS: I have two recommendations. If you don't want to eat it, if you've decided that this rice is too old for you to eat, two things. Number one: Leave it in your fridge, if you've got roommates, as a deterrent for them eating your food. They're not going near that. It'll teach them a lesson. And then number two—

DM: Wait. But they're gonna go for the good food. They're gonna be like, "Well, I don't want that rancid eight-week-old Chinese food, but look at this: last night's pizza. I'm gonna help myself to some of that."

KS: Put the Chinese food onto the pizza, spread it around. Don't let anybody get near it.

DM: All right. Excellent. Yeah, I didn't know if that was implied.

KS: Well, you have to kind of develop a taste for the old Chinese food. But if you really don't want to eat it, then take that brick—that cube of rice—and throw it at a wedding of some people you *don't* like.

DM: Yeah.

KS: Hey, you're throwing rice, right? They can't get mad at that.

DM: Right. In a frozen cube.

KS: Yeah, you could just say, "I didn't know." That's a good excuse for anything.

DM: All right. Problem solved. @POSIDUCK says, "What should I get my brother for his birthday? He doesn't like having too much stuff cluttering his apartment. Also, his birthday was a week ago." Well, @POSIDUCK, I sympathize with your brother. I don't like having too many things. Like, I think I have probably all the things I need, so I get uncomfortable when people give me things. Because I don't want more things, and I have no place to put things. And I probably don't want the things they gave me, because everything I want, I just get.

Now, you don't mention what kind of relationship you have with your brother. If it's an antagonistic relationship, you can get him anything and it'll go through those same steps that I just outlined. And that will encourage a sorta bad relationship to continue in a bad way. So I don't know if that is your goal. If that's your goal, go to Barnes & Noble, pick something off the 70%-off remainder stack, and say, "Ehhh, I thought you would like this." Your horrible relationship will continue unabated.

KS: I like those semi-used origami kits, and stuff like that.

DM: Yeah. Anything that requires some sort of crafting or one of those things where it's like, "Here's all the things you can fold with a dollar bill. Also, it comes with a dollar bill!" But you have taken the dollar bill, or you find the cheap one where the dollar bill is no longer included.

KS: Or, it's fake.

DM: Yeah. Or it's a photocopy of a dollar bill.

KS: Or it's just a piece of paper that says "front" and "back" on it.

DM: Yeah. It's a piece of graph paper with a penciled "front" and then you just kinda wrote "B-A-" and then you kinda got bored.

KS: And you're done. Ah. Here's one: @YOHOTHEPIRATE asks, "My husband has a huge handlebar moustache that I hate. Short of duct-taping him to the bed and shaving it, how do I get rid of it?"

DM: How do you... So you are trying to change your husband? Husband, right?

KS: Well, just the facial hair. Yeah. Trying to get rid of that moustache.

DM: All right. So this question is predicated on the understanding that we should help her do this.

KS: Well, yeah. That's the advice as presented.

DM: Here's the thing, my facial hair sympathies are well-known. I'm going to try and not bring that into this conversation, but the tone that she strikes her is something along the lines of, "My neighbor's car is really annoying and he runs over my flowers: what's the best way to smash his windshield?"

KS: Oh. I see.

DM: You see what I mean?

KS: You're not about to give that kind of destructive advice?

DM: Well, here's the thing and again, even the moustache itself aside, the idea that, because she doesn't like it, she has the right to just say, "How do I get rid of it?"

KS: Yeah. You know what though? I think it's about diplomacy. It's not about force. Maybe you could deny him sex.

DM: Maybe you could be very passive-aggressive.

KS: Right. Maybe you could be mean to his family. That's a lot of things you could do short of shaving it off. Let's face it. He's not married to that moustache. He's married to you. So if you make his life miserable, that thing is going to be gone.

DM: Right. I think, ultimatum time.

KS: Yeah. But passive-aggressive.

DM: Yeah. Passive-aggressive, probably the best way to go. So @POSIDUCK comes back and says, "He doesn't want books or CDs or anything, what are non-thing gifts? I want to get him a good gift." Okay, so, non-thing gifts that I have gotten that I have really appreciated in the past. One: I kinda like a donation to the Dian Fossey Gorilla Fund. Like, a gorilla adopted in your name.

KS: Oh yeah. That's a good one.

DM: That's a good thing. And there's always a risk with the charity gifts. Like, "In your name, blah blah blah has been donated." That's a little bit chintzy?

KS: This one's rad though. How about—

DM: But I think the gorilla one is one that—I got that and I was like, "Awesome! I do appreciate it."

KS: How about this: "In your name, Coldplay is now carbon-neutral."

DM: *(laughs)*

KS: Is that cool? Or not? That's pretty rad.

DM: Definitely find something that is in alignment with your brother's political beliefs. So yes. "Ron Paul Blimp: Five Gallons of Gas" certificate.

KS: I like it. It's like, "Thanks to you, these children in Honduras can now eat for a week and as a token of their gratitude, here is some stuff that they got," and it's just like tons of blankets and knit things.

DM: Right. Here's forty-eight destined-for-Wal-Mart-but-slightly-factory-reject shirts with the American flag emblazoned all over them.

KS: Incorrectly.

DM: The children in Honduras give them to you as an expression of gratitude. They were able to steal them from work. Or, legitimate sort of non-thing but very useful gift: Gift certificate to grocery store. Always useful.

KS: You know what else though? He's your brother right? Why don't you give him a dead-leg. Why don't you give him the old—why don't you tell him, circle sign? "Oh hey, what's this?"—BAM!

DM: Why don't you give him a noogie?

KS: "I love you, bro." There's nothing wrong with that.

DM: Next question...

KS: I got one. @HUGPARTY asks, "Dear Tweet Me Harder, how does one talk to cute guys on the bus without being creepy? Sincerely, Girl In Transit."

DM: I think—this is something that I imagine girls know by now, but the truth is, no guy will ever be creeped out by a pretty girl talking to him unbidden. That just does not happen.

KS: That's true. That's absolutely true.

DM: It's a phenomenon that does not exist in nature.

KS: Yeah.

DM: Now the reverse is—here's the thing—the reason that's true is because the reverse is almost certainly the opposite. It's not a 50/50, sometimes people are creeped out, sometimes they're complimented. It's basically: 100% of the time, guys like the attention. Nearly 100% of the time, girls hate the attention. So, this is not universal blanket advice for guys as well. But for girls—here's the thing—I don't know if you are attractive or not. Let's assume you are not hideous, because that's really all it takes. Attention being paid goes a very long way.

KS: She's pretty good-looking. But you know what else? I—this is part of a discussion I was having with some people, the idea that—let's say you've got a bet. "By the end of the night, this has got to happen." Do you think that it's easier for a woman to get laid than a man? Under any circumstance? I'm talking about two single people who are starting from zero. Like, "Here's your target. It's a bar. Get in there and figure something out." And I say yes. For the reasons you've described. Absolutely.

DM: Easier for a woman than for a man to walk in from zero and go home with someone?

KS: Right, because a man will go, "Well, maybe it's not ideal, but it's in my *lap* now. How can I turn this down?"

DM: Yeah. Absolutely. Absolutely.

KS: "This could be an omen of my life turning around. You know? This could be just the tip of the iceberg of good luck that's coming my way."

DM: Yeah. I think that is true. I can kind of conceptualize some ideas where, or some situations and scenarios, where it would not be a slam-dunk. But still, on balance, if it's a comparison, absolutely the girl has the upper hand. Like, if there's two bars next door to each other, the girl walks in one and the guy walks in the other. And we have the counter in the corner of the screen as they each, you know, try whatever they can. The girl is going to walk out of the bar before the guy. They may not—she may not be out of there in five minutes, depending on the circumstances, but she's gonna be out of there. If you do the trial 100 times, over 74% of the time, she is gonna go out of there before the guy.

KS: I mean, can you imagine a scenario where a guy goes into a bar—it's last-ditch-effort time. This is Hail-Mary time. He goes into the bar and he goes, "Hey. Who wants some sex tonight?" Is that going to work? That'll never work. I can envision where a girl goes in there and does that, and it'll work.

DM: Right. And here's the thing. She's going to wind up with a skeezo.

KS: Sure.

DM: Probably. But if that is not a problem that we have to deal with? And, she can sort of do it more subtly and wind up with someone probably a little bit nicer, because she'll probably have her pick, is the thing. If she is aggressive, then she will have her pick.

KS: Yeah. So don't be shy—not that sex was the goal, but it is a bus. So...

DM: Right.

KS: I don't want to speak to motive. But I think it's gonna work out.

DM: Yeah. In terms of particular techniques, I think we could recommend probably commenting. If he's doing something, reading a book, comment on the book. If he's got, looks like new shoes, comment on that. Like, they're conversation openers. All of these things require a baseline level of confidence that simply cannot be tricked or techniqued out of. You just have to man up and do it. So to speak.

KS: I, ah—related story. I was at a supermarket buying groceries. And a man was looking at the, you know, the cheeses. Not the good ones either.

DM: Right. Cheap ones.

KS: The Kraft singles and stuff, and some of the Mexican, you know, the very cheap, you know. That one in the round plastic.

DM: Oh, yeah, yeah.

KS: The one that kinda tends to get recalled. But he sees me passing by and he says, "Hey, is this good?" And I'm like, "What?" And he's like, "This cheese? I don't know anything about cheese." And he *drops* the cheese, like he fumbles it. And I sensed nervousness or something, and I go, "Oh I dunno." And he goes, "Hahaha," he starts smiling. And I'm like, "Oh my God. I'm getting hit on. By this dude."

And I just keep going and I'm like, "Sorry, I can't—I don't know anything about cheese." And then as I walked on I thought, what a wretched opening line. "Hey, do you like varieties of *cheese?* Because I'm lookin' for a good cheese. And if you're lucky maybe we could have it *together?*" I don't know. *Cheese?*

DM: Is the guy cute? Or... or what?

KS: Eh, no. Well, I mean, he was all-right looking, but I think the anxiety was what kind of—like the bottom of my stomach just dropped out. Like, "Oh wow, this is happening. What do I do?" I think I literally went (*up-and-down rollercoaster with his voice*).

DM: Well, you know, he's found you. On the Twitter, we have @BRETTDONNELLY saying, "How do I become the meat in a Kris-David sandwich?"

KS: Ha. Well, you need a little bit of that cheese. Lay that down—

DM: That's all the time we have, folks. Uh, I'm not going to help you... Just come on over afterwards, it's fine.

KS: It'll be good.

[CLOSING MUSIC STARTS]

DM: Well folks, you can subscribe to the show using iTunes automagically, *tinyurl.com/tweethard,* or you can click the feed link at *tweetmeharder.tumblr.com.* Next week's show: we would like you to send us your obligations. Stories of things you have been forced to do. Whether it's work, whether it's a task of some sort, whether it is—even someone has asked you to feel a certain way and you don't feel motivated to. Give us stories of obligations that have been thrust upon you, against your will.

KS: I kinda want to hear the caveat *for what period of time.* What was the longest obligation you've had to endure? That you really didn't want to do.

DM: We're going to have a little bit of a contest. To see who has endured some sort of obligation the longest. So, of all the voicemails, of the tweets, we are going to see who has endured the worst and I think it's going to be a weighted scale. So it's going to be the worst obligation for the longest time.

KS: Right. It can't just be like "my marriage, for twenty-five years." That's a real low-lying one.

DM: Right. We want to be entertained, and the whole point of this is that we are asking for you to share your tales, such that other folks in other situations can heave a sigh of relief and say "at least I don't gotta do that."

KS: Yeah, we don't wanna make people sad. We want to make people happy because *you* were sad.

DM: Right, so give that gift to the world with our next show. Use hashtag T-M-H-5 for that. Or you can, of course, call us at anytime on our voicemail line. Kris, do you want to give the voicemail line number?

KS: If I have it. I did—well, you know what, I don't have it. What a brilliant thing.

DM: All right. The voicemail is 206-337-8560. An easy way to remember that is: you can just remember the Cessna Skymaster was Cessna model 337; 1985 was the year I went on a trip to Vancouver; And 60 will be the age we get to when we finally get around to answering all of your tweets. So. 206-337—

KS: I *thought* that you picked that on purpose. Sounds like you just reverse-engineered that one.

DM: Right, yeah. So, 206-Skymaster, Expo Vancouver, and Tweet number. We hope.

KS: At age. Yes.

DM: Just type it right in and you'll get to us.

KS: And off you go. We'll see you here next week, everybody.

Feed My Turtles

KS: Hey, everybody. Welcome to Tweet Me Harder, the world's first, best, only, and last talkback-enabled interactive audio podblast. I'm Kris Straub.

DM: I'm David Malki !

KS: You are listening to the fifth show. If you want to participate live right now, you should use hashtag #tmh5.

DM: T-M-H-5. This is the show about lengthy obligations, so we want to hear you tweet about things that you've had to do for extended periods of time. The more miserable, the longer, the more horrific, the better, in my opinion. And we will—

KS: That's good advice anytime.

DM: Yeah, exactly. Anything that builds character is probably something that is good for you. I mean, your parents were right.

KS: I was gonna say, you are using, like, Dad Logic.

DM: Yeah. And there is a reason why dads throughout history have used that logic. There is a threshold that you pass at some point; I think you're probably about, what would you say, like, twenty-two? Where you go, "You know what? My parents were actually pretty smart."

KS: Yeah, I think—

DM: You remember that moment?

KS: That's true, yeah. Well, it's the moment when it transfers from dogma to belief, you know? Because all the time I thought my parents were smart, but I disagreed with them when it suited me. Because they can't be right all the time. But, you know—now they *are* right all the time.

DM: You're right. It's one of those things that there's a moment when you internalize it. And it's not even necessarily limited to, you know, your parental instruction. But any sort of thing where you come to the same conclusion that you have always been told. And you *understand* it, rather than just believe it academically.

KS: Yeah. Absolutely.

DM: All right.

KS: So we love our parents? Is that right? Is that what I'm hearing? Everybody loves their parents?

DM: Yeah, I will go with that. I'm fine with that. For the sake of the show, we'll...I just don't know who's listening.

KS: Yeah. Well, I know my parents are listening.

DM: I love my *mom*.

KS: But I think that my parents had an easier than usual upbringing in a lot of ways, because my brother and I really didn't fight back most of our childhood. And I think—

DM: You just gave in.

KS: Well, it wasn't even a giving in. It was like, "That is the thing to do. Why would you not do that? Mom and Dad said we should do that." But I think you could really find the point—I think she would really know to the month—when suddenly my arguments were like, "Wait a minute! I don't want to have to do any of this! It's my life!"

DM: Well, my life—speaking of the obligations, my relationship with my dad is—whom I love dearly, he passed away some years ago. He is very tied in with the idea of an obligation. Because my dad is very, very old school. Was the oldest of eleven children. They grew up in poverty, he had to go to work when he was in seventh grade, dropped out to support the family. He was basically a father figure to many of his siblings. And so, of our entire extended family, he's basically the patriarch, he was the guy. He was the one to set up his siblings in businesses that would fail, and he would sponsor them for immigration. You know, he was a very authoritative figure.

And he, you know—hard worker. He worked every day of his life. Started his own business in 1960, which is still operating today. A car repair shop. And, every day of my life, he expected me to work in the shop. Because that is what you did. And you had to earn any time away from work. And he was not the guy to stay there until ten o'clock at night. He always wanted to leave at the dot of six o'clock, and my mom, who handled all the books, the paperwork, that was never possible. So he was always very frustrated. His idea was you came in in the morning, you put in a full day's work, and then you went home and you were done for the day. And...so, he expected every Saturday, every holiday, if there was a day off school, the bedrock expectation was you would go in and help in the shop.

KS: Yeah.

DM: And if you wanted to stay home, you had to do chores. He'd say, "That's fine if you want to stay home, but you are going to be weeding this entire field." Or, you know, you are going to be—it was mainly pulling weeds. It was mainly pulling weeds, was the stay-at-home job.

KS: Was it a literal *field*?

DM: Yeah, well, my parents lived in this house, kind of in the foothills. There were some people who kept horses and stuff. We didn't, but we had about a three-acre plot, that was, my dad grew some trees and stuff there. He had a garden with some fruit trees. And there was this one field that would always be overrun with weeds that, he wasn't really trying to grow much there, but he wanted to keep it clear, because it was kind of a fire hazard. There's always brush fires that come through there, so the fire department would come up and cite you if you didn't keep your brush clear.

KS: Right.

DM: So the idea was that you had to pull the weeds, so then you would pull them out by the roots. And then they would not grow back, whereas if you had merely cut them, then they would just grow back.

KS: Sure, yeah. We've all had *weeds*, my friend.

DM: Let me explain the concept of a weed. A weed is a plant that you *don't want,* you see.

KS: You know what? I was always upset when I had to pull weeds when I was younger, and now I don't ever want to have a lawn again. But the idea that, you know, a lot of weeds are kind of attractive weeds. You know? Not all, but some—

DM: Well, that's the thing. If we were mustard farmers, if we were farming mustard seeds and mustard plants and dandelions, boy, it would be lovely.

KS: Bumper crop.

DM: People would come from miles around to see our array of yellow-colored mustard plants.

KS: Well, yeah. I mean, why not enjoy that?

DM: Seriously! They're wildflowers, right? This is nature giving us its beauty and its bounty.

KS: The bane of my dad's yard has always been spurge. It's a little tiny weed.

DM: Is that a word? Because it sounds like a euphemism.

KS: It's not. I hope I'm not messing that up.

DM: It sounds like, "I had to wipe up some spurge from the window."

KS: No, it's this little tiny-leafed, flat-growing weeds, and it grows everywhere! But you know what? I bet if you had a yard full of it, it would look pretty good.

DM: It's mainly the uneven coverage that—

KS: It looks terrible with a patch in the center, you know, but you let that bloom...

DM: Our goal—sometimes it was me staying home, and sometimes it was getting roped into some scheme. If I had a friend over or cousin staying over, like, it was typically my older cousins who would say, "I don't want to stay at home." Like, "if we are going to stay at home, I want to go play video games or go down to the corner store and rent a movie or something. We don't want to pull weeds." And so they were always trying to get out of this obligation, typically by saying "let's just *cut* the weeds. Doesn't your dad have a Weed Wacker?" And, you know, it would spiral. There would be eight iterations of complications of the plan, where it would be, like, the Weed Wacker needs a special type of fuel that's gasoline mixed with oil.

KS: It's like an adventure game.

DM: It is. It's like you had to go and find the scroll, and then talk to the people in the right order, and then it would end up with "We've used up all the string on the Weed Wacker because we let too much of it out when we were hitting rocks and bricks the whole time, and we tried to mix our new oil-gas mixture in the precise proportions, and we ended up destroying the engine." Then we'd try to go to the store, and get a new thing, and then we'd end up stealing a car, and running over a fence, and blowing out the transmission.[30]

KS: And all you had to do was pull the damn weeds.

DM: Yeah. And we could have just pulled the weeds. So this is one of these things where you make more work for yourself, not because your method is superior necessarily, but because it's *your* method. And you don't want to do something someone else tells you to do. You'd rather do something of your own volition.

KS: I've got a wild ride of a story to tell you on that score, son. And it happened just today. I went to a website. It was kind of interesting, somebody tweeted it. And it was about the idea of the inherent, the symbolic failure of the word "fail," you know, as it has become an Internet meme. How negative it actually is, how detrimental it is to actual discourse.

DM: Right.

KS: And I thought, this is actually really interesting. I actually really agree with this guy. So I go to his comments section, and, you know, a lot of places now you don't have to make a login. You don't have to log in and register for his site, you can use OpenID. And if you have a LiveJournal account, or a Flickr account, or any of these, you can use that as your OpenID. Or—

DM: That's like Big Brother, right?

KS: Uh, yeah, probably. I mean, eventually. Not yet.

DM: Right now it's like Little Brother.

KS: Right. Right now it's like Baby Brother that we love. We love him.

DM: He's so cute and adorable—

KS: He's always looking at our websites because he's cute. But then I find out, you can use your *own* OpenID. How'd he do that? Then I go to this website, and it's like, yeah, you can make your own *site* serve as your credentials. If you add some code, and you do this stuff. And I was like, "Yeah, I want my own website to be me on the Internet!" The whole identity thing, I don't want to have to log into Yahoo to say who I am. I *got* a website.

So I spend about...I spent about an hour and a half configuring this OpenID protocol, this server, on my machine. On my account. And I'm like, "Ah! Finally I got it working." After struggling with PHP and all this other garbage. Now I can finally go back to this guy's website, and log in as myself, who I *really am*, and leave my thoughts with you. So I write a big long post, and I hit "send," and it says "authentication failed—"

DM: *(laughs)*

---

30 This last part is true.

KS: —and I lost it, and it was a gigantic waste of time. It would have been fine if I used Google Mail to do it, but whatever. You know why? It's because everybody else's name was showing up as like, *google dot com slash mail slash a-bunch-of-numbers slash a guy's username.* I was like, "No. I want my name to be sitting really pretty right there. Maybe a link back to my site—"

DM: You spent all this time branding yourself.

KS: Well. You got to keep your eyes open for that stuff.

DM: Always got to watch to see when you're gonna get stung.

KS: Branding is where you *find* it.

[*ACCORDION STING*]

DM: Let me ask you this. Recently I went on this trip. I went to the Napa Valley. Had a great time with my wife. We had an anniversary trip. And we don't know anything about wine, my wife and I. We know zero. I mean, we know some of it's red. Others of it is kind of yellowy.

KS: You can drink it. Put it in your body.

DM: We know you can drink it. We know that people bring us wine when we have a house party, and we know that recently we have discovered that the proper response —because when people bring us wine for a house party, what we do is we just slip it into our wine rack that someone else gave us as a wedding gift, and we are like, "Awesome! Thank you so much for the wine." And then some other time in the future we might say, "Oh, yeah. This recipe needs some wine. Let's open up some wine." You know, for like a spaghetti sauce.

KS: "Is wine good for plants."

DM: Recently we discovered, however, is what you're supposed to do is when you are having a party and someone brings you a bottle of wine, you are supposed to then open the wine and serve it.

KS: Oh.

DM: This is a new concept. So we are sort of steadily increasing our wine-related knowledge. And, apparently, the thing that you do in Napa, is that you tour wineries. Which I guess makes sense.

KS: Yeah.

DM: We had always heard, hey, Napa's kind of a fun place to visit. And so we went there. And we're like, "All right, we're here. What are we going to do? Oh, wineries. All right. Awesome. Let's check it out."

This is what I want to talk about briefly. There is a point in your life at which you are fine with something. All the wine in your life—and this can be applied to wine, it can be applied to pretty much anything. There is a point in your life at which you are fine with all the wine you drink. You know maybe "I like this more than that." You don't know any of the terminology, you don't subscribe to any newsletters, you don't have any receipts from winery tours in your wallet. But you have no problem with the fact that you are lacking all that stuff.

KS: Yeah.

DM: Then, you go on the winery tour. You meet the enthusiastic guide who has so much to tell you about the difference between a Cab and a Pinot, and you see the video of the wine-making process. You go on a guided wine-tasting tour, where you learn to swish the wine around to aerate it. To put your nose in the glass like they do in *Sideways*. The whole deal. And by the end of four days, you feel like you are, if not a wine *expert*... there are unfathomable depths that can be plumbed on this subject, as many others, so you are by no means at the bottom of that well, which has no bottom. But you are at least dangling on a rope four feet into it, whereas before, you were ambling casually by the outskirts of the well.

KS: At the bottom is a dead guy.

DM: Yeah, the bottom is alligators.

KS: He's incapable of understanding anything.

DM: Yeah, it's the kind of thing where as you ratchet yourself further down into the well, you will starve to death before you reach the bottom.

KS: Yeah.

DM: And every subculture and every subject has these depths, and everyone—there are fanatics of every stripe. And through life, we seem to choose the things that we are fanatical about, and the things that we are fine not caring about. So here's my question. When you encounter one of these circumstances, where you learn more than you cared to know, let's say, or you just develop more of a taste for something that maybe you didn't before: are you ruining your life? 'Cause now you can never be satisfied with a simple thing that before was perfectly fine. Now, you can't—if you learn more about specialty cocktails—you can never just go out and have a beer. You have to have a $14 cocktail. It makes your life tougher. And you notice when it is worse.

KS: That's true.

DM: When it's not up to your standard.

KS: I had that experience in college with sushi, which I did not like before that. Then my friend took me to a place in Westwood, which is no longer there. And we got his favorite, which is yellowtail, and it became my favorite. And oh my God, I couldn't believe that I would like to eat raw fish. It was crazy. And then we were going there every week! We were going there *twice* a week. And another place opened up in Westwood a couple months after that. And it was kind of like, "Look at the prices! Who's gonna go there? This is ridiculous! Not me. Good old Cowboy Sushi for me." And then we had friends saying "Hey, you should try it out. It is really good." And I think eventually we relented. And it was *really* great. And that made us realize that Cowboy Sushi was, like, fish that other fish restaurants throw away.

DM: It's like when all the sushi chefs show up in the morning at the harbor, like, "Let's choose the cuts for today's sushi."

KS: Yeah.

DM: The guys who got there at four A.M. are getting the stuff fresh off the boat, and all the stuff that they pour in a big pile in the center of the fish market are the ones that—Cowboy Sushi is just rolling up on his horse, like, "Let's see what we got here, pardner." He's got, like, a branding iron; he's fishing through the stack of fish.

KS: Yeah. Literally fish that they are wanting birds and cats to take away. And then after that, this sushi that we loved, we couldn't eat it anymore. It was just like, all the colors are wrong. It's gray. And that's not how it's supposed to be. And I got canker sores one time. And that's not natural. That's not okay.

DM: All those eggs, you're supposed to swallow them. They are not supposed to take up residence in your cheeks and gestate.

KS: Right. I thought that's what caviar was for a while. But apparently it's supposed to be fish's eggs, not cockroach larvae. Hmm. Interesting. Yeah, so sushi has now been spoiled for me. And it's been a little bit better living in Dallas. But living inland is not a good sushi proposition.

DM: Sure, absolutely. You definitely want some place that is within, maximum, a truck's drive from actual fish.

KS: Yeah. You gotta drive for about a solid twenty hours, you know, overnight, if you wanted to get to Dallas from the sea.

DM: Here on the Twitter, we've got @PISTOLPIXIE. She says, "Life's too short to drink boxed wine." So I have three immediate responses to this. One, I think that's a saying. Way to be clever. Number two is, I heard that some boxed wine is not actually bad, because the bag inside the box will keep the wine longer. Keep the wine from—

KS: Yeah.

DM: I don't know what happens. When you open a bottle of wine, and then eventually—

KS: It oxidizes.

DM: Yeah, anyway, so I don't know anything about wine.[31] But number three, is this true? If this is true, if in general as a metaphor, then we should be striving to have the best of every experience. We want the *best* of everything! If there is *anything* that can be improved, we should make the effort to find the best of it so that we get the maximum experience out of it.

But that will ruin your life! That will absolutely ruin your life. Not only because there are mountains that you can never reach in one subject, but because you just don't have time. You have to discern. You have to make a compromise. You have to make a decision that says, I care about A, and B, nah. Don't care.

KS: That's why I think being a sommelier would be a really good racket, you know? For people who really don't know. Because now you're trading something you *do* have, money, for that guy's expertise. You don't have time to learn about wines. But *he* knows, and he's going to bring me the best one for my dinner.

DM: Well, that is sort of an institutionalized and accepted racket that I think exists in every field.

KS: Sure.

DM: Every field has experts hawking, you know, especially in the realm of get-rich-quick books, where it's like, "Hey, I know everything about the stock market. You buy my book for $8.95"—or more likely, $44.95—"and attend my seminar for $600, I will teach you all the stuff that you don't know you are missing."

KS: Yeah, but those guys—'cause they have to avoid the certification process. There's no agency that will grant them permission to say these things. They have to be like, "Look. Nobody wants you to know this, but I'm the maverick. I'm the only guy who figured it out. I'm the one you give the money to." I want to be the maverick sommelier. I want to be like, "No, no. C'mon, man. I know you're paying me $300 an hour, but I'm telling you—PBR, that's gonna do the trick."

DM: So what you have to do is seek out the people who don't know any better. They obviously have no idea. They wouldn't know one wine from another. You're at the restaurant—you're not even employed by the restaurant. You just sneak in there. You're wearing the sort of sommelier, you know, tuxedo, and you're like, "Is that the wine list? Let's take a look at that. Let's see what you got."

KS: Right. Yeah.

---

31 David's confused on this point because on a winery tour in Napa, they told him that wine is *supposed* to oxidize. That's why you let it air out before pouring. So many *rules!*

DM: "What did you order? Pasta?"

KS: You know what?

DM: "What kind of pasta? Linguine? All right, what kind of sauce did you get? Oh, artichoke tomato. All right, let me look at that list. Here's the thing. Here's what they're not going to tell you. They want you to buy that $65 bottle. But guess what I've got in my car? For just $34—"

KS: What you actually have in your car is a half-drank cherry Gatorade. You're looking for the kind of people that don't know that a sommelier does not advertise in the *PennySaver*. That is the person you want.

DM: You're looking for the person who does not know that a sommelier is supposed to wear shoes.

KS: You're looking for the guy who is saying, "I really need a soma-*leer*." That's the guy you need to find.

DM: "Excuse me. I'd like to speak to Denny, please?[32] I'd like to get his recommendation on the wine." So we have some people weighing in here on the Twitter who agree with the fact that life is made harder. We have @RICO516 saying that "Working at a coffee shop has ruined coffee for me, I can't drink restaurant coffee. It's all crap to me now."

This is something that I hope never happens. Because I like coffee. I love good coffee. But I am also fine with sufficient coffee. There are some things that are, as long as they are above a certain acceptability threshold, they are fine. Like, I was at IHOP this morning. I had their coffee, it was not the best coffee I've ever had. It was perfectly fine.

KS: Yeah, or you know those people, oh, the thing about Starbucks. "Oh, they burn it. They always burn it. You don't know what coffee is if you like Starbucks." And that might be true.

DM: Yeah. And that's the thing. Maybe it's true. And we've got @CEPHALOPOD_GAL saying, "In my opinion, part of enjoying life is being able to enjoy stuff that's not the best *because* it's not the best." So, is this the root of hipster irony?

KS: Yeah, it is.

DM: Doing something that is very deliberately not high-fashion.

KS: What you're talking about is the difference between enjoying something because it's not the best, and enjoying it in spite of the fact that it's not the best. I am a big Taco Bell fan. And I know that I am going to have colon cancer.

DM: *(laughs)* You know that you, at the moment, have colon cancer.

KS: I have it right now. And it actually, at the first stages, helps you digest the Taco Bell. So at first it's kind of a symbiosis.

DM: You actually have to absorb the Taco Bell bacteria into your digestive system so that it can then break down future Taco Bell products. It's sort of like, you have to mix the two chemicals to get the thing?[33] You have to start with the starter

---

32 Owner of Denny's, presumably.
33 The epoxy concept, is the aim here.

taco. The starter taco has—

KS: It just launches off the entire thing.

DM: It's got the initial culture in it, and that will make a receptacle.

KS: They know if you've been there before, too. They can tell. They know you. So they are like, "We need to give this guy, you know, the booster up front."

DM: And that way everything after that just slides right through.

KS: But like, I mean, I got to the point where I went recently and I'm like, "They did not put scallions on my Nachos Bell Grande." They have changed the recipe. And I started wondering, is that an economic concern? Did something change? But I know that's awful. Those chips that they serve are not even, I don't even know what that is. They're like cereal. They're like what a chocolate chip cookie is to Cookie Crisp, a real tortilla chip is to whatever Taco Bell is serving in the nachos.

DM: Okay, so you enjoy Taco Bell despite the fact that it is horrible. And is that because that bacteria has taken over your brain stem? Or is it because it's forty-nine cents for meat product—which cannot be a good situation if there is a meat product that costs less than, you know, the cost of the metal that went into the quarter used to buy it. It's probably not the greatest.

KS: It's just the right combination of salt and fat. And I like Mexican food. And this is near enough to it that I'm fooled.

DM: But there is something attractive about it then. You're not eating it *because* it's horrible, you're eating it because you like it *despite* the fact it's not good for you. You do enjoy the taste of it, clearly.

KS: I do, yeah. I'm not going, "This is so dumb, guys. We're eating Taco Bell. I'm going to throw it up later."

DM: But there are some other things, like we've got @SEKELSKY here on the Twitter saying, "I wish I could go about my day without cringing every time I see a poorly chose typeface."

KS: That's a great one.

DM: Good job there, "chose typeface."

KS: Haaah, *chosen*. And use a hyphen next time.

DM: And @KORYBING says, "Learning about graphic design has made every billboard in the world an eye-searing terror for me." These are things that are different from food that you eat even though it's not good for you. These are things that clearly make your life worse experientially. Would you agree?

KS: Yeah, no. They're bad. There's problems. And I didn't care about it so much until maybe about a year ago. And then I got obsessed with it. You can definitely choose the wrong font.

DM: Oh, absolutely. And the thing is, you cannot—the only response when you see a badly-designed billboard or poorly-chosen font, is merely to get incensed. It's almost like how an individual's impact on the global economic market is zero. It's that sort of helplessness. Where you can get really mad! You can get *really* mad!

And it changes nothing.

KS: And the worst part is that everybody you know doesn't care. So you're like, "Look at that! Look at that garbage! Look at the kerning." And they're like, "What? I don't get it. What's wrong with it?"

DM: So, back to my initial question. Does knowing make your life worse?

KS: I think it makes you crabby.

DM: Yes. And in fact, I hate to sound like one of these guys, but I stopped watching the news, and I stopped reading the news headlines that I get in my e-mail, and I actually got a lot happier. Because I didn't get terrified that the world was going to end. And I say that not in an exaggerated way. I was literally trying to figure out how I was going to survive in my world of Chinese-made disposable products that I couldn't repair like you can repair a 1920 Soviet tractor.

KS: Yeah.

DM: And I was trying to figure out, how is my life going to progress? Like, is it morally wrong to have children? You know, and raise them in a world that's going to be a searing nuclear terror and also they're going to add the carbon footprint. And I just had this...once I put it all away, I've actually been much happier. Because it's not like I can do—that sounds so horrible—it's not like I can do anything about something massive.

KS: It's your kids' problem.

DM: Especially when it comes to politics. And I'm all about being involved politically, but there was so much fervor around the national election last November, and it went on for so long, and we got so involved, and I was so involved... I was so interested in following the polls and everything. And the bottom line was, for every new story that you saw about "oh, this candidate is saying this, and that's been debunked by the independent research and they are running these attack ads, and isn't it shameful? And then *this* rumor came out"—all this stuff, you get so worked up about it.

KS: Yeah.

DM: And it makes you miserable. The only result of that is it makes your life miserable.

KS: Yeah, unless you go out and change it, then there's no point. Exactly. Here—I could go a lot of different ways on this name. It's either J. J. ACKUNRAU, or it's J. JACK UNRAU.

DM: It's J. JACK UNRAU, I know this guy.

KS: I think it's J. JA CKUNRAU. He says, "my buddy gets angry at poorly-designed bathroom doors. *Incensed* angry."

DM: Yes! *Yes!*

KS: But what are you referring to?

DM: I love—I don't know. And that's why I love it. I love it because I have no idea what makes a good bathroom door and a bad bathroom door. And I mean, I can maybe guess, and obviously you want it to work functionally, but this is something where I have no deep knowledge of this subject, and the fact that someone else does, and there is something out there—

KS: You're saying—

DM: —That someone else gets so mad about but I'm fine with. I'm totally fine with.

KS: I'm actually more excited that I could potentially get upset about it later if I wanted. Like, there's such a world out there to learn about, that even the bathroom door, someone's burning up over. Apparently there is a level of complexity there that, you know—I could really dive in.

DM: Okay, I will go with you there. I love the idea that you can drill down. I was just at this pancake breakfast for the fire department fundraiser thrown by the Rotary Club in my neighborhood. And I went and looked at the fire truck. I never looked at a fire truck close-up, I don't think, in my life. And every gauge has a manufacturer's name on it. I think the manufacturer's name is "PumpCo" or something really fire-truck-related. And I got really excited at the idea that there is some company out there, and some factory, that employs all these workers just to make gauges for fire trucks. I love that.

KS: I love the idea that, they've kind of...it's a buyer's market, so they really have not had to get clever. Because there's really only two manufacturers of gauges, and it's PumpCo and it's ValveCo, and they're the only ones who—you know, they don't have to get flashy. Let the products speak for themselves.

DM: Exactly. So from an academic standpoint, I do love that idea that you can drill down all the way into, you know, any subject as deep as you want, and there are unplumbed depths there. However! The fact that there is something that I am still fine with, that my life is not as ruined by knowing too much, could be also a reassuring concept.

KS: That's true.

DM: And now, @JOEHILLS says, "A bad bathroom door has no discernable gender assigned to it." I'll buy that, but I'm actually hoping—and actually, @JJACKUNRAU, please do not disabuse me of the notion that that is not what you were referring to. I want to think that there is some sort of hinge, some sort of a latch mechanism that your friend could go on a tear for an hour about, and I don't know anything about it. I want to keep that.

KS: He's already sent a follow-up that's, like, "Oh, that's not what I meant." You're like, "No!"

My first girlfriend was—she moved here from Russia. And one of the things I hadn't thought about until she brought it up was the design of sinks. She moved here when she was like twelve, and she said one of the things that she had to get used to was when you go into the bathroom and the faucet basically juts out two inches from the back of the basin. In most sinks, it's just a real short little faucet. And I'm like, "What's wrong with that?" And she said, "Well, when you're washing your hands under that, you're putting your hand up against there." That's a relic from when people would use that spigot to fill the basin and wash your hands in your face in the basin, and then you drain the basin.

She said in Russia, all of the faucets—they arc up, and you can stick your hand under the running water, you've got as much space as you need. You know, like a doctor's faucet. Where you—

DM: Right, right.

KS: You know? And that makes so much more sense! Yeah, our short faucets are stupid! That's a functional thing that has become a stylistic thing for no reason.

DM: Well, thanks. You've ruined it for me now.

KS: Well, yeah. See, I was gonna say that's gonna poison you, because you're going to be washing your hands tonight, and your hand is going to hit the back of the sink, and you're going to say "it doesn't have to be that way!"

DM: Well, I'm never going to wash my hands ever again.

KS: Finally.

DM: I will just avoid the whole problem.

KS: A voice of reason.

DM: I'm never gonna wash my hands. I'm never going to drink wine. I never gonna have, like—some of the other people on the tweets are talking about movies that people have different opinions on, and that's something I've had to resign myself to as a matter of taste. You can't argue that one way or another.

  @DRHASTINGS talks about having to give the elaborate instructions when he orders a cocktail now, and then, you know, that's great, and I would never know the difference, so I'm happy. So there's some things like ordering a cocktail, the bathroom door thing that I hope you don't disabuse me of—I'm gonna keep those. I'm gonna hold on to them. I'm just going to go and do those things a lot. I'm not gonna wash my hands. I'm not going to drink wine. And those two together, I think will just avoid that heartache for the rest of my life, I hope.

KS: I'm not gonna fight it when.I go into a bar next time, specifically. I'm just gonna say "Give me *something,* in a glass." And we'll see what we get.

DM: Yeah. You should just order by color. Just bring in like a swatch book and say "give me something this color." And they're like, "We don't have anything that color." And you're like, "Well, mix it."

KS: Well, yeah. I don't mean out of the *bottle.* I know you don't have that.

DM: At Home Depot they can make that color. They have a base, and they put some sort of coloring agent into it.

KS: I know how it works.

DM: And they mix it around, and they result in a mathematically-precise match of that color.

KS: Right. You're like, "I know it's going to have milk in it. I know. Because you've got to start there."

DM: Aaah, @JJACKUNRAU, you talked about the— you told me about it! I'm going to know this bathroom door—@JJACKUNRAU says, it's all about the handles and hinges. He gets mad about sinks, too. Well, now I'm going to start paying attention to hinges.

KS: Oh, it's a pollutant. You can't get away from them once you start thinking about them. You're right. Just don't go into the bathroom.

DM: Knowledge is an infection.

KS: Just dig a hole from now on.

DM: Right. So now I can't go into bathrooms. So now I'm never going to wash my hands, I'm never going to go into bathrooms. It's okay, because I'm not going to be drinking.

KS: I can't read words now, because of the fonts.

DM: Right. I can't read anything. I gonna just stumble around with my eyes closed, bumping into everything, hoping—

KS: Hoping I'm bumping into food, because I'm really hungry. I don't know what to do.

DM: Okay, let's wrap up this conversation with a question from @PISTOLPIXIE. "Should we only learn about products that we are willing to be passionate about, or just deal with the ill effects of our knowledge?" Clearly, you cannot limit the things you know about. In this conversation, I've learned all about bathroom doors now, and I didn't want to. So you clearly have to just take it as it comes.

KS: Well, yeah. I mean, @PISTOLPIXIE, that, I would say as far as testing purposes, is what we would call in the computer-science world an NP-incomplete problem, because what we are going to have to do now is follow Malki around the rest of his life, and see whether or not you have a good life with this new knowledge that you've learned tonight.

DM: Well, that's kind of what @DHARMAKATE says. She says, "You can be incensed about billboards, bad fonts and bathroom doors, and love expensive fish and cheap Mexican, and still be a happy person." Well, there's two things I'd say to that. One, what we're talking about is sort of a metaphor for—there are many more things besides just these. And number two, you have just described Kris Straub. So I'm asking you, Kris—I know that you are incensed by bad fonts, I know this for a fact.

KS: Yeah.

DM: You have in the course of this conversation become incensed about bathroom doors, just because we know too much, now. You love cheap fish and bad Mexican, as you've detailed earlier in the conversation. Are *you* a happy person?

KS: Ehh, I can't complain.

[ACCORDION STING]

DM: So we're talking about lengthy obligations on today's show. These are things that you've had to do that have been forced upon you, and have made you miserable.

KS: Yeah, yeah. Yeah. You know what? I'm getting miserable thinking about them. I'm not having fun.

DM: Well, let's see some of the stories people have shared with us. We've got @MAGNOLIAPEARL with a multi-part story. She says, "My old landlord was part of a local theater company. Every weekend they put on stage readings of dry dramatic plays. Which meant they would sit on the stage and read from scripts, occasionally miming an action. Interesting, but not exactly my thing. She gave us free tickets to most of these." I don't know why you would need tickets. This just sounds like a rehearsal or something.

KS: "Psst! These are *free!*"

DM: "We couldn't say no to our landlord, so most weeknights"—*most weeknights*—"we politely sat through her shows. I did learn a little about theater, which was good, but most of the time I was wishing I could just go to a movie instead." Oh, no. *Weekend* nights. She says "most weekend nights, we sat through these shows." You can't say no to your landlord? Is she letting you live under the stairs for free? Say no to your landlord!

KS: That was in *The Big Lebowski*. That creepy landlord had a dancing show, like some Grecian thing.

DM: Oh, is Magnolia just making things up from stuff she's seen in a movie?

KS: No, no, no. It was sufficiently different. But I was gonna say, if it was every night, then she wins. I don't care what anyone else's story is. "I gotta live somewhere. I gotta go to these shows every night."

DM: I still can't get past this idea that you can't say no to the landlord.

KS: Well, I don't know. It might be an intimidation type of a thing.

DM: But every single performance? Every single show? You go once to be polite, I understand. Or was it the kind of thing where she just didn't say—she couldn't back out of it after the first one. Like, the landlord was like *(in a strange accent)* "So, what did you think?" And then Magnolia's like, "Oh, I thought it was great. I thought it was really interesting." "Oh, then you will love—I'll give you tickets every single weekend because we love having people who enjoy what we are doing. So many people don't understand what we are really trying to accomplish, and clearly, in the space of this sentence, you have indicated that *you* are our audience."

KS: I like how she went from immigrant American to German to Indian. That's why. She's like a shape-changer. And I'm terrified. I gotta go to the show.

DM: She's an actress, Kris. She's multi-facial. She's like Vin Diesel.

KS: She's like, "Why are you doing that?" *Acting!*

DM: "This is the thing that we do!" Reminds me of Jim Carrey in that *Lemony Snicket* movie.

KS: Oh, yeah. That's right. He was in that.

The example I have, and this might be a special case, of these obligations, is yet another one of my ex-girlfriends, because apparently they are making the rounds in this show. She worked for somebody who... her manager decided to start a Mary Kay business. She invited all of her workers—yay! All of the people that work under her. It was kind of like *(sigh)*, "I don't want to be rude." It's the first thing that you do when you're starting the thing, and—you know, it's all real no-guilt, sort of "we are just going to sit around and mess around with makeup," but there is an understanding that if you're not walking out of there with fifty bucks' worth of lipstick, then something is wrong. And I'm sure that nothing would've happened if she didn't buy any, but there was such a pressure to do it. You know?

DM: Right.

KS: So why, I mean, yeah. In those circumstances, yeah, it's an obligation. Just the same as you couldn't say, "Well, this has been good, but I'm going to go ahead and leave early." Because the second they say, "Why? How come?" Then you go, "All right, I'll sit down. It's fine. You know what? I've been having fun."

DM: "Have we been doing something wrong?" All right, we've got, @MEANDERING_MUSE says, "I offered to feed a friend's turtles while he was out of town, not realizing that he would never return and they would outlive me." He would never return?

KS: God!

DM: You've opened up a can here, @MEANDERING_MUSE. I want to know more about this guy. Now, was he running away? Was he like, "I've got to pack my bags, I'm gonna ride the rails," and you're like, "Oh, you need someone to watch Michelangelo?" He's like, "Yeah, absolutely." Or was it like, "Hey, man. Just watch my turtle. I'm gonna go to my girlfriend's house in Modesto for the weekend," and then on the evening news, "Missing."

KS: I was gonna say, it's not that they eloped. It's that he's *dead*. "And *I'm* stuck with his turtles! Come on! FML."

DM: Yeah, I can just imagine, he's running for his life, he's got the crazed killer chasing him over a mountain, he's in a blizzard with a grease-stained rag pulled over his face to shield him from the snow blasting at him. And it's like, "Oh, this is horrible!" And then it cuts back to @MEANDERING_MUSE in his dorm room like, "This is just too much! I can't take this stupid turtle!"

KS: He's got like, shackles, in some guy's perverted dungeon, and he's praying, "Keep my turtles safe. Lord, just keep my turtles safe. Make sure he feeds them."

DM: "As long as something good has come out of my life, I will have done enough." So I want to know more, @MEANDERING_MUSE, I want a follow-up to this. I want to know more about why—where did he go, why did he disappear? And your current—how long has this been, and how is your continuing relationship to the turtles?

KS: Yeah, and exactly when did you flush them down the toilet is the question? How many days after?

DM: @MRBILDANGO says, "I worked retail for years, delaying other ambitions out of loyalty to a manager who quote, 'needed me to be there because he didn't know how to do certain system things in the store.' He then quit, and I was stuck for even longer."

This is a really, really tough situation. And this is why I advise never making yourself indispensable in a job. I know too many people that have done so well at the job that they are irreplaceable. And therefore they are never promoted, and they're never able to quit without this huge problem. The thing about working a job that you dislike but that there is a lot of pressure in, is that the minute you quit, you feel all that pressure *lift*. Because you don't care one white grain of rice for the company after you are no longer employed. But, up until that moment, you are deeply invested in the success of your job.

So, you're unable to realize how much you'll just stop caring about all that interoffice political B.S. And everything seems so important and crushing, and when you're stuck in that position, you feel like you are obligated to stay because "what will they do without me?" This is a bad situation to find yourself in. So my advice to all aspirants in any sort of job is to either train someone immediately to replace you or, stop doing good work. Only do mediocre work, such that you are not integral to the success of the company. Now, if you want to stay with the company your whole life, God bless you, Godspeed. If you want to go somewhere else, you have to stop doing good work.

KS: Yeah.

DM: Is my advice.

KS: Well, like, I wish that when *I've* quit jobs that I've needed to quit, that the guilt would go away. Like, "Ah! I don't have to worry about it." It's almost like you don't have to worry about it in the same way you don't have to call your mom anymore because she's dead. You know? Like, I couldn't leave the job and feel good about it, especially not during the last two weeks, where I had been working seventy or eighty hours a week at that job, and after I gave my notice, you know, I wasn't going to do that anymore.

And yet, at the same time I was thinking about the people I knew who would have to take it on. And, even just the act of, "this was my charge. And I'm not doing it anymore. I told them I'm not going to do it." I felt they had a hold on me. But I think that's when I was younger and much more naïve.

DM: Yeah—

KS: Now I'm very detached.

DM: Now you don't care at all. That's the point that you want to try and get to. In fact, @FROSTYPLUM says it well, I think. "When you think you're irreplaceable at your job, think of how fast they'll find someone else if you quit." That's true. They have to fill that job somehow. And they were going before you arrived, in many cases—although, every now and then I meet someone that worked recently, or currently works, at a place I used to work and have not worked in many years. And they say, when they meet me, "Oh! Oh, you're Malki. Oh, all right." Like, they're still using the manuals that I wrote for the job, you know, things like that.

KS: You become like a godlike figure.

DM: There was a little bit of, "Couldn't you do it like Malki used to do it?" So that's nice.

KS: Like, "I thought that was the name of the company!"

DM: So we have some new comments. Magnolia says, "We were on friendly terms with her, and she was a pretty good open-minded landlord." I don't know if that's code for group sex, or what. "We felt ungrateful turning her down."

KS: Now I understand why she had to go to the show.

DM: The whole time? Really? Okay, @MEANDERING_MUSE writes back and says, "It has been seven years since he left. The turtles are still getting bigger." And then he drops the big bomb. "He was deported."

KS: He was deported! Yikes. But imagine how happy he'll be when he can see the turtles again.

DM: Eventually the turtles are gonna cross the ocean, going back to meet him in his native land.

KS: It's a one-way "Gift of the Magi" sort of thing. Where he's like, "I've taken care of your turtles for thirty years. And now that you can come back, here they are." And he's like, "I don't want these."

DM: "Those turtles—really? You're still—? I was raising those to *eat!*"

KS: "And now they're too gamey." Or he's like, "Why didn't you turn the note over?" "Why?" Look at it, and it says "If I get deported, just throw them away. It's fine."

DM: "All right. Here's my instructions. Step one: feed the turtles. There's eight boxes of food underneath the sink." So @MEANDERING_MUSE goes, "All right, eight boxes of food. That should last a couple days." And then the friend doesn't come back and doesn't come back, and he's all, "I'm gonna run out of food here. I'm gonna need to go buy some more." So he goes to the pet store, and he brings the empty box, and "Oh, this food is discontinued. This is some kind of weird foreign brand." He has to special-order—I don't know if they're on some kind of hypoallergenic diet or something, but he has to special-order from some other country, pay all these customs charges. He finally gets this specialty food, now the turtles are happy as a clam eating the special food, blah, blah, blah. But on the back of the note was, "Once you get through all eight boxes of food, they are ripe. Cook them, sautéed with butter."

KS: I was gonna go *Twilight Zone* with it, and say, "Whatever you do, please remember to feed my turtles." "I did!" "No, look—feed my turtles *to my beloved snake! Oh no.*" And it's just snake bones.

DM: The snake, the snake is just dead. Oh, man. All right, let's play a voicemail.

> Back when I was in high school, this is about 2003, I somehow, through the student union associated with my high school, got roped into teaching a Introduction to Computers course at the senior center. There were about four people, all of them probably over the age of 80. None of them had ever touched a computer before. This went on for maybe a month or so, and it was the typical tech-support hilarity. Some of my favorite moments including, saying to a lady to point and click, forgetting that these terms are second-nature to anyone of my generation. She picked up her finger, pointed it at the screen, and clicked. Meanwhile, the woman next to her picked up the mouse and was using it like a remote control pointing it at the screen. It was something I ended up having to do once a week for a month or two and...not too fun.

DM: Yeah, this is similar to the time I had to introduce my dad to a computer. You remember, the description of my dad, very kind of old-school...

KS: Yeah.

DM: So the idea that you had to move the mouse to make the cursor hover over something—that requires some dexterity that we take for granted nowadays, I think. We have pretty fine motor control over our mousing hand, in a way that we probably didn't the very first time we used a computer.

KS: So you're saying that if you had somehow rigged your family computer to work with like, a plow, that your father would have been an expert.

DM: He would have done great, yeah. If it had been a diesel-powered Caterpillar tractor, he would have gone all up and down AltaVista all day long. However—

KS: He would have been able to be a hacker by the time.

DM: Right. He would have been the equivalent of a hacker, if we could have just made those giant gearshift levers, where there's like four of them, and some of them are kind of angled, and they're in a big gearbox? If we could have made that work WinAmp, I think we could've had a real—

KS: "Son, before I use the computer, I want to be outside climbing up into something. Before I start to use it."

DM: I had that Super Nintendo game, *Pilotwings*.

KS: Yeah.

DM: I don't know if you remember playing it, but the very first level is a very easy level where you just have to go up and down. You don't have to turn at all. In fact, if you turn, you end up ruining your chance for a perfect score. And so my dad would—my dad was a pilot, and so he liked to watch me play a little bit, and then he wanted to try. He wanted to "land the plane." So the game was just the first level of *Pilotwings*, which I guess is all he was interested in. And so he couldn't quite understand, or it was difficult for him to manage, the standard flight-simulator convention of a the game controller, where you press up on the controller to go down, and so on.

KS: Yeah.

DM: And so he would hold the controller upside down, which is fine, because he's not turning this level. And then, A and B are, you know, the throttle control in *Pilotwings*, or whatever the two buttons are. And as I've learned, becoming a pilot, your actual altitude control is controlled not by the angle you point the nose, but rather the amount of throttle you give the engine. If you want to climb, you get more power. If you want to descend, you decrease power. That's how airplanes fly. So, that's how he worked it, whereas I had always done it strictly directionally, and had always flown very fast down the runway. But every now and then, he would come in and say, "Hey, let's land the plane!" So we would fire up *Pilotwings* and we would fly that one level, and he would hold the controller upside down, and we had a great time.

Basically what I'm saying to the caller is: sometimes it doesn't take much.

KS: If I could go out on a tangent, I want to say real quick, the failing of any kind of modern technology, and now I'm gonna add that one to the ball. My biggest, top-of-my-list complaint is braking a car. How do you get a car to stop? "I don't know, we've got this advanced engine that gets it moving. I know, we'll invent two things to push on the wheel until it can't turn any more. How about that?"

DM: Right.

KS: "All right. That's a great idea. We're so advanced." But what kills me as you're describing this plane—you throttle up and that's going to give you altitude, and if you want to stop, you cut it. So it's like, if you want to go down, the plane crashes. But we'll make it crash really slow! In a controlled way. And then you can go down at the rate you want.

DM: Well, there's a law of physics that makes what you said sound retarded. But I agree with you on the braking thing. The fact that it's strictly friction-based, and that the advancement in braking technology has been to make the brake pads more durable and better at grabbing onto a brake disc, instead of some alternate deceleration technology. Although the Mercury Mariner, as a hybrid, has...

KS: Plug.

DM: ...It re-captures braking power to charge the battery. And I don't know—this is what I would like to know; maybe someone can let me know about the mechanics of it. Does it involve some sort of mechanically-geared thing, where—

KS: It does.

DM: —Where it actually saps energy from the wheels? Or does the actual braking of the wheels turn a brush or something?

KS: Well, I mean it—it's just a bunch of electrodes down there. It's two sweaters, and then the static—

DM: The entire axle is wrapped in copper wire.

KS: Yeah. No, it's on the Prius, too. The same thing, braking spins up some flywheel in the back of the car, and that will help charge the battery. It's cool that it's on that car.

DM: But does the flywheel sap energy from the wheels, thus slowing them? Or is it the actual brake-pad braking of the wheel that then does something else?

KS: You know, I want to say it's the energy of the braking. I don't know. Is there, like, a—"Well, here's the problem. Your braking battery died."

DM: Right, so you can't stop!

KS: "We don't talk about that."

DM: And that's the thing about friction brakes, is... I think, because you need to be able to stop a car in three seconds in an emergency, I think any sort of mechanical deceleration-type thing—you have to be able to put the brakes on and it just grabs the wheel and it stops moving.

KS: Yeah. I always think, "How do you fire alternating magnets to get it to stop?" But that's really complex. You know, you'd make it like one of the machine guns that can shoot through the propeller on a biplane?

DM: Right.

KS: Just time it right, and you could really control it.

DM: Yeah, you just gear it correctly. And in fact, in the early days of World War I, their idea, before they figured out how to gear it to the propeller—they just put armored plates on the propeller. So any bullets that do hit it just bounced off.

KS: There you go!

DM: That was the first breakthrough in machine-gun-through-the-propeller technology.

KS: That's just doing the bare minimum. That's like, "We ran out of time."

DM: "All right. Here's the situation. We want to shoot through the propeller. But we shoot the propeller *off*, is the problem. Because the bullets are going really fast. So, let's just make the propeller stronger so the bullets will just ricochet off it. And maybe they'll hit some enemy off to the side. It'll be a double advantage."

KS: It's like getting the spread gun in *Contra*.

DM: Right!

KS: In fact, the propeller is now a disc. We *want* that to bounce off!

DM: @Sciencedog, our favorite dog of science, says, "Hybrids run the generator in reverse using the wheel motion to charge up a battery."

KS: Yeah, but does that mean they're running—

DM: There's probably still brake pads involved, is my guess.

KS: Oh, there absolutely is, yeah. I don't think you can recapture all of the energy. At some point, a plastic thing is touching the wheel.

DM: I want the fully-electric-braking-energy motor to go haywire. And not in the way where it leaves you with no braking power, but in that it is *always* braking. So if you're not accelerating, you're braking.

KS: Well, that's just it. "How do we recapture the energy from braking?" Well, the fact is, the flywheel is strung so tight, the car is literally *always braking*. It's always stopped. The answer is to make a super powerful electric engine that can overcome that.

DM: Right. It's the same problem in reverse. So we have—the electric motor controls braking, and then we have the super-powerful forward motor so that it's stronger now than the actual braking power, but that makes it *too* strong, so now we need a *third* braking mechanism. And this one is actually just a grappling hook that you stick into the concrete.

KS: Right. And then you have to—clearly, you can't just wreck the concrete, so around the city, they've installed Prius-brand grappling towers that you have to fire it at.

DM: The Honda Corporation is like,[34] "Okay, first you have to guide your car into one of the channels in the road. And then there's going to be a series of lights that illuminate in a proper sequence." When you are angled correctly—because the light shines through a lens that has three prisms on it. So if you are too far to the left, it shines green. Too far to the right, it shines red. So you want to be right the center where it'll shine pure white. Then you know you're aligned properly with the tracks in the road.

KS: Now, the problem is, when you're coming up on it, though, you're going to notice that the drum in the engine is rotating so fast you 're gonna get gyroscopic effects. So you're not going to be able to turn the wheel. So you're really going to have to lean on it. You're probably going to need a friend.

DM: You're going to have to use the side grappling hooks, to first straighten the car out. There are several miniature grappling hooks that you can use like braking thrusters in a rocket, where you have to shoot small grappling hooks in increments to align you properly with the grappling-hook track in the street.

KS: Once you have managed to stop the vehicle, the car is going to resemble a spider with diarrhea. That's basically what it's going to look like.

DM: Now, here's the thing. You may encounter other cars on the road that have already deployed their grappling hooks. So we have equipped our car with a razor blade pointed forward so that you can simply power through other people's lines without fear that it's going to arrest your travel as well.

KS: It's a buzzsaw, the chain of which is attached to that wildly out-of-control engine. So yeah, don't worry. You're going to be able to cut through anything.

DM: So if you encounter a traffic jam where there are too many grappling hooks—so that your braking power is able to continue unabated from other cars' buzz saws,

---

34   Er, Toyota, of course, for the Prius. Unless it's a partnership!

we have titanium-plated *your* grappling hooks.

KS: Every single group we produce is a little bit stronger than the last one.

DM: So it's to your advantage to buy the newest car on the market. This is the definition of planned obsolescence: Where every other car has a buzzsaw that can cut through the braking grapples on your car.

THE REDESIGNED FORD HOOKSMAN 2010

WE LISTENED. MORE HOOKS. MORE BLADES.

KS: And for all this: 42 city, 48 highway. What do you think about that? That's not bad.

DM: Also, we need the government to give us $48 billion.

KS: Not for research, but because we're running out of titanium.

DM: Because we just—for *some* reason, these cars are just piling up on the showroom. We can't sell them. So what we need to do is, we need the government to seize all the homes around the dealership and declare eminent domain and pave them, so we have a larger dealership to park our cars on.

KS: Together, we are going to make this work. USA!

DM: All right, thank you for listening to Tweet Me Harder. This has been the world's first, best, only, and last talkback-enabled interactive audio podblast. We have two things we want to say regarding next week's show and the shows to come: Next week's show is going to be a special episode exploring the nature of memory. We're going to dig out some stuff from Kris' past. I think it'l be a really fascinating hour of humiliation and so on.

KS: It's actually going to be very good.

DM: So no dedicated topic for next week, but we had some fun answering your questions and requests for advice last week, so the voicemail line, I think we will leave that permanently open as an ask-us-a-question. Whether it's a request for advice regarding a situation in your life in particular, or some other question you'd like us to answer. If there is ever a dedicated topic for the show, you can use it for that as well, but in general, feel free to leave us a short voicemail asking us a question. Try to keep it around thirty seconds if you can, and we will address those intermittently. The number again: 206-337-8560. You can easily remember that number because 206 is the model number of the six-seater Cessna airplane. 33 is a palindrome. 7-8 is two numbers in sequence. 5-6 is the previous two numbers in sequence. Zero is the check digit at the end. So that should be a pretty easy mnemonic to remember.

KS: I like to remember the zero as the number invented by, I think, the Mayans.

DM: Was the Mayans, or was it the Arabs?

KS: You know what, I don't know.

DM: Dude, let's claim this one.

KS: The answer to that is probably contained in the other numbers of the voicemail line.

DM: Right, it's probably numerologically encoded. If we were to put it on a grid and transmute the numbers to Hebrew, I'm sure we could dig up all sorts of Nostradamus predictions.

KS: Why Hebrew? Why not ancient Incan? Of course if you translate it to Hebrew, it's going to be, "Oh yeah, Arabs did it." Yeah, it's from the region.

DM: Well, I was going back to that whole Bible code stuff. You ever see that stuff?

KS: Yeah, I did. That's no good.

DM: Do you think the Incans had their own Bible code? Just, "We don't have the Bible? So we can't encode it? We can't decode it?"

KS: Yeah, I think it was *as* dumb, too. It was *as* accurate and good.

DM: Do you think, you know, the Bible code is this thing where thousands of years later some guy who thought he was really smart figured it out—"Hey, let's try and decode this ancient text." Do you think the Mayans had that for their own sacred text? Like, there's just some guy saying, "Hey, guys, guys. Check it out. Check it out. If you write the hieroglyphs, or whatever it is, in a particular order, and then you circle every one on a diagonal, and then you disregard every fourth one, and then you put in the ones from the corners at the end—then it makes a recipe for chocolate."

KS: "Yeah, 'cause that's how I *wrote* it." Their ancient stuff was written three weeks before that discovery.

DM: "We're ancient *now*, man!"

KS: "A *delicious* recipe!"

6

My Dear Minnie

KS: Hey everybody, welcome to Tweet Me Harder, the world's first, best, only and last talkback-enabled interactive audio podblast. I am Kris Straub.

DM: I am David Malki !

KS: And you're back with us for our sixth episode! That means if you want to interact with us right now on Twitter, you can use hashtag #TMH6.

DM: T-M-H-6. That's how it goes.

KS: You're gonna like it. You are gonna like what you get.

DM: *(laughs)* We offer no guarantees, however.

KS: However—but you will like it.

DM: As is. No warranty. You will like it.

KS: You'll absolutely love it. But we cannot promise.

DM: There is no assurance that we are actually telling the truth. We 100% guarantee that you will fall completely in love with this. However, it's not entirely certain whether or not we are, in fact, lying.

KS: A lot of people have been sad. When they have left. I mean, they left early.

DM: But this is anecdotal evidence. It's purely anecdotal. Some people—maybe they had some sort of bladder problem. We cannot take responsibility for their sudden vomitous revulsion.

KS: I want to say—at the top—yeah. We have not been reviewed by the FDA. Or actually any government body of regulation.

DM: We cannot diagnose or cure any disease.

KS: Despite what we will be doing later on.

DM: Which is curing—diagnosing and then curing diseases.

KS: So stay tuned, if you're dying. That's basically the message.

DM: Ah, we have a voicemail. Let's listen to the voicemail.

KS: Let's tuck in.

> *Hi, Tweet Me Harder. I just have a quick question. How can I get motivated?*

KS: Ooooo. How can he get motivated?

DM: This is a very, very tough question.

KS: Yeah.

DM: The thing I imagine someone must struggle with.

KS: A lot of people.

DM: I don't.

KS: Yeah.

DM: I'm sure someone might.

KS: I don't either. I mean, I used to.

DM: But then you developed your technique.

KS: I—you know, I really like the movie, what is it? *The Road to Wellsville?* You know that movie?

DM: Is that a Bing Crosby movie?

KS: No no no no. Close. But it's the remake.

DM: *The Road to Albuquerque?*

KS: It's the one with a—where they were doing the whole thing with Doctor Kellogg—the guy who made up cornflakes. You know that?

DM: I know cornflakes.

KS: And then he had, like, an asylum.

DM: I do know cornflakes.

KS: You know about cornflakes. Well, Dr. Kellogg was a nutbag. He basically thought that cornflakes, were gonna, you know, restore all of your bodily humors.

DM: Uh-huh. Right.

KS: And so—

DM: Your black bile, your—

KS: Yeah, yeah, yeah. You know, your aqueous humor, your vitreous humor.

DM: Right. All the standard humors.

KS: All the other things that elves secrete. So I, basically, I start my morning with an ice bath in a copper tub.

DM: Right.

KS: And then, you know, electrodes. You know just stick 'em on there. Anywhere. I mean, it's attached to a car battery. You're gonna get a ground at some point.

DM: And the copper just really helps, you know.

KS: It just shoots through.

DM: It's conductive.

KS: Yeah. That's the key. I was using a porcelain tub for a while, you don't get nothin' off of that.

148

DM: Right. Because there's a lot of induction.

KS: And then, believe it or not—

DM: I believe it. Whatever it is, I believe it.

KS: After about three, three and a half hours of that.

DM: Yeah?

KS: You're gonna get some ideas.

DM: They're just going to come to you. They are gonna start flowing.

KS: And if you're like me, you're gonna want to get out of that tub.

DM: But you can't, because all of your muscles are frozen.

KS: You have to wait until the battery dies. Talk about a motivator.

DM: So, yeah, you get so full up with ideas that you're thinking, "I can't wait until I get muscle control back!"

KS: Yeah, that's basically where the—

DM: And then it lets you down gradually, as the current—the voltage—dies down.

KS: Yes.

DM: Then ultimately you are able, sort of, first slowly kinda move your elbows a little bit.

KS: 'Cause you're clinched.

DM: Well, yeah.

KS: Because there's still the residual—it's like all of your muscles and your bones, it's like a dielectric. You're still feeling it.

DM: It's almost as if they're all shouting out in pain. Just crying for their lives.

KS: I like to think of pain as a physical idea.

DM: Pain is an actual substance that enters your body, and you have to just squeeze it out. You have to squeeze it out your pores, your fingertips. It's a long process. It involves a lot of very complex massage techniques.

KS: It involves laudable pus. I think we can be agreed on that.

DM: And depending on the school that you subscribe to, either cooking implements, or in some cases, simple cooking utensils.

KS: Yeah. But then—

DM: Sometimes it's the spatula; other times you go all the way out and use the colander, let's say.

KS: I don't wanna say—I mean, a lot of people would say maybe that what I'm doing is creating an aversion to not being motivated. But I think that you get a lot out of the pain. And don't just think about it as a negative. You know? That's selling yourself short. You're only getting half the benefit, if you dislike pain. I'm saying that you also have to like *not* having pain.

DM: Right. You actually have to make not-pain its own—It's sort of like how there is steam, but only until it condenses into water can you actually use it to power, I dunno, a mill or something.

KS: Yeah.

DM: You have to take the abstract concept of not-pain, and you have to coalesce it. And you have to make it into something that you could use to power... a mill, or something.

KS: Or just the body, *as* mill. Which is actually the name of pamphlet I'm working on.

DM: Right. It's a metaphor. It's sort of a metaphor.

KS: Well, yeah. I mean it is a metaphor... Unless you do connect your body up to a wheel. And use it to grind things.

DM: Let's say you have some wheat.

KS: Yeah! Exactly. There you go.

DM: You could grind that stuff up.

KS: Take care of that at about 5:30 in the morning. 'Cause you can't sleep because of the electricity.

DM: Yeah.

KS: And the dreams. But, you know, that's my take. What—do you have any methods that you use to get in the mood when you're not feeling it?

DM: Well, there are a couple. It's interesting that you talk about the whole idea of creating aversions, because if I was a real Pavlovian individual, you would think that all the problems I've gotten into from not being motivated when I was supposed to be, I would have developed some sort of brain-stem biological aversion to not working.

KS: Makes sense.

DM: You would think so. I'm still confused as to why it hasn't quite happened that way. I did try and develop some techniques that I hope will help the caller. The first was, when I found out that you left your webcam on when you were doing the car battery thing—and I was able to just watch you. That was kind of fun too. I didn't get the physical, visceral benefits in the same way that I'm sure that you did, but I did get kind of a kick out of it, I have to admit!

KS: So you felt a motivation surging through you body. Not an electrical one but...

DM: It just sort of made me happy, you know, to see you, just, kinda flopping a little bit—the water's kinda going over the edge.

KS: All splashing on things.

DM: When you see stuff, you know, making a mess, it's always kinda funny.

KS: I hate that. I hate that when that happens.

DM: The pie in the face, and all that kinda stuff.

KS: It's just a lot of fun. It's just fun.

DM: So, I hope that helps the caller.

[ACCORDION STING]

DM: This is a special episode of Tweet Me Harder. This particular show is going to be about Kris. And it's going to be about all of us, if you use Kris as a metaphor. So we'll see just how apt that turns out to be.

KS: I don't know whether or not I like that, but I guess we'll find out.

DM: So let me ask you something, Kris. Is there anything in your life—and this goes out to the audience too, if you want to tweet with us using hashtag #TMH6, we'll be able to see that, and you can see what everyone else is tweeting as well.

Has there been a point in your childhood when you thought something, or you had some memory that became a memory of a memory and so on... and then at some point later in life you were able to revisit that, and it was different than the way you imagined it? Or maybe it was the same! The whole idea is that you revisited your childhood memory to either confirm or disconfirm—if that's a word—what you had had in your mind.

KS: It's actually—I think it's been kind of rare that I've been able to go back and confirm any one of these things. I mean, I think that maybe the most benign is if you're in a room you remember spending time in when you were five years old, and you go back and everything seems small.

DM: Sure, sure.

KS: Because you were small back then. But a lot of that—

DM: Right. Your eyes hadn't fully grown.

KS: Yeah. Because you grow as you age. As a human.

DM: Right. Your eyeballs sort of—there's a refraction.

KS: There's—I'm sure it has something to do with quantum mechanics, but that's beyond the scope of this program. But a lot of my childhood memories have to do with my brother, and there's a lot of stuff that he and I have—we joke around together and we basically would do bits together, and make up things, and a lot of them I don't remember where they were generated, but we'll repeat them today and ask, "Why is it like that now?"

And every once in a while we can trace it back to a specific reference or a movie or something and go, "Oh yeah, that was the line," and then we'd said, "Wouldn't it be funny if this guy had said it instead," and then we went way out on a limb with it, and now here we are six months later driving our parents crazy because we won't stop saying it. That happened a *lot,* a lot a lot a lot.

DM: We've got @SEVENF on the Twitter who says, "I heard every time you remember something you are actually creating that memory and re-remembering is creative." This is something I have heard as well. Where the idea is, you have to reconstruct a memory from its, its sort of atoms, as you recall it. And so every time, it gets a little more corrupted. And in fact, the purest memory is the memory that you don't remember. Because it's uncorrupted by the process of remembering.

KS: So is there a—there's a storage type for an experience I've had that I have not yet actively remembered?

DM: Well, all the, you know, whether that's stuff that maybe you can recover in hypnosis, or something will trigger a memory that you don't remember actively—you know, like, it was not in your basic default memory bank, but you hear that sound or you revisit some place and that memory comes flooding back? If this is a memory that you haven't experienced recently, rather than your favorite memory that you replay over and over, that revisited memory is going to be one that is closer to the original then the one you replay in your mind over and over. Because that gets corrupted over time. You start to remember the memory.

KS: Right.

DM: Rather than the initial thought.

KS: No, I agree with that 100%. If there's a—I mean I guess it's the purest form before you've actively remembered it, but I dunno how pure that is. I think it's as pure as any memory before, over time—

DM: Memory is subjective. Of course.

KS: Yeah, yeah, exactly. But—

DM: @Sciencedog says, "I went back and watched *Power Rangers* and it was surprisingly not as badass as I thought." All right. You know, I had the exact same situation with the *Ninja Turtles* cartoon. That—I'm sorry—I loved that as a kid and it just doesn't—It's not entertaining to me anymore.

KS: I would say any cartoon I've seen as a kid, well practically any, has fallen short.

DM: I think *Garfield and Friends* holds up surprisingly well, but you definitely have to buy into what it's doing. There was a period recently where I had to watch a bunch of them for a project I was doing for work, and I don't know if it was the selection of episodes that was provided to me or if they were all like this, but they were *all* self-referential. They were all meta. They occupied this universe that understood itself in a way that I never noticed as a kid. And it's things like talking to the camera, talking about that process—that it's a television show, talking about how to structure a joke, *as* they're doing it. And about writing comedy and all these sorts of in-jokes and existential recirculation that made it so I really enjoyed coming back to that. Because it was almost a cartoon show *about* it being a cartoon show.

KS: Yeah. I think most episodes were like that. The only thing I didn't like about *Garfield and Friends* is when they'd ditch out to U.S Acres. I couldn't care less about those guys. I kind of liked Wade's design, but, you know...

DM: @Koeso1 says, "What about U.S. Acres?" I wonder if that was just to make that show an hour long? Like, you couldn't take an hour of Garfield and Jon and Binky the Clown, and so we had to change the setting a little bit.

KS: I'm surprised it was an hour.

DM: Yeah. A cartoon show was an hour! And it was a sketch show basically—although I guess a lot of cartoons will have the 15-minute episodes, or the 10-minute episodes in between commercials.

KS: I guess.

DM: Like *Animaniacs* and all that kind of stuff.

KS: *Animaniacs* was only a half an hour long. I mean, you might have three vignettes in there, but...

DM: I wonder if the whole process of pitching *Garfield and Friends* was, "We can give you an hour's worth of material," and it's such a known property that people are going to jump at that. They're going to sell more ads and fill more space.

KS: Yeah. That's true. They probably said, "Look. For 20% more effort we can fill a whole hour."

DM: Right. Not knowing, you know—the network didn't know. It was all, "What's this pig? What's this duck? What's going on?"

KS: That's right.

DM: "Oh, but we'll make the comic strip too." Did you see how they did the comic strip?

KS: Now, I thought—I thought the comic strip came first.

DM: Aw, maybe it did. I don't know.

KS: I don't remember, but I do know it was one of Jim Davis's things that didn't seem to do as good as "Garfield."

DM: Right. You know that Jim Davis did a "Mr. Potato Head" comic strip? Might *still* be doing it.

KS: I remember it.

DM: A licensed "Mr. Potato Head" comic.

KS: And it was pretty rank, I thought. But, you know what? His hands are tied. Can you honestly make Mr. Potato Head funny? He could store things in his body. That's about it.

DM: Well, *Toy Story* kind of made him into an interesting character. I guess, in contrast with all the other characters in that world, for sure.

KS: Well, I would say though, that "Mr. Potato Head" the comic strip was not like *Toy Story* where they got permission to use Mr. Potato Head and used him towards a particular end and a sense of humor in the movie. Whereas the comic strip was probably labored over by Hasbro executives going, "Now, I don't think we should show his eyes coming off, ever. I mean I know that's part of the toy, but it could upset the children. So let's—"

DM: "What is that little thing right there?" "Well that's just a French fry..." "That's placed in a very inappropriate place."

KS: That's a little racy for Mr. Davis, but...

DM: We have a couple more tweets. @KOESO1 says, "U.S Acres did have that good bit about gravity being called 'grabbity' because it grabs." Yes. There was the one highlight. That's nice.

KS: All right. That's plenty. I mean in seven years of a show, you get one good line. I guess that's okay.

DM: @KEDOTEGE says, "What I've noticed is that as I've gotten older my memories of things change focus, like with *Batman: The Animated Series*." Tell me—I'd like to get a follow-up on this. Explain exactly what you mean by "change focus." We can speculate, but let him clarify that, because I think that might be interesting.

KS: I think it's as he got older he—I mean when you're younger you're like, "Yeah! Batman. Do it." And then when you get a little bit older watching *The Animated Series* you're like, "Oh. Catwoman. Oh my goodness. Poison Ivy. I like these Bruce Timm ladies."

DM: "I like this sexualized cartoon character."

KS: "Batman is doing everything *I* want to be doing."

DM: So, Bruce Timm—we've got these humanoid characters in sort of a more—slightly more—adult cartoon world. But that sort of sexualization of cartoon characters starts fairly early.

KS: I would say.

DM: Wouldn't you say?

KS: I would say that that's a great segue, because one of the things my brother and I—it's one of the ones I have *not* been able to revisit. This would have been about, like '92, '93, which would have made me maybe thirteen at the most, and my brother's three years younger than me. But I remember reading in the *LA Times*, the Calendar section on Sundays—it used to be a big fat section—it's like its own book. With like, you know, the movie listings, but there were a lot of articles and play listings and stuff like that. They probably still do it.

DM: There are still newspapers. At least for the next six months or so.

KS: Oh yeah, the Sunday may have more content, may have less. It's like—it's just this little paper inside that says, "Eh, you know what? Go out, enjoy your Sunday." No paper today.

DM: "It's a weekend."

KS: "Wheeeeee. Uh, you know what? Even God rests…" All right.

DM: "Here's a bunch of grocery store ads. I hope you like 'em. Pretend they're comics!"

KS: "Hey, coupons, right? Everybody's got to go shopping."

DM: It's got word balloons on the broccoli.

KS: But in the Calendar section, they used to put a half-page ad, and it was an ad that was designed to look like an advice column. It was either called "Ask Minnie" or "Dear Minnie", and it's where people would write in questions to Minnie Mouse and she would answer them. And inevitably the answers were all like, "Well, if you need to get away from it all, you could, ah, try going to Disneyland." You know, it was advertising.

DM: What were the questions about?

KS: The questions were like…ahhh. I wanna say they weren't as hacky as, "I'm looking for a great place to take my family." You know what I mean? I think that the questions were more like—they tried to be more sly than that—like,

"I'm really stressed out but I don't know where to take my family on a budget."
You know? And then her answers were always, "This is my favorite thing at
Disneyland and right now you can get—the kids get in at half price,"—whatever,
whatever. And that was a whole half a page.

DM: But it was standard advice-column type questions from—do you think it was
actually from readers? Or do you think they wrote them?

KS: No, no. I mean, this is going to be a manufactured memory, but I want to say
that even the submitters' names—the people who wrote the questions had fake
pun names. But I don't know that that's true. They were supposed to be actual
questions, but it was obvious the way they were asked that this whole thing was
written by one guy.

DM: Now was this something that recurred a lot, do you think? Like throughout time?
For how long? For a month? For a year?

KS: I'm going to say that there was a period of at least... it came out weekly, on the
Sundays, and I want to say there was a period of at least two months. Because I
know there was a relatively good run of them. And the reason why I remember
them is because I'd read the Calendar, just because—I think the comics might
have been in that section back then. But I'd read the Calendar and I'd always read
the Ask Minnie column. And I started to notice a pattern in the way the questions
were presented.

DM: Right.

KS: And the way that Minnie would answer back. And it was always—I swear—I
would bring Kurt over to look at it, and we would laugh at it. At that point we'd
wait for that Calendar section to show up, just so we could dig in. But we swore
that everything that Minnie wrote back with was just rife with sexual innuendo.

DM: *(laughs)*

KS: It was stuff like, "One of my favorite things at Disneyland is to visit the..."
friggin', the old thing, whatever that Haunted Mansion was made out to look like,
that old plantation—"And I know that there's an old cannon in front. And I know
Mickey just loves to shoot his cannon. And while I'm at it, let's go over to the hot
dog stand and get some of those delicious foot-long wieners."

I mean, there was nothing like, "And then Mickey and I would get in the back..."
You know? It wasn't like that. But I had this theory that this had been a project
handed to, like, a junior-level ad guy at Disney, and they said, "We're writing
an advice column. Make it fun. You know, just talk about—here's your talking
points for this week and what offers we have, and go ahead and run with it." And
I felt—I mean now, knowing what I know now about Disney, I don't see how
that's possible. But at the time I thought, "There's nobody reading this! Nobody
is governing what this guy is writing, because every one of Minnie's responses is
talking about some kind of a phallus! And how much she enjoys it! And how you
could come to the park and do the same things with Mickey and Minnie."

And Kurt and I would just die laughing at it. And it's such a powerful memory.
I'd be ashamed to find out later that it's just like, "Oh, those were just coupons.
There's no advice."

DM: So how old were you at the time?

KS: I was probably—I wanna say I was between 11 and 13. Or maybe 12 and 14. And that would have put my brother at 9 to 11. So, pretty juvenile. Not quite at puberty.

DM: But this is sort of prime seeing-sexual-innuendo-in-things age.

KS: Potentially, yeah. I mean, it was the cusp of puberty, definitely. And it was just at the age where instead of going, "Wieners? That's gross, I don't wanna think about that." Now it was like, "Wieners? Tee-hee-hee!" So there was a lot going on, I thought. I think.

DM: You think.

KS: I mean—I maintain.

DM: And this is roughly when? Like era? Era-wise.

KS: It would have been early nineties.

DM: Early nineties. Okay.

KS: Yeah. I believe.

DM: Okay. Real quick, we have a response from @KEDOTEGE: "Well, yes, Kris, Poison Ivy is a naughty, naughty girl, but what I was getting at was themes, uses of music and color, and voice work." 140 characters, and he manages to be extremely patronizing.

[BOTH HOSTS LAUGH]

DM: And then he goes on to say, "When I was younger it was all about the punching and the kicking and that little bit of blood in *Mask of the Phantasm.*"

KS: I just want to say that I also noticed the color and themes and symbols, whatever. At the time.

DM: So you didn't need to wait to get older to appreciate all the colors and themes.

KS: No. Actually, him saying that makes me want to go back and watch it. And now pay attention to that, because, I think until I stopped watching it—when did that go off the air? I dunno. I must have been like 17 or 18. I was just like, "Maaan, he punched him hard."

DM: You missed all of it. Even the second time around. Even as an adult.

KS: Yeah. I just thought, "It's a good Batman show!"

DM: And, ah, I think—@BRETTDONNELLY puts it an interesting way. He says, "I think it's interesting how nostalgic characters retain the pedestal you place them on in your childhood. You feel a sense of awe you can't feel for comparable characters in your adulthood." This is true. This is something I was thinking about recently when I was on a UStream and I was sharing the music video from the *Ninja Turtles.* It was for the first *Ninja Turtles* movie.

KS: Oh yeah.

DM: "T-U-R-T-L-E Power."

KS: I vaguely remember that.

DM: And this is a bad song. It has horrible lyrics. It's things like—I think here's one of the lyrics: "I was mugged/ Give me a quarter/ I'm-a find a phone booth/ Call me a reporter." Things like that.[35]

KS: And at the time you'd be like, "Reporter/quarter. Yes!"

DM: But it was *so* awesome. Like, watching it I felt such a nostalgic wave of "Yes, I love this so much." And it was hard to differentiate between enjoying it for any merits it might've had, versus enjoying it for nostalgic reasons because I truly, truly love—especially the second *Ninja Turtles* movie. I think the first *Ninja Turtles* movie is very good. I think the second one—I love it as a fun movie. I would never be able to—well, I don't know. I have tried to defend it to different people. I won't shy away from that. But I was having a hard time differentiating between, like, "Couldn't I just enjoy the nostalgic fun without having to label it as 'oh, you only like it because you were ten when the movie came out.'"

KS: Yeah.

DM: It's still legitimate enjoyment I'm getting from it. Right? It's still making, like, my blood pressure rise and making me feel happy. Can't I keep that? Can't I enjoy that?

KS: You can keep it. But I don't think you have a right to demand that people don't make fun of you. Or at least, not the right to demand that people interpret it as great. You know, now that they're seeing it for the first time. You know? Not to get nerdy about it, but I know that that's been an argument with *Star Wars*. Like, "Yeah, you like it because you saw it as a kid. But the original trilogy's crap. It's not very good."

DM: That's a tough question, because maybe there's someone who feels that same really warm nostalgic feeling for something that I wasn't ten years old for when it came out. Either I was too old to like it, like *Power Rangers*. Or it was before my time. But somebody else is like, "Oh I just really, really love this." And to me that seems like, "Oh come on. Dude. Seriously? Like, grow up."

KS: We got, like, I don't know, maybe another ten years to go. Where everyone was like five or six when they first saw the *Star Wars* prequels.

DM: Right. Yeah.

KS: Where they'll be of age to be able to discern, you know—because they may be like, "No. I remember we went to see it. It was awesome. I got to see Jedi. It was great." You know, "My dad was there." All these memories tied in.

DM: Yeah. I wonder how critically thinking the seven-year-olds are. Or if they got jaded—seven-year-olds are pretty media-savvy nowadays. If they got caught in with that swell of, "No, everything sucks."

KS: Right. I wanted to push it younger because, yeah, if it's like a ten-year-old who, back when the original *Star Wars* came out it was probably the most amazing

---

35 Actual lyrics: "The crime wave is high with muggings mysterious/ Our police and detectives are furious/ 'Cause they can't find the source of this lethally evil force/ This is serious so give me a quarter/ I was a witness, get me a reporter/ Call April O'Neil in on this case, and/ You'd better hurry up, there's no time to waste/ We need help, like quick, on the double/ Have pity on the city, man it's in trouble!" ©1990 Partnerz in Kryme

thing in the world, but if you're ten now looking at it you're probably like, "Meh, it sucks. There's so much better." And you get back on your BlackBerry.

DM: We also have @TPARADOX, who says "My first memory used to be going to meet my newborn brother. Then I was told I couldn't have been with my mom, and then it changed." This is true. There are things—either I've seen a picture of myself when I was a kid, or I've heard the story so often that I feel like I remember it. I'd be interested to hear, @TPARADOX, what your memory changed to.

KS: Yeah, it's not nearly as fun as my vision of Minnie as some oversexed trollop.

DM: That's true.

KS: But my first memory, I've always maintained, is being baptized. And I was baptized at like 6 months. And my parents say, "No, there's no way. There's no possible way." But I described him—I described the guy—and I didn't see pictures of it. At least I didn't think I had. And I remember the water going over—my theory is that I dreamt about it like a year later, and I'm remembering the dream.

DM: Oh sure. Yeah. And that's tricky when you have those—especially when you're young and you have those dreams, and then they seem like legitimate memories later because you can't really differentiate. It's all so cloudy from back then. Well, here's the thing. I was at the library recently.

KS: Oh yes, yes.

DM: And what I did was, I decided to look in the microfilm archives to see if I could find the "Dear Minnie" column, because I've heard you talk about this before.

KS: Right.

DM: So I said, "Let's either verify or disprove Kris' memory of the Minnie Mouse advice column."

KS: Likely disprove.

DM: So I did a search in the *LA Times'* Calendar section. I started in—I wanted to give myself some range, so I started in 1992 and I looked through about 1997.

KS: I'm sure you must've hit somethin'.

DM: So, results are going to be after this short break!

[ACCORDION STING]

[The podcast version of this show included a delightfully laugh-free sponsorship segment here, which we have excised for length.]

[ACCORDION STING]

DM: So here's the thing. With the L.A. Central Library, they have a huge periodicals collection. And I go there all the time; I like to look through old books. And so I have a—

KS: I've never been to that one. I remember going to the Powell library at UCLA.

DM: Oh sure. Yeah. And so they keep the *LA Times* on microfilm. They have the microfilm reader, and you have to spool the film on there and everything. And they can only fit six days of newspaper on a roll of microfilm.

KS: Okay.

DM: And I was looking through years' worth of stuff. So I tried to be smart. First I said, "All right. Start with—"

KS: Ugh. Does that Sunday, like, drift across, then? Like they do six and then, "Here's Sunday. Starts on that one." And that means that Sunday's going to be two deep on the next one. And three deep on the next one.

DM: Yes.

KS: Ugh.

DM: So I had to kinda guess where the Sundays are.

KS: That is rotten.

DM: But at first—here's the thing. With the books I normally get from the library, you know the periodical indexes? I get old books from the 1800's, and they bind those books in hardcover.

KS: Yeah.

DM: And so you can get a giant book that's six months, and just flip through it. So I was thinking I'd just do that. But no, it's all microfilm, and it's all the very few days per roll.

So at first I said, "All right. January first, 1992. Let's just start at the top." And I quickly realized that it was not an idea that would scale easily. So what I did instead was, I picked sort of representative random dates. Like, here's April of '92, and then maybe we'd go with November. And we'd go with May of '93 and stagger it a little bit to try and pinpoint—like, if it's gonna be a several-month-long thing, it'll probably be in one of these dates.

KS: Yeah.

DM: And I also had the idea that maybe it was a summer promotion, because of, you know, summer, traveling and vacations. So—

KS: Oh yeah, that's smart too! Plus, my brother and I would have been home and been able to read it.

DM: Sure. So I definitely looked through June/July/August, those sort of things. And the way that they scan these papers is, they scan everything. They scan all the real-estate supplements. They scan all the grocery coupons.

KS: Right.

DM: Every single thing. Now, the thing that made this feasible is that the Calendar section is a shorter section. It's not the same height as the newspaper page.

KS: So you could find it pretty easy.

DM: You could scroll though the microfilm at high speed and see when the pages changed shape. So there were a few of these short sections. There was, like, the book-review supplement in the Sunday, and that sort of thing. And the Calendar was like the second chunk of short pages. So I able to zip to it pretty quickly, and I was able to find a fair number of dates that I could investigate.

KS: Okay. Okay.

DM: So. The column was called "Dear Minnie."

KS: So it *was* called that!

DM: It was called "Dear Minnie." It was a vertical column, as you remember.

KS: Yes. *Yes!*

DM: It took up—It was typically on the right hand side of the page.

KS: Okay.

DM: The border of the column was a red—sort of a polka-dot, like Minnie's dress.

KS: Of course.

DM: And it said "Dear Minnie" at the top and it had a little portrait of Minnie. And at the bottom it says "Disneyland." It's a Disneyland ad, obviously.

KS: I'm enthralled!

DM: And what I'll do after the show is I'll scan some of the pages, because I printed out what I found. I'll put up some images and I'll link to it on the @TWEETHARD account. So you can take a look at this a little bit later. Get your eyeballs on it.

KS: *(giddy)* Oh man. Oh man. Kurt is going to flip out.

DM: So. As best as I could tell, it ran in 1995 only.

KS: Okay.

DM: I didn't find it in the summer of '96 or in the summer of '94. So—and I only did spot checks.

KS: Seems likely.

DM: But I did find it in 1995. It seems to have run from June through September.

KS: Okay.

DM: Every Sunday of 1995. So, I didn't go before June—there may have been a May or something, but I figured, if your hypothesis is right and you think the person writing this column is getting more and more deranged as the days go on, it's going to get the weirdest at the end.

KS: Because I remember at some point, we went to look and it was gone. And I thought, "Oh, they caught him! They must have found him."

DM: I'm going to read you a sample question.

KS: Oh, yes!

DM: "Dear Minnie, My husband and I will be taking our five-year-old daughter to Disneyland in a few weeks."

KS: Okay.

DM: "Like her parents, she loves fast rides, but she sometimes gets cold feet at the last minute."

KS: *(giggles)*

DM: "What are our options if this happens? Or if she doesn't meet the height requirements?"

KS: Okay. That's like a real piece of advice.

DM: Signed, "Looking for Solutions."

KS: Okay.

DM: "Dearest Looking"—I'm not going to do the Minnie Mouse voice. "Dearest Looking, Oh my, I'm so glad you wrote in! With so many exciting attractions like the Indiana Jones"—TM—"Adventure, Splash Mountain, and the Matterhorn bobsleds, it would be a shame for you to miss out on the thrills."

KS: Okay.

DM: "That's why we have what's called ChildSwitch. While one parent or adult waits with the small child or shy child, the other adult in the party can go on the attraction. When the ride is over, you quickly switch and the next adult goes on. If you're interested, just let the host or hostess know you'd like to do a ChildSwitch."

KS: That kinda sucks. Just as an idea in general. It's not—it wasn't very sexual.

DM: This is from Sunday, August 20th, 1995. And each column had sometimes two, sometimes three—typically there're three short little question/answers.

KS: Right.

DM: Actually, ahh, maybe it's two. There's two, and then there's like a little note. Here's the next one. "Dear Minnie, My kids love sleeping out underneath the stars, especially on these warm summer nights. But we're looking for some other nearby sights. I know Disneyland has accommodations for RVs, but what about casual tent campers like us?"

KS: Okay.

DM: "Signed, Tents-R-Us."

KS: I wasn't old enough yet to think about tents as an innuendo. I don't think I would've been able to figure that one out.

DM: So this is—I mean, these questions are about Disneyland in particular.

KS: But it's not like a McDonald's ad where it's like, "I'm bored. What'll we do? Oh, go to McDonald's." It's like, "What can Disneyland provide me beyond what I know already?"

DM: Yeah. Exactly. You're providing information that people might not have thought about, or maybe concerns that they have. But there's a reason they are asking this question to Minnie, and not Dear Abby.

KS: Right.

DM: Because they *are* talking about Disneyland. Here's the answer to Tents-R-Us. "Dearest Tents, I know just the grassy area for you, and guess what? It's right in our own backyard. You may have read about Disney's Vacationland Campground in one of my earlier columns, but oops! I must have forgotten to mention the delightful spaces set up for tent campers like you. Why, you're right near picnic tables and built-in barbecues. So you don't have to bring your own! But you may want to bring your bathing suit because they have a good-sized pool there, just right for a refreshing dip."

KS: *(weak laugh)*

DM: "And speaking of *dip,* I hear one of the most popular attractions of Vacationland is the all-night showing of—you've got it—The Big Dipper."

KS: What?

DM: All right. Here's the button at the end here.

KS: Okay.

DM: "Happy tenting."

KS: Ha-hah. Come on!

DM: *Happy tenting.* Is that a thing, do you think? Someone's "tenting," you know?

KS: Yeah. No, I could easily go there. I could've gone there. But the thing was—what was it? I think in my depraved state I would have latched on to, "And here's another attraction for you," you know? Like, I'm not even following sense. Like, "Oh my—she said it! Men and women are attracted." But no, okay, no. Happy tenting. Now we're starting. That's the territory. That was the level of things.

DM: Mm-hmm.

KS: I seemed to remember them compounding themselves.

DM: Here's another one, from August 13th. "Dear Minnie. We noticed a couple of mountain climbers scaling the Matterhorn Mountain. Who were they and how did they do it? Signed, On Safe Ground."

"Dear Ground, You have an eye for adventure! What you saw were the Matterhorn Climbers. What a talented group of men and women! These folks are top-notch pros and are at least fifth-class climbers. In climbers' talk, that's the second-most difficult climbing class, and they have at least three years' experience under their lederhosen. They know how to climb like the best of them in the world, but—oh my!—the Matterhorn can be tricky at times. No, there aren't any built-in steps to make the climb easier, but I bet they wish there were. It would sure make waving to guests a lot easier. Now, if one of the climbers you saw looked like Mickey, it was! Matterhorn Mickey, as he likes to be called, can occasionally be found climbing that mountain, and like the Matterhorn climbers, Mickey proves that he too, is an entertainer of the highest degree."

KS: Eh.

DM: We getting anywhere here? Or is this... I'm wondering...

KS: I'm not aroused right now.

DM: Your reaction to this—it was not something you were searching out. It was something that you latched onto, that you found. Right?

KS: Yeah. It wasn't like—I didn't approach it with the hypothesis that there is some kind of deviant—some sex-obsessed maniac writing this, and I'm gonna prove it. I was reading it idly and I thought, "Jeez, there's a lot of that stuff." And I would laugh about it to myself before I brought Kurt in.

DM: So I'm wondering if maybe there is some stuff buried in here. Here's September 17th. This is a little later than the August ones.

KS: Okay.

DM: "Dear Minnie, My husband isn't exactly a morning person, but my family wants to get an early start on our day at Disneyland next month. Is there some place you can recommend that serves great pastries and cappuccinos before the park opens? We'll be staying at the Disneyland hotel. Signed, An Early Bird."

KS: "I don't know how to help you. There's *no* place that serves coffee or breakfast in the park."

DM: That's actually—@SEVENF here says, "I bet Minnie doesn't answer any questions where Disneyland didn't accommodate."

KS: "Sorry. You're out of luck. Wheelchair access is very limited."

DM: "Dear Minnie, Is there any way to avoid the long lines? My husband is asthmatic and my child, um, also has some sort of immune disorder. Can we somehow bypass the lines, because we don't want to spend 14 of our 16 hours at Disneyland just standing in your friggin' line? Signed, Seriously." "Dear Seriously, them's the breaks."

KS: "Dear Seriously, Mickey and I like to get it on." I *knew* it!

DM: "Dear Early"—er—"Dearest Early, What good timing! Just this month The Coffee House opened at the Disneyland hotel. It's a delightful place next to Stromboli's Ristorante. It welcomes customers as early as 5:30 A.M. I hear they have scrumptious fresh-baked muffins and Danish, biscotti, espresso beans, coffee-based chocolates and other goodies." Except she calls them "expresso beans." I wonder if this is a regional thing or some sort of—

KS: Nah, I think they just did it.

DM: —Branding thing. Or it's just 1995.

KS: Yeah.

DM: "You may want to take some home with you. And their fresh-roasted beans make some of the best coffee and specialty drinks anywhere. I just love the smell of fresh ground coffee. Sounds like even your husband will want to rise and shine early that day."

KS: I could've gone somewhere with that!

DM: Yeah. That one I flagged as a possible. "My Uncle Sherman will be visiting"—but here's the thing that makes me wonder if they are, in fact, real questions, because some of these are so obscure. Like, "Dear Minnie, My uncle Sherman from Minnesota will be out visiting in October. He's an avid collector of Disney merchandise. You should see his keychain collection, and I know he'll be looking for more of the rare and unusual. Which direction should I point him in?" Like, is this some Disney staffer saying, "I know, how about a question from a guy with a keychain collection?"

KS: No. It's gotta be—I mean look at the breakfast thing. They're like, "Oh, what a coincidence, it just happened to be open." I'm sure it's like—it's probably some inter-department thing where they say, "Uh, hey, what's not selling? Keychains. We cannot move these things for the life of us. All right. Let's see what this drums up."

DM: All right, let me see what else we've got. Okay. This is June. This is early in the cycle.

KS: This is earlier? Okay.

DM: Yeah. "Dear Minnie, I live near Disneyland. I can see the fireworks from my front porch. Mom says I can watch them if I go to sleep right after that. When will you have fireworks in the sky every night? Me and my mom really like them a lot. Signed: Yours truly, Daniel."

"Dearest Daniel, Well, the performances of Fantasy In The Sky fireworks are now nightly. So you and your mom should be able to see them every night right through summer. Did you know that this fireworks show has been brightening the sky for—let's see—Oh my, 38 years now! And the fireworks come from places as far away as China, Australia and France. Ooh-la-la."

KS: That's sexual.

DM: Yeah. The China part, or...?

KS: Yeah.

DM: The "Ooh-la-la?"

KS: No, just China. Just mentioning other countries as a foreign venue.

DM: They're exotic!

KS: For debauchery.

DM: "I'm glad you and your mother enjoy them so much. You know what I always say? The best fireworks are the ones you share with someone you love."

KS: See—!

DM: Yes? No?

KS: Look, I can go there. And the fact is that, like—I swear to God, there was one with hot dogs. But that was about the level of which, where we were like, "No. Come on. There's too many of these things." Couldn't it be that my brother and I were just mistaking familial love for sex?

DM: The love between a humanized mouse and its opposite-gender, humanized, freakishly life-sized, man-sized mouse partner.

KS: "I bet they're doing it."

DM: Bonded for life...

KS: "That means they're gonna do it."

DM: I wonder if Minnie had a hysterectomy or something. It's like, why are there not more mouse children?

KS: That's true. Did they ever say that? "Is Disneyland a romantic place to take my husband? I really want kids. And frankly I'm getting kind of sick of this."

DM: Ah, "Dear Minnie, I'm thinking about having a hysterectomy, have you had your tubes tied? What can you explain about it?"

"Well! Oh, my! Oh, dear! Well, let me see. When I had the surgery, it was 1944, so things may have changed. Disneyland has their own staff of doctors in-house."

KS: *(laughs)*

DM: "If your kids get—if they're driving you nuts, you just walk in here, take a load off, and we'll make sure no more of those nasty brats ever come squirtin' out of you again."

KS: "And also, enjoy our pastries!"

DM: Here's one that might have sparked something with your...your wiener fetish.

KS: All right. I'm ready.

DM: "Dear Minnie, What's the name of the fast-food barbecue place at Disneyland that serves chicken and vegetable kabobs, and where is it located? We're coming to the park next month, and would love to get some of those kabobs to eat while watching Fantasmic. Signed, Kabob Bob."

KS: Really? Yeah, that's real.

DM: "The way I can remember the name of the place you're talking about is to think B, as in Big Bobbin' Bengal Barbecue. Oh, but I hear lots of my friends say the food is A+. This delicious food find is in Adventureland. Why, you can get beef kabobs there too." Eh?

KS: That one didn't do it for me. Although, look. My tastes may have changed.

DM: "And fresh fruit with a raspberry yogurt dip, or fresh vegetables with a tasty dill dip. Whatever sounds Fantasmic to you." Blah blah, it goes on to talk about sorbet.

KS: Ha. Now we're just talking about ice cream.

DM: This one doesn't really make a lot of sense—talking about the portrait artists? "As you may remember, they work in pastels and they work fast. It only takes 16 minutes"—or—"15 minutes for a profile, and 25 minutes for a front-view portrait." Yeah, like, "it takes 16 minutes, or 23.5 minutes—"

[BOTH HOSTS LAUGH]

DM: "Why, you can even get it framed right there and they'll hold it for you until you're ready to 'head' home." Head is in quotation marks.

KS: What? See. Like, I might have been able to pick up on that.

DM: Otherwise that's like the worst pun ever. If it's not sexual, I'm not sure why it's such a horrible—

KS: You know what? I think—I don't know how many of those you have, but I have a feeling that that was the caliber of the pun. And so you would end up with this thing where it's like, "Why did they do that?" You know?

DM: Like, you'd have to drill deeper and see if you can figure out some...

KS: Yeah! I mean, here I understand it's because they drew a picture of your head, but, you know, I think at the time I would've just been, "Why did she call attention to that? There's no way!"

DM: Here's one. This is from June again. "When does the Pocahontas stage show at Disneyland open? Also, what kind of Pocahontas souvenirs are available at the park? Signed, Excited About Pocahontas."

[BOTH HOSTS LAUGH]

DM: Um, all right, blah blah blah. "My new friends Pocahontas, John Smith, Miko and John Ratcliffe. Why, it gives me goosebumps just thinking about that show. Pocahontas and all of her friends are causing lots of excitement and activity here at the park. Why, let's see..." There's lots of "why, comma..."

KS: Right.

DM: "Why, let's see—Oh yes, the restaurant. Mmm Yums near Videopolis is now Miko's, named after our friend from the movie. The new Pocahontas 'Child and Chief meals' are really yummy, and I hear the Spirit Of Pocahontas shop has everything from pencils to Pocahontas dresses for little girls, in all the colors of the wind. Hope to see you soon." Would you get anything there?

Later in the same column, talking about parasols: "I hope your daughter has a wonderful birthday. Please give her a big birthday hug for me." So you're picturing—you're like, what? 1995. You're like 16. Right? 1995?

KS: '95? I might have been.

DM: So, I don't know if you're thinking about little girls in their Pocahontas dresses getting hugs from giant humanoid mice-women...

KS: That doesn't seem to go far enough. Now, here's the thing.

DM: Yeah.

KS: It might be the case where the things I found perverted at age, ah, I guess at that time I would have been age 15 or 16... but now that I've gotten older, I've had to replace them in my *mind* with things that I think *now* would have been perverted, actually. You know what I mean?

DM: You rationalize that if you had such a strong reaction, they must have been talking about, you know—

KS: They *must* have been bad, and what could they have been? Well, they didn't talk about anything dirty. They must have been weird uses of, you know, penis-shaped words, and things like that.

DM: Right. Yeah. Come play with Mickey's balls in the ball pit, or whatever.

KS: Exactly.

DM: All right, I'll share one more. This is from July '95. "Dear Minnie, My whole family loves the King Arthur carousel. What can you tell me about the horses? How do they keep them so beautiful? Signed, Just Horsing Around."

"Dearest Horsing, Did you know that there are 72 painted horses in the King Arthur carousel stable? And that no two of them are exactly alike?" Well, of course I didn't know, that's why I wrote the question.

KS: Nobody asked.

DM: "Why, most of these prancing ponies were hand-carved in Germany about 100 years ago." Germany? Is that a sort of sexual thing? "And their beauty secret for staying so young? Well, all of them are 'brushed' by a master painter." *Brushed* in quotations.

KS: What? Oh, okay.

DM: "At the rate of 40 painting hours for each horse, it takes a couple of years to get around to them all." To *get around* to them all?

KS: No.

DM: "Then the cycle starts all over again." See? I don't know.

KS: Period. Like a period.

DM: Yeah. So I dunno what all there is in here. There is this part: "As for the oodles of brass poles on the carousel, I hear the person in charge spends six hours polishing them every night."

[BOTH HOSTS LAUGH]

KS: I bet you I looked at that one.

DM: "That's a lot of TLC!" Here's the thing. This is July. If I might make some sort of a reconstruction. maybe... because that is the most overt of any of them.

KS: Maybe they're saying—

DM: Maybe you landed on that one. And then from July, August, September, you started projecting.

KS: That's like the only one that could possibly be sexual. And then the hunt was on.

DM: And so, your hypothesis for the reason that they ended was this guy got caught, right?

KS: Yeah. Because, I mean, even

Dear Minnie:

Dear Minnie:
My whole family loves the King Arthur Carrousel. What can you tell me about the horses? How do they keep them so beautiful?
—Just Horsing Around

Dearest Horsing:
Did you know there are 72 painted horses in the King Arthur Carrousel stable . . . and that no two of them are exactly alike? Why, most of these prancing ponies were hand-carved in Germany about 100 years ago. And their beauty secret for staying so young? Well, all of them are "brushed" by a master painter. Now, at the rate of 40 painting hours for each horse, it takes a couple of years to get around to them all. Then the cycle starts all over again. As for the oodles of brass poles on the Carrousel . . . I hear the person in charge spends six hours polishing them every night! That's a lot of TLC!

Dear Minnie:
Where are the best places to spot Pocahontas and her friends at Disneyland? My kids want nothing more than to see them up close and in person.
—Looking For Pocahontas

Dearest Looking:
My goodness! There are lots of places where you can find this very popular young lady and her companions. Let's see now. . . . You can see them at The Spirit of Pocahontas stage show at the Fantasyland Theatre. And another great chance to make their acquaintance is Goofy's Kitchen at the Disneyland Hotel. Why, at dinner time, they come right up to your table so you may want to bring along your camera and autograph book. And if you want to have an "animated" conversation with my other Disney friends, I hear lunch is now being served at Goofy's Kitchen through Labor Day.

Dear Minnie:
I heard there's a shop at Disneyland where you can trace your family history. What's it called and how does it work?
—Roots In Ireland

Dearest Roots:
You must be thinking of the Heraldry Shoppe right in the archway of Sleeping Beauty Castle. It's the cutest little place. Wait until you see what's inside! First, you find your family name in the shoppe's directory and then you can read all kinds of fascinating facts about the family history on the computer screen. You can even see what your family's Coat of Arms looks like. And if you want to purchase a beautiful printout of it, the folks there will even frame it for you. They have lots of other fun heraldry things like Coat of Arms T-shirts, rings, mugs, and even wall clocks that will take you back in time!

Editor's Note: For Character Meal reservations at Goofy's Kitchen, call (714) 956-6755. For details on other information shared by Minnie, call Disneyland Park at (714) 999-4565.

Disneyland

©The Walt Disney Company.

though I knew it was an ad, there was a part of me that said, "Well, look, if they're going to end it, they're going to be like, 'Well that's the last one...' " They wouldn't have done that if it was just advertising. I thought, "No. It was in the paper last week and it's not here—What would call for such an unceremonious, abrupt, drop of this *featured* column?"

DM: September 24th, 1995. "Dear Readers, All good things must come to an end. So it's with a tear and a smile that I say thank-you and goodbye to all of you in my last Dear Minnie column. Your letters have given me more joy than I could have ever imagined. I never knew I had so many friends, but now that I'll be writing less, I'll have more time to spend with you at Disneyland. And, as you know from my column, the door to Minnie's house is always open."

KS: There you go.

DM: "I hope to see you in the neighborhood soon." Then there's a note, "No masks. Costumes deemed unsafe or inappropriate will not be permitted. Advanced ticket purchase recommended for Mickey's Halloween Treat."

KS: Well, what have we learned?

DM: I like how that's the edit—like all the boilerplate fine print is, um—

KS: Like, "Do not approach Minnie."

DM: That's the editor's note. From Minnie's editor. "Let's talk about the rules of Halloween at Disneyland."

KS: From the editor. Like he's not—he's not sending her off. It's not, like, "Thanks for this column." It's just like, "All right. Let's get this over with."

DM: "Listen. Lawsuits on our hands, frickin' kids." We have @CEPHALOPOD_GAL who says, "Got a friend who was told by her parents that she was conceived at Disneyland." So, I'm interested to see if that's the Disneyland hotel, or if that's—

KS: The park proper.

DM: You know, behind the Pirates of the Caribbean ride, and possibly by a character in a costume.

KS: Yeah. I like to think that after reading all those columns... you know... Depends on how old her friend is. Because if she was born in '96...

DM: Maybe they got some food...

KS: A little romance started up by that... Nah. I think we've learned that I was a pervert.

DM: Well, I mean, I'm glad that we talked about your childhood, and something that's provable, and not *my* childhood, which will remain in the misty, you know—

KS: The deep recesses.

DM: —The hazy shores of memory that can never be retrieved unless you find any of the books I was... 1995? I wrote a novel. I wrote—yeah, I was always writing a novel when I was a kid. They were never any good.

KS: I used to—I wrote—and I know it wasn't as late as '95. It would have been about '90. I wrote a zillion time-travel stories. And I have some the them. And they're all written—

DM: Just trying to go forward in time to where you're old enough finally—

KS: To get it on.

DM: —To *do* something with someone. "I wanna take on the whole park! Line 'em up!"

KS: No. One of the stories was this: I had my time machine, and ran out of power, and there was no way to get that power. But I happened to be—you have to understand, I was like ten years old—I happened to be in Japan. In 1944.

DM: Oooh.

KS: So what I was going to do was find ground zero, and I could collect the energy from the atom bomb just in time to get out of there.

DM: Now, would that absorb the power of the bomb, so that the bomb would not destroy—?

KS: Oh, not at all. I just needed a sliver.

DM: So all those people, still totally dead.

KS: The other people—I used the mechanism of their demise to go safely back home.

DM: Back to 1990?

KS: Back to 1990.

DM: To watch *Garfield & Friends*. I wrote a novel when I was—I think—My first sort of what you could call a novel, I wrote about the same time, same age. 1990. And it was a novel about these guys, and they had fighter planes, and they were, you know, solving all kinds of crazy... You know, like, you go on an Air Force base and there's a Russian guy trying to steal a helicopter, so they gotta dogfight him, and this kinda stuff. And I realized about halfway through writing it, that it was just aimless, you know, action scenes—

KS: Yeah. You're just having a good time.

DM: And then, starting from about page 50 or so, I just started copying from a *Hardy Boys* book. Like literally propping the book open and re-typing it. Because there was one *Hardy Boys* book about, like, pilots, and this hotshot airplane, and there was corporate espionage and all that.[36] And *Hardy Boys* books are not very big, you know, 150 pages or so. And so I just made the characters *my* characters— like, I just changed the names.

KS: I like the idea that "Look. Any story about pilots is just probably going to be about the same. Eh, there's no harm in me just copying it. I mean ,there's gonna be flying planes, there's going to be a crash."

DM: I literally had no conception of the—the concept of plagiarism. *Utterly* unknown. Just not even a shred of it. And so I'm just reading—again—I have the book propped open next to the keyboard as I'm typing it on my mom's TRS-80. And I spent a lot of time trying to get, like—using spaces to get the lines justified and everything. Printing it on the daisy-wheel printer. I hand-bound a couple of them. I had to go through and—I photocopied the pages, and in the copier, like, they would offset somehow; some of the pages didn't turn out right. So I'd scroll

---

36 Hardy Boys Casefiles #47, *Flight Into Danger.*

those pages into the typewriter and re-type that line of the page that got cut off. I put a lot of effort into this novel.

But yeah, it was—most of it was just a *Hardy Boys* book. And I even went a little more extreme with some parts of it. I remember there was one scene where the characters were in the restaurant eating, you know, fast food. "They stopped at a fast food place and Frank grabbed a soda," you know, was in the *Hardy Boys* book. So I was like, "Pssh, look at these guys. They're skirting around the issue. Here's my book: 'Major Bob stopped at McDonald's and grabbed a Diet Coke.'" I'm like, "Brand names!" *(claps hands)* "Using 'em!"

KS: There we go, that can't be wrong! That's gonna—somebody's going to notice that, before they notice some guy grabbing a soda.

DM: Right. Then they're like, "Wow. This guy, he's takin' it to the limit. He's extreme. He's not afraid."

KS: "Did you notice we've been selling more Cokes?"

DM: "He's livin' in the world that *I'm* livin' in." That was my big thing. It's like, "These people live in *our* world." It's all the verisimilitude, you know? The urge for verisimilitude.

KS: It's like, "these people are just faking it!" A generic diner. A generic sandwich.

DM: And I could never quite bring myself, even later, to tell my mom that I had plagiarized the entire *Hardy Boys* book, and so I would skirt the issue a little bit. I'm like, "Yeah. I kinda developed the plot after like 40 pages or so... It took me a while to figure out what was going on."

KS: And to this day your mom is very proud of that story.

DM: I hope she never read it. There's a lot of gore in it.

KS: Oh, jeez.

DM: This is at a time where I wanted to write—I even had a little term for it—"I'm going to write Gory Stories." Not that they were horror or anything like that, but it was just like—

KS: Just why not write about some guy *blowin' up?*

DM: Yeah. It was.

KS: People like that!

DM: I had been reading some of those, like, *Mack Bolan: Executioner* type books and that kinda thing, so... there's a lot of violence in these things. All right. So what have we learned? We have learned that "Dear Minnie"—Mickey likes to polish his poles, or whatever it is.

KS: I think we learned—it's not as bad as I though it was. Although I'm wondering if there isn't one that's earlier than that. Because it seems a little late—it seems a little juvenile of me at age 16, to be reading that and going, "Woooo, *poles!*"

DM: Like I said, June was the earliest that I checked. So next time I'm at the library, I'll spool up May, April. I will take a look. Like, I will do this. We can come together, make an excursion out of it, if you like. Because I am, you know, I'll do whatever it takes to put this to rest. That you were just an extraordinarily pervy little kid.

KS: It's possible.

DM: Because 16 is not—now you had told me, you have a brother. You didn't grow up with sisters.

KS: Yeah. I have a brother. I'm kind of eager to see what *his* recollection is.

DM: Yeah. You should—actually, I would like that. Now that we know the score for the most part, you should call up your brother. Either let's get him on the show, or get some sort of a written thing, or get a recording. I think you should have him call in next week's show.

KS: Leave a voicemail or something.

DM: Leave a voicemail, or I'd like to ask him the questions too. So if he's available to do a live interview, let's get him. And then we, and the listeners who know the reality of it, can sort of see how his recollection jibes with both your recollection, and then the actual truth of the matter.

KS: That's what I like about Tweet Me Harder.

DM: We'll make fun of everyone.

KS: Is that we run down answers!

DM: We disabuse everyone of their foolish notions. So hopefully we can get that going on for next week.

[closing music starts]

DM: So, you've been listening to Tweet Me Harder. This is the Internet's first, last, only and best talkback-enabled interactive audio podblast. We thank you for listening. We hope that you will check out our Twitter account, @TWEETHARD. In the next hour or so I'll do some scans of these pages.

KS: I can't wait.

DM: So you can take a look at them yourself. And draw your own conclusions. We report, you decide!

KS: And if you're like me, you're going to be saving them and putting them in a special folder on your hard drive.

DM: Oh, I thought you were going to actually have a folder—You're going to carefully lick the back of them and place them in the photo album that goes on the shelf inside the box, in back of the closet behind all the coats—

KS: It's scrapbook I have. It's just called *Disillusionments.*

DM: I think it'd be funnier if there's a scrapbook that's just waiting for "Dear Minnie, one of these days... I didn't know I was going to meet you but—"

KS: I've just got a binder full of letters I never sent in.

DM: "She never answered my letters." I wish I had the presence of mind to make photocopies of the letters I sent to various people as a child. I never did.

KS: Oh man.

DM: This is, you know, pre-computer, where everything was just on a typewriter. Okay. Hopefully next week we'll have some more; we'll have Kris' brother talk about his recollection.

KS: That would be awesome if we could get him.

DM: You can call our voicemail, ask us any question, request for advice or other question. The phone number is: area code—You know what? I'm going to see if I can remember it from the mnemonic.

KS: It's not possible. But I'll bail you out.

DM: 206.

KS: Okay.

DM: 337. Six...four-five-zero?

KS: No.

DM: Am I off?

KS: It was 206, 337—you're right so far—8-5-6-0.

DM: 8560. 337-8560. The way you can remember that is: two plus zero plus six is eight. Three plus three plus seven is 13. Um, five? 8560... Eight plus five is 13, *again.*

KS: Uh-huh. Okay.

DM: Six plus zero is six. So you can probably dial, just, 8-13-13-6, we'll probably get that as well.

KS: Just mash the keypad and leave a message. And if we get it, we'll play it on the air.

Escape from the Dentist

DM: Welcome to Tweet Me Harder. This is the Internet's first, best, only and last talk-back-enabled interactive audio podblast. I am your host, David Malki !

KS: I am also your host, Kris Straub.

DM: We're co-hosts.

KS: Together, we host.

DM: Separately, we are...not the *most*. We'd be the least. Independently, the least. Together, the host. Sort of a brood kind of scenario.

KS: That's really like a Taoist—that's a really philosophical thing. Because you'd think, apart, we would have something. But apart we have nothing.

DM: No, we have *something*. We just don't have a lot.

KS: Then why would it turn into a lot when we get together?

DM: It's sort of the way molecules bond with each other. Where they have to fit into, like, the one... I will give you the caveat: Everything I've learned about molecular chemistry has been from watching, like, shampoo commercials and stuff. Where they have, like, the big round-y molecules, with the different things, and they interlock. And so, they're drifting in this sort of blue CGI void, right? And then they drift towards each other, slowly rotating, and then the one sort of module part clicks into the other, uh, puzzle-piece-looking-thing, and then it's strong as glass to make your hair shiny, vibrant and bright.

KS: Oh yeah. I learn more about chemistry from those ads than from school.

DM: Right.

KS: I thought you were trying to—I thought you were going to make the example that salt is made out of poisons.

DM: Oh, right.

KS: So. Together—

DM: It's made out of arsenic and cyanide.

KS: Together it's death. Separately, I mean, but then you bring us—Well, you know what? Enough *salt* will kill you.

DM: It's rat poison and strychnine. Together, it's harmless table salt.

KS: "Go ahead." "No, I don't want to." "No, no, go ahead. Have a little bit."

DM: "I made my own homemade salt, dear. I took all the household poisons from underneath the sink, and I just mixed them together."

KS: "I made something for you. That's proof of happiness in a marriage. Have some."

DM: "It's Orange Glo and Oxi-Clean. They're all, like, organic green chemicals, right?"

KS: You know, we forgot to do a little bit of business. Guys, you are all listening to Tweet Me Harder and this is the seventh episode, so you can interact with us right now on Twitter by using hashtag #TMH7.

DM: Any tweet that says #TMH7, we will read, and in fact we are reading some now. So, if you have something to say, that's the way to say it! And we will, uh, you know…

KS: We'll talk to you. For example, @LYMANALPHA says, "Mmmm, delicious #TMH7." And I saw it because of the tag.

DM: That's how it works. It's called the Internet. It's, um—I don't want to say the *future,* but it's a pretty cool fad for now.

KS: It'll do. Look, I know what *I'm* doing this summer.

DM: It'll do until Cranio-Net goes online.

KS: *Finally.* Did anything ever happen with Internet-2? I know that it was for schools.

DM: Well, it had a bigger budget than the first one.

KS: Yes.

DM: Because the first one was a cult hit on DVD, so they decided to get some stars for the second one. But the problem was, they wrapped up the story very well in the first one, and so the second one was just like, "Ehh, bigger explosions…"

KS: It wasn't like a real sequel, yeah. It was just sort of like, "We've got to do it again."

DM: Yeah. Plus we'll get Brett Ratner. And I guess that guy must have a lot of friends. You know he has a photo booth in house?

KS: Oh, rad.

DM: For parties.

KS: No wonder.

DM: Yeah, they published a book, a hardcover cloth-bound book, of the photos celebrities took in his photo booth.[37]

KS: Racy. I'm imagining. But maybe it's not at all.

DM: Not really.

KS: Is it, so…

DM: Someone gave me that book as a gift. It comes shrink-wrapped. It's like, *Art Book.* Capital 'A', capital 'B'. 'U' with umlauts. *Bük.*

---

37 *Hilhaven Lodge: The Photo Booth Pictures,* 2003. List price, $35.00.

KS: That's what I was going to say, is that you don't... I dunno why you would have run across that thing. And I was going to say it's not... it probably wasn't presented like some rag. Like, "Drunk Celebs!" Bullet point.

DM: No, it wasn't at all. It was very highbrow. It's like large, crisp, glossy white paper. The photo strip aligned vertically, you know, one per page. There's sort of a really light italic type at the bottom of the page with the person's name. There's no annotations. That's... that's the book.

KS: "This picture always makes me think of summer."

DM: The only one I can remember is Michael Jackson's. Because I guess he attended some party at Brett Ratner's house. So.

KS: Well, what a feather in his cap. You know what? How disgusting, that he would get that book printed before Michael Jackson died. Just to make a friggin' killing, you know.

DM: Jeez. Man, I hate people...

KS: Talk about...

DM: I hate people! There's no qualifier.

KS: I don't need the follow-up. I just don't like people to be here.

DM: @Professor_d says, "Interesting to think that we are the last generation to remember a time before the Internet. All those who come after will never know." Well, I think we are in sort of a middle generation. I think there was no-Internet, no-Internet, for thousands and thousands of years.

KS: Yeah.

DM: And then, you know, there's this really compressed time up to the present which is like, "Hey, Darpanet, Internet, whatever. Now, we are in Internet time." And then there's going to be the holocaust, and then it's going to be no-Internet, no-Internet for thousands of years.

KS: Well, I don't know if you guys remember *Escape From Los Angeles*. The sequel to *Escape From New York*.

DM: Directed by Brett Ratner.[38]

KS: Directed by Brett Ratner, and featuring as President of the United States, Cliff Robertson in a landmark "give me my money" sort of role. And Snake Plissken destroyed the Internet. So...

DM: Good for him.

KS: Yeah.

DM: He really took a stand against, um... eBay.

KS: At the end of the movie, he blew up every satellite in the world. And they're like, "What are we gonna do now?" And he's like, "I don't care!" And that was the end of the movie. Because he had his bike and his smokes. He was finished.

DM: "My ill-defined need for rebellion is more important than your commerce and

---

38   Actually directed by John Carpenter. Brett Ratner's pseudonym.

your need to have groceries delivered to your door by FedEx."

KS: "What am I *rebelling* against? Whaddaya got? Alright, see you losers later." *(Motorcycle sounds)* Gets home. "I wonder what they said about this on... Oh."

DM: Ha-ha! Wahh-wahh-wahhhhr. *(Ironic punchline sting)*

KS: "I changed my miiiiiind!"

DM: And then in Part Three, he has to blast back into the atmosphere... like, up into the upper atmosphere, to find all the pieces of the satellites to put them all back together again.

KS: Yeah and there this really madcap sequence where he's like, "Oh boy! I dunno if this one... this goes to here or... Hhhhh."

DM: He's got a giant net. He's trying to... it's like a giant space butterfly net... but it's all in space, so it's like really balletic. And it's like, *(hums Nutcracker Ballet)*. And he's like, "Ughrrrr!" Like, snagging satellite pieces, old Russian satellites. "This one'll work. It's the same. It's got vacuum tubes."

KS: Right. "I don't need much! But maybe I'll get a little Internet on this one."

DM: Uh, @MCGORGOMAGON says, "Oh, man, that was like that terrible new *The Day The Earth Stood Still*, where at the end they blew up all the electronics." Now, the blowing up electronics, blowing up satellites, blowing up Internet, blowing up, you know, the EMP bomb, *Fight Club* destroying, you know, skyscrapers and bringing the whole credit economy to a standstill: is this some kind of sublimated wish-fulfillment on the part of the world? Is it like, we know we kinda effed this up, and we wish there was a way we could go back...

KS: "I wanna take a break!"

DM: ...We can't, obviously. It's sort of like, when someone says "Think about your 10-year plan for your life. What are the most rewarding things you could possibly achieve, and then those will be your goals." And you think, "Um..." You *know* the real answer is "Nurture a closer relationship with your family, and volunteer your time to help others," because that is going to be the most psychically, like, soul-nourishing, rewarding thing you can do, but you always... sort of...

You know that's the thing you're *supposed* to do, but it's like, "You know, I just want to be really famous."

KS: You're like, "Publish that book about celebrity nipslips that I had that idea for. Get a lot of pictures. That would have been smart. Would have been a smart move."

DM: "Step One: find pictures."

KS: "Step One: I guess go to every celebrity event and try to get a picture or something. Hope you catch one."

DM: "I should concentrate on the ones *(a)* with women. That cuts my work in half, just right there."

KS: "It cuts my work in half... I mean, as far as, you know, being selective, but the men's are so much easier to capture!"

DM: *(laughs hard)*

KS: So, I guess, you know what? Maybe I don't have the budget right now. I'll start out with the men's nipslips. I go to any beach, I'll find 'em. It's gonna be perfect. And, then, when I'm famous and wealthy, you know, I can hire a team.

DM: How do you think that press tour goes? It's like, "Ahem, tonight on this show, we have the author of *Male Celebrity Nipslips.*" Except no one will book him on their show, so he has to just call in to Larry King.

KS: It's just CSPAN-2. He's on *Book TV.* You know how they read the books to the audience? This is just, "Here's one. Right? You all see that? Okay. Here's another one. This one was pretty funny. This one's..."

DM: He holds the book open and shows it to the audience.

KS: Yeah. "Well, you know what? I'm gonna pass it around. I'm gonna pass it around. Everybody take a flip."

DM: Okay. This is what I picture. He goes on... he's just like, "I'm gonna get publicity any way I can, because people are going to hear about the concept of the book, they're going to seek me out. I just gotta get that concept out into the atmosphere." So, you just hear, "Columbus, Ohio, hello. We're talking about how the Michael Jackson family has requested privacy. We are staked out outside their house to honor their request. What are your thoughts?" "Well, Larry, I have this book called *Male Celebrity Nipslips...*"

KS: "And let me tell you exactly where I am."

DM: "I sympathize with this problem, because Michael Jackson also asked *me* to leave him alone."

KS: "In fact, there isn't anybody who hasn't asked me to leave them alone. But guess what I'm *not* gonna do?"

DM: "Unfortunately, I discovered... shockingly... I don't mind giving this away to your listeners or to your viewers. Michael Jackson has not one nipple... not two nipples... not three nipples... not four nipples... not five nipples... not six nipples..." and he just keeps going and going. He just keeps going. And they're like, "I'm gonna change the channel. Let's go over to Wolf Blitzer. Uh, no, nothing going on." Come back. "Not 48 nipples... not 49 nipples... not 50 nipples..." "Well, how many nipples did he have?"

KS: "Not 50... Wait, oh, sorry. It's two. Sorry. Sorry. It was two."

DM: "Actually, it was two. Yeah. I don't know how I..."

KS: "I really miscounted, guys. I kinda blew it."

[*ACCORDION STING*]

KS: You know what? I want to mention some tweets here.

DM: All right.

KS: And I want to mention them as a special service that the show provides, that Tweet Me Harder does for the community listening. @PROFESSOR_D says, you know, as a tack-on joke to *Escape From Los Angeles,* he says, "*Escape to the*

Stratosphere: The Satellite Scrambler." And then @TMOVERBECK said "*Escape From Earth's Atmosphere.*" So, the two of you guys get together and make some friends.

DM: I think *Escape From Earth's Atmosphere,* or just *Escape From Earth,* is sort of the next iteration of that.

KS: I like the idea that everywhere that Snake goes, he messes it up. He just always has to leave.

DM: Yeah, it's like "I'm leaving Earth. I'm going to the idyllic civilization on Mars." And then it's *Escape From Mars.* The Martians just have these pitchforks and these torches and Snake is like, "See ya, losers!" *(motorcycle races away)*

KS: *(laughs)* And then the fifth movie is *Snake, Please Leave.* "We don't care where you go. Nobody wants you."

DM: Snake's just wandering the dusty highway. "Will *you* put me up for a night?" "No! We will not! Get outta here!"

KS: You know those hobo signs that they... you know, it's like, a smiling cat means this house is friendly to hobos. There's a cat with an eye patch with an "x" on it.

DM: The three interlocking circles means "no buggery here."

KS: Yeah. "Don't bring it up. She won't give you soup."

DM: "She'll give you soup, but not the euphemism soup. Just the food soup."

KS: "Just the actual food. If you are hungry for actual soup, go to the house. It's gonna be fine."

DM: "If you want buggery, or the euphemism soup, you want to go to the one with four interlocking circles."

KS: "You want to go to the one with the drawing of 48 Michael Jackson nipples."

DM: "A lot of people get confused with the drawing of 48 Larry King nipples, but that means something *totally* different. Don't go in there!"

KS: "You can tell the other one because the Michael Jackson one, I just drew a little musical note on top."

DM: "And the Larry King one is just... the nipples look kinda shriveled and wrinkly. It's hard to say in chalk."

KS: "There's two lines. They're suspenders."

DM: "If you can't... it's hard to explain, but you'll know what I mean if you see it."

KS: "That's what we talk about getting a feel for the road. You've gotta understand your hobo business."

DM: @PROFESSOR_D says, "David, you could easily participate in Kevin Pollak's chat show 'Larry King Game.' " This sounds like something I'd be interested in. I do not know what it is. I request a follow-up from @PROFESSOR_D. Please send us a tweet explaining what that is, because I assume Kris doesn't know either.

KS: I don't know either. I do know that Kevin Pollak has a show on UStream.

DM: It's not this show?

KS: No, I don't think he's been on this one yet.

DM: Not on our show. Okay.

KS: No. I also suspect that we won't be featured on their site any time soon, because of the lack of video. It's kind of opposite to the point of the service. "We just want the audio. That's fine."

DM: We should have, like, a slide show that goes along with ours, that updates like every five seconds. It's like a really slow animation. It's just like, "Hey!" and our faces are all happy. And then the faces are sad. And then we're kind of talking to each other, and looking ponderous.

KS: We can cue up emotions. We just take pictures of them, and then when we're talking about something and I'm mad, I just drag and drop it on there.

DM: We shouldn't even control it. It should just be on some sort of automatic cycle.

KS: Yeah, just point it at your directory...

DM: It's just changing as we're talking. We have no idea if it's going to sync up or not. If it does, it's almost like one of those things if you're listening to the radio, but you're watching TV, and sometimes they sync up. You know, it's going to be accidental like that. And oh-so-good when it does.

KS: *(laughs)* Ah, here's a tweet. @MCGORGOMAGON... that's it. I don't want to read the tweet, 'cause I don't care. That's the best part of the tweet. 'Cause it killed me the last time. Ah, but it's awesome.

DM: @ALSOBAGELS says, "Internet-2, to go back to that, was overly long and they killed Optimus, but then he came back. Predictable." I think you're thinking of *Unbearable Noise 2*. Similar movie, but different.

KS: I have not seen that film.

DM: *Unbearable Noise 2?*

KS: No, and I won't be.

DM: It's a lot like the title suggests.

KS: It's not a title that they really...

DM: Well, there's a subtitle, too. "Indecipherable Motion."

KS: *(laughs)* Nausea. "Epileptics, do not attend screening."

DM: @PROFESSOR_D follows up. He says, "The Larry King game. One: Do a bad Larry King impression. Two: Reveal something about yourself as Larry, but no one needs to know." Okay, I can see this. So, it's something like "I've got 48 nipples, but only three of them give milk!"

KS: We've been doing that, yeah. I mean...

DM: So, we're just playing the game. So basically what this guy... Kevin Pollak... is doing is giving names to things that people do already. He's like, "All right! I've got this great game! It's called "The Kevin Pollak Cereal Game." First you pour some cereal in a bowl, and then you pour some milk on top of it and you have a delicious breakfast."

KS: It's called "The Kevin Pollak Make Jokes Game." Okay. Here it is. You take something topical. Or, it doesn't have to be. Then you make a person laugh with it, and you're done.

DM: @JOEHILL says, "CamTwist can slideshow a folder of images you've got with a built-in plugin." I feel like we should maybe do a video slide-show version of this show, with our facial expressions changing at random intervals. But, then, how would people enjoy it later? They'd have to... we like to be piped into your ears. Right now, this is a special message... not to the people on Twitter. Not to the people on UStream. Not to the people with computers. Not to the people with Internets. Not to people with electricity. Not to the people with food in their belly. But to the people out there on their jog, on their drive to work, on their long ponderous walk on the beach at night, wondering what you're going to make of your life.

KS: For some reason, this was a good soundtrack for that.

DM: On your iPod that you're trying to get into a romantic mood with your girlfriend, but this came up on the shuffle and you just kept listening...

KS: Yeah, and it's got the remember-where-you-left-off, so it's just sort of, like, 18 minutes in and "Ah, that's where I stopped listening at work. Ah, well. Okay."

DM: So, this is a special message to all of you guys. Just imagine that we're doing funny faces. Like, I wouldn't want to leave those people out. Those people are our lifeblood, and...

KS: Well, look, you know, we're going to have to talk to a developer. Maybe we can come up with an app that will sync up the faces with the broadcast. Like, it could detect the ID4 tag, and when iTunes on your iPhone is playing this podcast, it would line it all up and it would work beautifully.

DM: I really like two things about this. One, the idea that it's an app that can sense the tone of our voice, so not only can it identify the speaker, but also it can judge the emotion and play the appropriate expression. I think that would be a bare-minimum feature of this app.

KS: It's like a predictive video technology.

DM: Yeah.

KS: You know, if you could perfect that, you wouldn't even need cameras on computers any more.

DM: Yeah, exactly, because it'll just *know*. "He's doing something kind of like this." "It's sort of... it's sort of interpolated. I'm not sure if this is rage or if this is lust, so we'll just kind of give him sort of... ehhh. This sort of middle-range face. Because it could work for either."

KS: Right. Your friend is watching you on the system and he's like, "Hey, I thought you told me that you were going to get a haircut." Oh, wait. We don't actually have cameras. That's right. This is a picture of you from five years ago, and the fact that I downloaded it when this started.

DM: So, that's number one. Number one is I'd want that predictive technology. Number two is... what did you say? This is on your iPhone. I totally had lost the thread of this. On your iPhone. This show. You're listening to it... um...

KS: Yeah, you're listening. You're running with it. You're jogging.

DM: Oh, gee. Hey, let's see what people have to say. @PROFESSOR_D goes on to say, "Then you go to the phones. It helps if the city is somewhat humorous, as well, and of course Pennsylvania has been used, so this is like 'Trenton, New Jersey. Hello!' and then you kind of..."

KS: Oh, like Larry King does!

DM: I've heard of that! And then he goes on to say, "You can submit them to Kevin Pollak's chat show via YouTube and get on his show." Eh, all right. This whole sort of user-participation is... I think it's on the way out.

KS: I'm gonna guess that @PROFESSOR_D is Kevin Pollak. I'm gonna go ahead and... he's like, "I've got a show coming up in an hour. I'm a little stuck for content."

DM: "See what I can do."

KS: "Let's see if somebody will come on."

DM: @JAYPROD says, "My request for advice... I just got three wisdom teeth removed, yet I still require nourishment. What can I eat?" He then goes on to say... well, actually, what would you suggest in this circumstance? What's your recommendation? Something he can eat with his wisdom teeth out?

KS: Uh, well, the problem is... actually, I only know this secondhand, because I have not had my wisdom teeth out.

DM: Oh!

KS: And if you ever get a chance to look at my teeth, you can understand that I did not get my wisdom teeth out, because my mouth looks like a box of knives. But as far as I understand, you're not allowed to eat solid foods, right? Because you can't get 'em back there. But you also can't drink liquids... well, you can drink them, but you can't suck 'em, because you'll suck out the blood-clot plug that's filling the hole. So, my advice is to eat blood clots, because even if you knock one out, you're just gonna get another one back in there.

DM: Well, it's kind of funny that you say that, because he says, "I solved my problem. I seem to be bleeding, which may tide me over until the law of diminishing returns kicks in." So, he's just going to cycle that protein through his body a couple of times.

KS: Yeah, you know what, blood is a good... it's kind of a variety food.

DM: There's a lot of vitamins in blood.

KS: There's a lot of vitamins in blood. When it dries out, it's a solid. You get something to chew on. That's satisfying. And when it's liquid, it's flowing down your throat. It's warm.

DM: Right.

KS: It's the perfect temperature.

DM: Lubricating.

KS: You're not going to burn your mouth. *Absolutely* lubricating.

DM: I have had my wisdom teeth out. I remember when I was preparing to do it, I was talking to my boss. I was working a job at the time. And he regaled me with tales of when *his* wisdom teeth had come out, and he's like, "I didn't want anesthesia." He was being manly, or I don't know, maybe it was back in the Middle Ages, I'm not sure what the situation was.

KS: He was a monk.

DM: But he said, "I could hear every tendon snapping and popping and echoing through my skull." And I was like, "Well, I'm not gonna do that. I'm going to get anesthesia." So I got my teeth out. This was a Friday—I took Friday off to go have it done, because I knew I could then recover over the weekend. The doctor said, "You might be out until Wednesday." Because, you know, they give you Vicodin and so on. So I called him up on Monday, my boss, because I still wasn't feeling well, and I said, "The doctor says I might be out until Wednesday. Um, I can't make it in today, for sure." And my boss goes, "I've had that done. You're fine." To be honest, I was trying to not go into work, because that was the last place I wanted to be.

KS: Absolutely.

DM: But this was... it was like his experience worked for everyone. His was the universal, like, "I had it the worst that it could possibly be. You can't possibly have it worse than I did, and *I* was at work, so you are not getting out of it."

KS: "And I was there that day." And, then there's like a really quick wipe and now you're looking at him at work and he's going "Ohhhhh." *(moan and groan)*

DM: *(laughs)* And drooling out of his mouth. I will say this: I was pretty puffy for a couple of days. You know, you get swollen. Your cheeks get swollen.

KS: Understandably, the body did not like what had just happened.

DM: I asked the dentist, "Can I have the teeth? Can I save them?" He's like, "Well, I had to pulverize them, so they're kind of in little tiny shards." I was thinking cool teeth, but no, it was little shards.

KS: "I had to pulverize them, and I actually powdered them and I stirred them into this water, if you want to just chug it."

DM: Yeah, that way you get all the enamels. You know, calcium back in your diet.

KS: *(laughs)* I'm a big believer in recycling and getting all that back in your system.

DM: Yeah, it's the sort of thing, like, we could go off on a whole tangent about the people that save placentas in their freezer, and they make sort of a paste with it and powder and make tea with it and get all those vitamins and nutrients back in their body.

KS: Why waste perfectly good teeth?

DM: Well, here's the thing. We drink cow's milk and we eat chicken eggs. Why do we not eat more placentas? Well, anyway. I'm not going to...

KS: Why don't we eat more teeth?

DM: *(laughs)* Yeah. Why don't we eat more teeth?

KS: It makes sense. They're in your mouth. Why don't we eat teeth?

DM: There's a lot of baby teeth in a little cup in my mom's china cabinet, and for years I've been thinking, "Why don't I just... it's like a little shot..." It's like a little egg cup, but it's the size of a shot glass. I could just slug that thing right back. One go. I've just been waiting for years to just knock those back.

KS: It's all natural. It's part of the body. I believe in that kind of thing.

DM: It's good that I have a gizzard.

KS: And then you could line your esophagus with other teeth.

DM: Anyway, so I'm all swollen, and I go to the library and I'm just sort of "blahhhh." I'm kind of feeling miserable, and I notice that the high-school and college-aged girls that were—I was like 21 or 22 at the time, so I was kind of that same age— and they were giving me the same look as they always did. Which meant either "I'm as handsome as ever!", or the initial look, the default look, is really not that high on the scale. The swollen, horrible-looking wisdom-teeth face is soliciting the exact same reaction.

KS: I'm going to go ahead and reveal something here on the show.

DM: All right.

KS: It might excite and interest you.

DM: Oh?

KS: Well, no, actually it probably won't. The last time I went to a dentist was... let's see. I want to say seven years ago. The time before that, probably six years before that.

DM: Is that because you got tired of the abuse? Like, "You need to come more often." You're like, "No way! You're not my mom!"

KS: No, because I'd go in there and it was like, "Your teeth are perfectly healthy and good and I'm glad..." And they would say, "It's good that you go to the dentist as often as you do." And I would say, "But I don't go to the dentist."

DM: "This is a total scam!"

KS: My mom, who is probably listening and will get mad—she is that way. She's like, "Those dentists! It's a scam!" Because her mouth is the same. Like, it's a resilient mouth. There's something about the ethnicity, or something, that creates just a robust saliva, a self-cleaning mouth. Like an oven.

DM: Well, my teeth are pretty robust, too. Like, I've never had to have braces or anything. My dad had wonderful teeth his whole life, until he got them knocked in when he was mugged. To be honest, I have not gone to the dentist in several years myself. And that's because I don't have dental insurance, more than anything. But there have been periods in my life when I just didn't go for a long time, and then I went in and it's like, "Well, let's check you for cavities. Oh, I guess you're fine."

KS: Right, yeah, which makes me think... I mean I know that's not the same for—it doesn't work for everybody. But what I'm saying is that it *does*...

DM: For people with congenitally bad teeth.

KS: Yeah, yeah. But I'm telling even *those* people, "Don't go to the dentist." Because I don't like to be wrong.

DM: Yeah, so no one should go to the dentist.

KS: Just blanket advice. No special consideration for anybody.

DM: Or do you think that the dentist should be like... everyone should be on the same level playing field. It's not like, "teeth cleaned every six months, eye-doctor every year." No. Let's just have one standard. You go to everybody every seven years.

KS: *(laughs)*

DM: That's it! Right? Eye doctor. Regular doctor. Dentist. Urologist. Pap smear.

KS: Whatever.

DM: Some kind of oil change.

KS: There's no way that can backfire.

DM: Seven years. Let's just go on a cycle.

KS: You know what I hear? I understood this to be a real statistic—is that, you know when you eat food, and cells in your body die, and they are replaced by nearly identical cells? Or they're practically identical.

DM: Slightly mutated.

KS: Right. So, I heard the statistic was, I think seven years—or maybe it was four years, and I'm misremembering—*all* the cells of your body are replaced, so there's no matter left over from four years ago today. So, I would say that means that you only have to go to the doctor once every four to seven years. Whatever that statistic is.

DM: Just to check each set of cells.

KS: Right, because I could say today, "I checked that stomach, you know, five years ago, and right now I've got a new one and I'm going to go get it looked at." If it's fine, it's going to be fine.

DM: @Tmoverbeck says, "One time I went twelve years between dentist visits, and strangely enough, I had no cavities for all that time." See, I think with fluoridated water now, I think cavities are almost a thing of the past. I think, probably, poor people in countries without fluoridated water, south of the border...

KS: It's also free will.

DM: There are some countries that do not have fluoridated water, and their toothpaste is overly-fluoridated to compensate. So, it's like... I don't know if it's urban legend or if it's just a thing from Consumerist or what, but you know, don't buy toothpaste from a 99-cent-store because it might be from South Africa, and it might have nine times the fluoride of American toothpaste, and give you fluoride poisoning.

KS: Well, that's something... my dad explained to me the reasoning behind this, but when I was a little bit younger, I said, "Look, why don't they put... I like to eat candy bars. Why don't they put vitamins in it? That way, I'm eating a candy bar, but I'm getting some vitamins too and I don't have to eat any damned vegetables." And he said, "Well, that's a good idea, but they don't want people to overdose on vitamins. Because if there's vitamins in everything, you can't predict a person's diet and they might end up getting 600% of the iron that day because of what they eat, and they had no idea."

DM: Right. So, we have to just concentrate on only things that are fine to have in huge doses, like sugar and sodium and corn syrup. Those we just overload. But vitamin D... no, you've gotta be careful, because it's going to turn your skin orange.

KS: Although they did make... what was it? 7Up Plus? And all that. It had vitamins in it. But it's always a disappointment. It's always like, "2% vitamin C. Hehhh!" Well, why bother?

DM: There are certain vitamins that they really overload, like on the multivitamins you see it's got 1000% of your RDA and that sort of thing. So you never know, like, which one—is it just that they had too much? Is it like, "Well, we ground up all these beets, and so we'll just pour in all this manganese, otherwise we're just going to throw it away."

KS: I think I have niacin here. I wish I had it on the desk so I could look at it, but it's something like one tablet and it contains 32,000%, which makes me think that, like, the day's dose...all your body needs every day is one molecule of niacin, but we can't give you one molecule. We can't break it down like that.

DM: Yeah, the smallest available unit is an entire visible speck, and because we can't actually pick it up with the tweezers...

KS: Right. It's just easier for us to make a regular-sized pill.

DM: Just take one every ten days.

KS: You'll be fine.

DM: The other thing with the sodium. Obviously, every processed food is so high in sodium—it's like, your Hot Pocket has 33% of your RDA, but it only has 3% of your protein or whatever. Here's my thinking. Thirty-three percent of your RDA? I eat three of those a day. I'm fine, right?

KS: Right.

DM: Now I have enough sodium.

KS: They do that with V8. Have you seen that? I like V8. It's delicious.

DM: V8 is super high in sodium, so they have the more expensive, low-sodium V8 right next to it. It's like, "Look, here's the thing. We ground up all these vegetables that were so good and organic and growing in the garden and so good for you. Somehow—we don't know how—they got dumped in a massive vat of salt. We're just going to give you that. Look, if you want us to pick through that vat and pull out a couple of carrots and a stick of celery and a turnip or two, we've gotta charge extra, because we've gotta pay some guy overtime to actually wash the salt off the turnip."

KS: Do you remember Cap'n Crunch cereal? "Oops! All Berries!"

DM: *(laughs)*

KS: That's what it's like. "Oops! Salt! Oops! They fell in the vat of salt."

DM: Some guy got fired over that one.

KS: You know what? I think the kids are going to like a lot of these berries.

DM: Uh, @PREMISEBEACH says, "My town doesn't have fluoridated water. The city's trying to bring it in, and folks are going nuts." So, this is interesting. I would like to hear what the objections are to fluoridated water. Like, literally. Is it a Communist plot? Is it Big Oil? Is it going to addict you to toothpaste?

KS: "I don't want anything in my body other than the trace metals and the lead and the deposits on the insides of the pipes. That's all I want."

DM: "I want nothing unnatural. So, let me just adjust my contact lenses so I can see more clearly what they say."

KS: *(laughs)* Oh, man! No, I have no problem. You can put everything you want in my water.

DM: So, @PREMISEBEACH, I hope you write back to us. We also have lots of people who want to grind up baby teeth and make *teethade.* That was from @MRBILDANGO. Oh, so, the initial question was, what to eat on wisdom teeth. Here's the thing about wisdom teeth that I didn't realize until... no one told me ahead of time. It leaves a hollow in your gum.

KS: Oh, yeah.

DM: They give you a little squeeze bulb, and after you eat, like after every meal, you have to flush that hollow of the food particles that crept in there during the meal.

KS: Yeah.

DM: It's literally like someone pried the manhole cover off and there's a sewer in your gum, and so, until that swells up and closes, which it does in a couple of months, you have to flush. You get these big old chunks of, like…"oh, I guess whatever sandwich I was eating, there's like a full cubic centimeter was lodged in my gum."

KS: It's like a perfect imprint.

DM: Right. I could make a cast of it.

KS: What kills me is that… I know we talked on a previous show about how brakes work on a car, and now it's just like, "We'll just invent something that grips the wheel and we're done." It kills me. It's like, "We've gotta get these wisdom teeth out." "Well, then what happens?" "Well, then I guess you got a big hole in your mouth. I don't know what to do. Good luck! We'll give you a syringe."

DM: Would you rather that they want you to come back for a follow up visit every three days, with a $40 co-payment and bill your insurance?

KS: Why can't they invent something that goes in the hole? Why can't they take my tooth out, reassemble it like on *CSI*, like they're doing some ballistics or something, and then make a perfect polymerized plastic tooth that they can just stick in the same spot?

DM: Well, they can, but it costs $10,000. Well, they'll bill your insurance $10,000, because the process actually costs $500.

KS: But I want it *now!*

[ACCORDION STING]

DM: So, on last week's show we talked about the "Dear Minnie" column. You'll recall this was—Kris, do you want to talk about it? You told me after the show how you were feeling during this whole exploration. Do you want to give the listeners more of a sense of it? Because if you listen back to the show, you're pretty deadpan. You really take it in stride, but can you give us a sense of what was going on as you felt the past come back and get thrown in your face?

KS: I didn't… I mean, I thought at the time, after the show was over, that I should have revealed more of it on the show and it would have been better, but I was… my face was red. I was warm. I felt foolish. I felt like a pervert, which some will attest to, but I don't like feeling like that. Like other people know. I felt like a dumbass, I'll be honest. I felt like I had completely fabricated this thing from some weird mid-puberty fetishism that I was going through, and it was awful. It was not good.

DM: So, the way to see if that was true or not, was… like, to see how much of that was pure fabrication or how much of it was understandable that you would feel that way, we wanted to talk to your brother Kurt, who sort of experienced the same phenomenon along with you.

KS: Right. Kurt is hard to get ahold of, I'll tell you that.

DM: Busy guy?

KS: He's a busy guy. He's working. He's doing his research. He's important. He's a big wheel. And literally—we had a week between that show and now, and we talked to him earlier tonight. In fact, we talked to him immediately before we started this show tonight.

DM: Right.

KS: It's when he could squeeze us in. And that's what Minnie said. That's what I swore Minnie had said.

DM: What does he do that keeps him so busy?

KS: Uh, he works in a lab and they do research on parasites. Specifically, toxoplasmogondi. They inject mice, and I don't know what they do beyond that.

DM: Toxoplasmogondi. Is this like a new, more virulent strain of Gandhi?

KS: Yeah. They're finding a way to...

DM: They're finally weaponizing Gandhi.

KS: They're very passive, though.

DM: After all these years. It's been so difficult, but they finally figured out how to weaponize Gandhi.

KS: That is the parasite—I only know this because of all the time I've spent with my brother, as he is a member of my family—but that is the parasite that is commonly found in cat poop.

DM: Oh, good.

KS: And that is why they say to pregnant women that they should try to avoid changing cat litter, if you have a pet cat, because you might end up with it and I guess it's not good for you when you're pregnant. But the rest of the time, if you're not pregnant, go for it, because only good things can come from that parasite. It's the best. But, anyway, yes, we did talk to Kurt.

DM: So, let's listen to that real quick before we launch into it. The follow-up from @PREMISEBEACH is, there is a Facebook group for his city rallying about fluoridated water. Basically people are upset because it's not proven 100% safe. My feeling is, if all they're doing is having a Facebook petition, I think you're probably safe.

KS: It just says, "Keep fluoride out of our wells!"

DM: "Let's get indignant!"

KK "Ahhhhh, I'm mad!"

DM: I'm sure there's a lot of totally legitimate objections that we're totally trivializing. But let's move on.

KS: Let's go on and listen to our discussion with my brother, Kurt, about my perversion.

[ACCORDION STING]

KS: Hey, all right. We are with Kurt, who is my younger brother.

Kurt: Hello. How's it going?

KS: It's going good. How much younger are you, Kurtis?

Kurt: Well, it oscillates between two and three years.

KS: That's right. It's two years and eight months, and that's proof that this is my brother.

DM: You sound like a scientist, Kurt.

Kurt: *(giggling)* Sorry. What can I say? I just came from the lab.

DM: Does that you mean you have a very analytical way of seeing the world?

Kurt: Hardly. I guess to some extent. If we start talking parasites, yeah.

KS: Well, this is perfect.

DM: Maybe so! Exactly. We're talking to the right guy for this subject, then.

Kurt: Oh, you guys got infected!

KS: Yeah, that's what this is about.

DM: This is sort of a cry for help in a certain way. Um, I've been eating a lot and not gaining weight, and I'm fearing the worst.

KS: What do you know about lampreys?

Kurt: *(laughs)* Well, you have to understand that the tapeworm, it has to get at least six feet long before it's had its fill. Okay? It's got to wend its way all the way through, and then loop back in on itself through your intestinal tract.

DM: Is the thing I've heard true, where if you feed yourself with an IV and, thereby, starve the tapeworm, then you can dangle a leaf of lettuce over your mouth and it'll jump out after it? And you can grab it and pull it out?

Kurt: I'm sure that's in an independent film somewhere, but not that I know of.

KS: It sounds like a student film.

DM: I had a teacher that actually described this method to me as "this is how they do it." But maybe she left off the end of the sentence, which was "in a remote tribe in New Guinea."

KS: Right. No, the secret is that, "Yes, it will work, but the tapeworm, at that point, becomes invisible and you will continue to lose weight."

DM: There's a lot of chanting involved as well.

Kurt: This is as far as medical science can progress on this. I'm sorry. It's cured by leaping, okay?

KS: Books are closed, friends.

DM: There's just a big chapter entitled "Anecdotes." It's the list. This happened to one guy. This happened to this other guy.

KS: It's, like, there's this one guy, and he fell on his head, and he only knew cuss words from then on. I don't know. Something going on there.

DM: This other guy slipped on a spider, fell down his basement steps and then he could speak Chinese.

KS: "Must investigate for... well, you know what? No, that's fine."

DM: And then Chris Carter got the book and wrote a whole, like eleven seasons of a TV show about it.

KS: *Millennium.* No. So, Kurtis.

KURT: Yes?

KS: You're a smart man.

KURT: Thank you.

KS: And a healthy man.

KURT: Thanks to the parasites, yeah.

KS: Yeah, exactly. Do you have their... it's a symbiosis.

DM: Yeah, he's got the good kind.

KS: I'm gonna go out on a limb and say that these parasites that you work with have given you a great memory, as well.

KURT: *(giggling)* Uh-huh.

KS: Because on last week's show, David and I explored the limits of memory and how your remembrance of things changes as you age. And I was regaling him with an advertising... well, it's not a supplement, but it was a column in the *LA Times* Calendar called "Dear Minnie" and it was an ad for Disneyland, but it was in the format of Minnie Mouse giving advice.

KURT: *(laughs)*

KS: Do you remember?

KURT: Very vaguely.

KS: Really?

KURT: But the name sounds familiar, definitely. But what can I tell you as far as impressions? I remember...

KS: Just give us the shape of the time. It might just be... like, there might be aromas. Sense memories.

KURT: All right.

DM: It was a heady time. There was a lot of Christian Slater in the movie theaters.

KURT: The king had just been beheaded.

DM: Keanu Reeves was rising to stardom.

KURT: I remember the ink from the paper bleeding into my fingers.

DM: *Universal Soldier* was up for Best Picture.

KURT: *Universal Soldier? (laughs)*

KS: Oh, yeah.

KURT: You interrupted my reverie.

DM: I'm sorry. Ink was bleeding through your fingers. Tapeworms were absorbing through the newspaper.

KURT: No, no, no. Let me finish. As I passed my hands over the paper, as I sat hunched over on the toilet reading the *LA Times,* hoping for my dear Minnie to speak to me…

DM: So you're in the bathroom, at this point, on purpose. Okay. This is a good scene that we're setting. Never know what's going to happen. You want to be ready for any eventuality.

KS: I want the audience to be aware that… I lived there, too, and that was a very low toilet. So, imagine a high degree of squat.

DM: Knees up above your shoulders. I imagine Kris is pounding on the door, saying "I want my turn with the Calendar section!"

KS: Imagine a contortionist's toilet.

KURT: That's right. As Kristofer pounded outside the door, I pulled my knees up higher to get a better view. And that's when I read, "Don't worry, Kristofer, your Mickey will soon come to you. Now go out to Disneyland and go buy something."

…I don't know. I don't remember it being a commercial, truth be told. I just remember having…

KS: Wait, you do or you don't?

KURT: Well, what I do remember of it was that it didn't… it never advertised Disney or anything like that. But it offered lots of, you know, banal advice, like "I'm sure you'll get a new mouse." Or something like that. And it wasn't… there was no romance, right? It wasn't anything like that kind of column.

KS: No, no, no. I mean not in my… well, it wasn't romance.

DM: A matchmaking column, if that's what you're getting at. It's not like one of those pen-pal columns where you write in and you talk about your five favorite books and then it's like, "Oh, this person in Connecticut also likes *Catcher in the Rye.* Here's their address." It was nothing like that. That was *Wizard* Magazine.

KS: That's right. I remember the bottom of the *Wizard* Magazine, where it's like "Pen Pals," and it's twenty guys who like *X-Men* and one girl—and I'm sure that she was inundated.

DM: Well, I mentioned that once on Twitter and one of those girls, I guess, who had put in for a pen pal, said, "We got a lot of letters from jail."

KURT: I was going to say, do you think that "Dear Minnie" raised and then dashed the hopes of a lot of furries? By any chance?

KS: I don't know. That's probable.

DM: Do you remember any sort of particular spin that the column may or may not have had in that direction?

KURT: On furries? You mean, like, innuendo, or…?

KS:　Yeah, like just a broader...

KURT:　I don't remember her advising... "just tug on his ears," or something like that, "and he'll squeak," I don't know.

DM:　He's nailed it! That's exactly what it said.

KS:　That's good advice anytime.

DM:　That's good advice for life. Try the ears first!

KS:　So, I'm guessing, Kurt, that you don't remember what I recall to be a highly sexually-charged atmosphere, in which Minnie Mouse dispensed advice about Disneyland... in the *guise* of advice about Disneyland, when, in fact, she was meting out prurient juvenilia for the masses who were smart enough to see it.

KURT:　I remember that was what we joked about. That's the way that we spun it.

DM:　You didn't realize that Kris was actually being very serious. He's like, "Don't you see it?"

KURT:　"C'mon! Validate me!"

DM:　This is a great picture I'm painting in my mind. You guys were in front of the hearth and Kris was like, "Yeah, don't you see it?" And Kurt is like, "Yeah, totally, man! Uh, huh." And Kris is like, "Yeah, huh, huh." And neither one of you know which one is joking and which one is serious?

KS:　But all I know is that it was...

KURT:　He pulled a knife at my throat, later that night!

KS:　"It's real! She is real!"

KURT:　"She is hot for me!"

DM:　"She's talking to me, guys! I have the decoder. I got it for $48 at Disneyland!"

KS:　And it's just a Disney Dollar. The secret is written around the edge.

DM:　You hold it up to the light, and you put it up against a bottle of Ovaltine.

KS:　It says, "Kris, I need you. Come to Mickey's Bounce House."

KURT:　Do you think that anyone following the advice of Dear Minnie, you know... mild as their problems may have been or whatever... they later went to Disneyland and then saw whatever guy they were paying $5 an hour in the Minnie costume, and then he tried to have, like, a heart-to-heart with the guy in the costume?

DM:　"Remember what you told me? I just wanted to give you a follow-up."

KS:　"I was 'Excited in Encino.' Do you remember me?"

DM:　"I thought the alliteration would make me stand out, but then I realized that everybody does that. I should have done it the other way. I should have been 'Excited in Tarzana.' "

KS:　I should have gone with my original. 'Depressed in Encino.'

DM:　Kurt, do you remember the type of questions that people were asking Minnie?

KURT:　Like I say, nothing that ever would stand out to someone who is 10 years old, or

12. How old were we? This was like when I was 12, that kind of thing? Or 13?

KS: I want to say that, but I think that David may have found it to be a little bit later. I think I was twenty-two.

KURT: Did you find it? Did you look it up, David?

DM: I did indeed look it up.

KURT: Did you access the power of microfiche to find "Dear Minnie"?

DM: It was micro*film,* thank you very much. There was whirring. There was less of 'placing under a sheet of glass' than 'spooling into a projector.' Thank you very much.

KS: That is a little more challenging. You do have to spool it.

DM: It's not the 60's. This was... well, at the time, it was just this year.

KS: We're not talking about 1960, Kurt. We're talking about 1962.

KURT: I'm sorry. I was going to ask earlier whether or not they had a daguerreotype of the first "Dear Minnie" column, but...

DM: "Dearest Minnie: I write you today hoping you'll respond to my earnest entreaty."

KURT: I thought it was going to be "Your creator has not been born yet."

KS: "Dearest Minnie: The war is not going well."

DM: "I gave birth to you. I am your mother." So what I did, Kurt, was after I heard Kris explain his recollection of this, I went to the library and I looked up the archives of the *LA Times,* and I found the actual columns. They were from 1995.

KURT: Uh-huh.

DM: So, that would have placed Kris at about 15, 16. So, if you're oscillating between two and three years younger, you'd probably have been around 13 or 14.

KS: He was 13 or 14, yeah.

DM: And Kris had a very, very strong recollection of the sexual innuendo inherent in the "Dear Minnie" column, and he described in great detail...

KS: With great relish.

DM: Relish. Talking about hot dogs, talking about sauerkraut, and talking about all the different...

KS: No, that's not what I meant.

KURT: Minnie talked about sauerkraut? Wow!

DM: Minnie loved to... uh, was that another in-joke, you guys? I know you guys are of German descent. Was that, "Oh, he's a real sauerkraut over there!" Is there anything in that? You laughed at something that wasn't funny, so I didn't know if it was an in-joke.

KS: No, I'm just excited to hear my sweet brother's voice. That's all it is.

KURT: I was going to say, of all the ethnicities, we've never tapped into German background for a joke, I don't think, Kristofer.

KS: Certainly not as deeply.

KURT: For all the dumb skits we've done...

KS: Well, you can't really... there's nowhere to go but Nazis. Where else can you go? We had helmets.

DM: You can talk about how well you build cars.

KS: That's true. "This car's not going anywhere."[39]

DM: Play-act a Mercedes engineer.

KS: Exactly.

DM: *(German accent)* "Nobody understands. There is such precision. We are down to the thousandths of an inch here. Nobody gives us zat much credit!" I'm really just spit-balling here. You guys can take that and spin that someplace else.

KS: Let's run on "Fahrvergnügen" for a little bit.

DM: Do you guys remember Fido Dido?

KS: Yes.

DM: That's kind of the same era.

KS: Fido Dido, I always... even at that age, I got the impression that... because I remember that he was like in bumpers for cartoons and stuff like that, but he didn't really cross into a show.

DM: Because he was also in those Slice commercials.

KS: Yeah, that's right. But I sensed that his creator was just champing at the bit to go further, you know?

DM: Well, that's what I wondered. Do you think that was some, like, you know the 1991 version of a webcomic? Like some independent thing, where the guy is like, "Awesome! They licensed my character for Slice commercials." And then it's just Fido Dido, the guy who says "After these messages, we'll be right back."

KS: Yeah.

DM: And that was as far as it went. He's like, "No, he's got a whole backstory! He's got schoolteachers! He's got cousins! He's got a wacky dog!"

KURT: I just remember him in bumpers...

DM: "He went to Mars this one time!"

KS: Kurt, please. Yes. Go ahead.

KURT: To get back to the... I don't know! I certainly don't remember "Dear Minnie" in general as strongly as Kristofer does, and what I do remember is that we joked a lot about the sexual innuendo, but that if you really looked at it, it was just, like, boring problems and even more boring advice. But, like, "everything is going to be fine." You know. "Have an apple. You'll feel better."

KS: Actually, it wasn't nearly as trenchant as that.

DM: I'll buy that. So, in your recollection, Kurt, anyway, the joking about the sexual

---

39   Kris thinks David's being ironic, but no! Germans build good cars. Does Kris know??

innuendo and all that sort of thing was sort of like, "Let's see if we can find something in here. Let's *make* it interesting, because it's just so blank, we can project a lot onto it."

KURT: Mm-hmm.

DM: Okay. So, whereas Kris thought it was real.

KS: Yeah.

DM: You thought there really were, you know...

KS: You know, it might not have been I thought it was real. It might have been that I *needed* it to be real. There's a big difference.

KURT: But what *did* you find, though? What was it like? Can you read us any? Do you have it with you?

DM: I posted some online actually. I'm not going to read them right now, because we read a bunch of them on the show last week.

KURT: And it's too hot. For the Internet.

DM: Right. Too saucy for the Internet. It's Disneyland ads, and the advice... the questions are all things like, "We love eating at this place, but where do we find that great barbecue the last time we were at Disneyland?" And Minnie says, "Oh, you must be thinking of the Big Bob Bengal Barbecue, which is over by New Orleans Square." And so it's questions about Disneyland, specifically. Like, "Is there a place we can bring our kids where they can... if they're too scared to go on the rides?" "Yes, we have a thing called, whatever. And the parent steps aside with the kids."

KS: "Dear Minnie: I am at my wits' end. I am trying to figure out where in the hell I can get some kind of mouse-shaped pancakes. I don't know how you make 'em or where you get 'em, but I have got a hankering and I don't know where in the hell I ate 'em, but..."

DM: "I've seen kids wear those black caps with the sort of two round, like, satellite dishes on them and I definitely need this hat to receive alien transmissions, to line them with tinfoil and put sort of a screen on there and get microwave reflections. I have been to every Gap. I have been to every Abercrombie & Fitch. I have been to every hat store. I have been to every specialty haberdashery, and I cannot find those round kinds of hats. Do you have any idea of how you can help me? Signed, Frustrated in Encino."

KS: And Minnie says, "Uh, well, fifteen bucks is fifteen bucks. You will absolutely hear the aliens when you come to Disneyland. These hats are amazing! And you're going to want three of them."

DM: "We have one version that sells for $400. It's... let's say it's fur-lined."

KS: "That's the one you're going to want, because you're going to get cold out there on the top of those mountains listening for the aliens."

DM: So, our conclusion, after looking back at the actual historical record, was that Kris seems to have built up this thing in his memory over the years, into something that... if it was there, it was certainly very subtle. I mean, there was a couple of lines. There was a "happy tenting." There was "the best fireworks are the ones you share with the ones you love." Like, there were a couple of those things here and there.

KS: Yeah, what about the one...

DM: But there was no, "Mickey loves shooting off his cannon full of sausages." That was a fabrication on Kris' part.

KS: But what about the one with the carousel, saying that they polish the poles every day.

DM: Okay. So, there was a thing where it's like, "the guy who polishes the poles and spends like 36 hours a night on it and he really like has... he gets sort of a shiver of joy when he finishes."

KURT: *(laughs)*

DM: There was some of that. But that was sort of in June. That was at the beginning of the run. It definitely did not get deranged over time. Kris had this whole elaborate backstory that the guy was realizing that nobody was paying any attention, so he's trying to push the envelope and eventually he gets fired. The guy storms into the office and slams the door and says, "What have you been putting in our newspaper?" And the guy is just out on the curb, bouncing along with his pink slip flapping in the breeze. None of that stuff ever happened.

KS: No, it didn't.

KURT: So the real history would suggest that the writer, after initially sating his pole-polishing finish, was gradually beaten by the editors into, just, various questions about Disneyland itself, or something like that.

DM: It's like—I can imagine the editor probably took the writer aside and said, "Look, we all have this impulse at the beginning. I did, too, when I started writing copy for Disney advertising. Everyone wants to make it about pole-polishing. I let that one pass. You got it out of your system. But we really need to talk about the clam chowder at the Pirates of the Caribbean restaurant."

KS: "I understand that you're twelve and a half years old, and that makes you the youngest Disney copywriter that we've ever hired. I know you're going through some changes right now, but you need to keep that stuff out. However, you've got to keep it professional."

KURT: "Just listen. Okay. Carl Barks, the guy who came up with Uncle Scrooge and Donald and all that kind of stuff..."

KS: Yeah?

KURT: "Listen. The first issue that we never published of *Uncle Scrooge*, Duckburg was ACTUALLY written 'Dickburg' in the script. Okay. You have no idea how hard he fought for that. Sorry. They had to smack him down."

KS: "And that was Carl Barks and you're nobody. So, what does that tell you?"

DM: "But, you know what we left in? You know, 'Duckburg'—this is a city full of Jew ducks."

KS: "We're okay with the racism."

DM: I can imagine that that whole cycle of, like, "I'm going to try to push the envelope. I'm the young, creative guy"—and is, like, beaten down by the Disney machine? That whole accelerated cycle took about... four weeks. Sometimes that takes a career. Sometimes it takes ten years of like, "You know what? I better pick my battles. I want to buy a house. I don't want to make waves. I'll just write Disneyland ad copy." In this case it was "Summer internship! All right! Start out. We go in fast. And then we burn out fast. And then we're just talking about New Orleans Square."

KS: It might have been, like, a conceptual art performance piece, sort of a deal. "This is a commentary on commercialism."

DM: Consumerism. Yeah, it's just this sort of klatch of conceptual artists. You know, they're out of Berkeley or something. And they're like, "Let's really just mess with the system. We're going to write this totally realistic looking 'Dear Minnie' column. We're going to get Disney trademark logos everywhere. We're even going to buy ads in the *LA Times*. Everyone's just going to... we're going to blow their minds!" It's just like... Disneyland is like, "Huh, wonder why our sales are up this year. We haven't really done anything special."

KS: Right, and then at the advertising office, it's like, "Is this you? Did we get permission to run this? I mean, it's doing well." And the guy is like, "Uh, yeah."

DM: "Yeah, boy, good job! Good job! Bonus for you!" And those guys at Berkeley, they're like, "We're just too... I guess we're so... um, the verisimilitude! It's so subtle."

KS: "I'm making a comment on the ownership of sexuality."

DM: "Twenty-five years from now they're gonna be like, "Who were those culture jammers?"

KS: *(laughs)* "Why did Disneyland burn to the ground in 1996? Because of us!"

DM: "We're making fake history here." Yeah, like they're writing a whole, like... their whole plan was to gradually extent it over like four years and have this really subtle transition, because they're like, "The first five months, we're going to do it totally straight. Totally deadpan. Never give it away. That way we gain everyone's trust and they think it's the real thing. And then, eventually, we're just going to make it *twisted*. And everyone's going to be like, 'Whoa! The Disneyland thing is twisted, man!' " And then they ran out of money after like three months.

KS: And it's like, "Aww..."

DM: It's like, "My mom said I can't pull from my trust fund anymore. I'm going to have to go back to work. So...let's just put this on hold? We're going to come back to it, and let's just reconvene and take some time off. We're just going to come back to it and brainstorm a little bit in like six months."

KURT: "No, man! If you leave now, Team Minnie is dead!"

KS: "Fine!"

DM: So, the one guy is still writing them and he's waiting for the money to come in and he's still writing them. "I've got the backlog ready to go. We've got six more years ready to go. Every week with Minnie. And I'm going to build this whole character of Minnie as this chick who's just so frustrated with this thing, man! Mickey never gives her any respect!"

KS: Even after a time, he's had to pay the rent and he can't, so now he's trying to convert it into this character called "Miney," but he can't sell it to anybody.

DM: And he's at some party and he's like, "I spent a lot of time developing this character. I kind of made the most rookie mistake in the book, man. It was a character I didn't own, so I can't really sell it, so I'm trying to adapt it to something original, but it's tough, man, because it's so similar to this really popular property." And his other stoner friends are just like, "Parody, man! Fair use! You can do anything under Fair Use. Just do it, man!"

KURT: "Oh, yeah!"

KS: And then he just draws a joint in Minnie's mouth. Everywhere.

KURT: "It's done, man!"

DM: And the best part is when he's had to do all this research and he's just like, "I just gotta make it just... in order to make it believable, I gotta just really get all the details right." So, he takes all these fact-finding trips to Disneyland, and he reads all these books and he's like, "All right, so portrait artists are there for 25 minutes. Awesome! All right. I can put that fact in the column. All right. Let's check this out. Oh, wow! This lamppost is from France, like 1865. That's... *kinda* cool! And they brought it over here, and we'll put that in the column." And so he just develops this real deep-seated appreciation for Disneyland and the craftsmanship. He's like, "Wow! These brass poles require a lot of polishing, man. Someone's getting paid... it's their job, they're the polisher." And, then, that person, ladies and gentlemen, is Cory Doctorow.[40]

KS: *(laughs)* I like the way that you wrapped it up.

DM: Thanks so much for talking with us. It's been a real pleasure.

KURT: My pleasure. No problem.

KS: So, I am a pervert.

DM: And the conclusion is, you're a pervert, and Cory Doctorow wrote those columns—that was his first published work.

KURT: Very good, gentlemen. Go enjoy yourselves in Dickburg.

KS: *(laughs)* Go back to your parasites.

DM: Everything's a dick blur, around me.

[*ACCORDION STING*]

KS: And we're back.

DM: So, that was our conversation with Kurt.

KS: Yeah, it went a lot of different places.

---

40 Author, blogger, famous lefty intellectual–property advocate and, incongruously, the hugest Disneyland fan on the planet. Also let's say he's a deep–sea diver, why not.

DM: Yeah, I think we covered a lot of good ground there. We answered a lot of questions. We raised some others. Answered them and then moved on to Dickburg.

KS: Yeah, by the way, I didn't get a chance to tell him when he was on, but I really appreciated how he basically threw me under the bus there.

DM: *(laughs)*

KS: "Hey, do you remember this thing we did?" "No, I don't remember that at all. I was studying. I was reading history books and informative novels. You were enjoying a little..."

DM: Do you think he was trying to save a little face, or do you think that was his actual recollection?

KS: You know what? It might have been, but it might have been more, like at the time, my sense of humor and not so much his. So, it might have been like, yeah, it was funny then, but just because Kris is having a good time with it. So, he's like, eh, it's all right. I don't care that much.

DM: Well, if he's twelve and you're fifteen, he's probably not... even if it was in the text, he's not going to look at it the same way that you do. So, he's going to take your lead from... you know, the interpretation of the material.

KS: That's true. Yeah, that's true. That's a good way to put it. And you notice something—that he didn't put it that way. He just let me twist in the wind.

DM: "Yeah, no. You know what? Now that I have you on the line, there was a lot of other weird stuff that Kris did when he was fifteen."

KS: You just call him back after this.

DM: Tell me everything. I want to hear it all. I want to make sure I'm not the only one who was that weird.

KS: "Kris, I know you're busy next week. So, no show." "Oh, okay." And then it's just you and Kurt. "What else did he do?" "Oh, God!"

DM: "Dish. Do dish."

KS: *"Do tell us. Delightful!"*

[ACCORDION STING]

DM: Well, this has been Tweet Me Harder, the Internet's first, best, only and last talk-back enabled interactive audio podblast.

KS: Oh, no. I wish this wasn't.

DM: You wish this was not the Internet's, or the world's, first-best-only-and-last talk-back-enabled interactive audio podblast?

KS: Yeah, I got nothing to hide behind. That's the problem.

DM: This is you. Yeah, you're really putting yourself out there and letting everyone scoop out their chunks of flesh...

KS: I bleed like everyone else.

DM: I will say, for the record, um, I've had a lot of fun making fun of your bizarre pervy self. I feel a little bit bad that you've had to endure all this abuse and I've been the one mocking you for it, and sorta taking all the glee and all the delight and all the pleasure and so forth.

KS: Yeah, yeah. Uh, huh.

DM: And the after-the-fact moral high ground. I mean, it's certainly... there are some indefensible things in my own past. But! I'm happy to leave it there.

[CLOSING MUSIC STARTS]

KS: Like, "So, we've all done that. Anyway, good night everybody."

DM: So, I'll just say, "Eh, me, too."

KS: It's like, "I feel your pain." "Oh, really?" "Uh, yeah. But not really."

DM: Uh, next week, it's going to be kind of a weird-scheduled week, so you'll have to watch the Twitter account and watch @TWEETHARD and we will let you know when the next show is going to go up. We have to do some schedule shenanigans and as soon as we have a time settled, we will let you know and hopefully we will be able to do something kind of fun. We'd like you to keep sending in your voicemails and requests for advice or other thoughts. You can contact us at... all right, I'm going to try again to remember using the mnemonic. I'm not gonna look it up.

KS: You're going to do the voicemail, right?

DM: Yeah—I remember 206.

KS: Yeah.

DM: I remember 337.

KS: Yes.

DM: 8560.

KS: Yeahhhhh. You did get it!

DM: You know how I remembered?

KS: No. Tell us how we can remember.

DM: All right. 206-337-8560 is my height, weight, wedding anniversary and butt size.

KS: *(giggling)* Just like, somehow multiplexed. Like, run through an assembly adder.

DM: Yeah, it's an app. I just sort of feed the numbers into this kind of... it's like a crypto thing and it comes out the other side.

KS: All you need to do is give this app every single detail of your life, and then it will find a mnemonic for anything you need.

DM: It's one of those things where...

KS: Everybody remembers their butt circumference.

DM: If you know all the other variables, you can solve for the missing one. So, if I forgot my wedding anniversary, I just put in my height, weight, butt size and the Tweet Me Harder phone number.

KS: And then, eventually, you know what? You don't need this app anymore, and then that's when it deletes itself and says the magic was inside you.

DM: *(laughs)*

KS: See, you could remember. You knew.

DM: Our mission is done. Everything is done.

KS: By the way, this app provided by Tony Robbins. "Omigod! I can't believe this!"

DM: A single tear rolls down the cheek.

KS: I love him!

DM: "And now, all you have to do is sell this app to 20 of your friends and become an affiliate."

KS: *(laughs)* Oh, I'm on board now.

DM: "We have a two-tier affiliate program. So, if all your friends help their friends, you can get a quarter of their affiliate fees, and that way, come to our seminar."

KS: "It's what we call a rhombus scheme."

DM: "Look, 'pyramid scheme' gets tossed around a lot these days. The correct term is actually 'Friend Pile.' "

KS: "Isn't that better? You know what? When I think about pyramids, I think about in Egypt, old stuff. That's the old way. Who's buying pyramids these days? Are you? Anybody? No."

DM: "Yeah, with the real estate market the way it is, am I right?"

KS: "Arf arf arf arf. Let's get on the friend pile!"

DM: So, if you want to join the friend pile, check out our Twitter account, @TWEETHARD. Our website is *tweetmeharder.tumblr.com*, at which you're probably listening to this now, or you can listen live at the next show if you're listening to this after the fact.

KS: We'll give you details coming up.

DM: If you're at the gym; if you're jogging; if you're trying to make love to our sweet, sweet voices, just know you can listen to us live and tweet back to us next time at *tweetmeharder.tumblr.com*.

KS: I think that would be a great service, if we could just kind of slow down the pace of our voices. Just kind of get a little husky.

DM: Just want to make sure you're really enjoying yourself.

KS: Having a good time tonight? That's good. That's real good.

DM: I like that. You haven't done that before, have you? I'd like you to do it *every* time.

KS: And by "every time," I mean join us for the show.

The Centrifuge Method

8

DM: Welcome to Tweet Me Harder. This is the world's first, best, only, and last talk-back-enabled interactive audio podblast. I'm David Malki !

KS: I'm Kris Straub.

DM: Thank you for joining us on this special episode of Tweet Me Harder. We are broadcasting live, in the same room, for the first time.

KS: Feels good.

DM: I know, look at this.

KS: I know, look at you!

DM: You're just inches away.

KS: You're all clean-shaven and everything.

DM: You're all scruffy and horrible.

KS: Exactly. You have considerably less gray hair than I thought you would.

DM: I'm really excited to—I mean, they're coming in though.

KS: Yeah?

DM: I can't wait for them.

KS: They're—only when the light catches them, can you see them on me. I hope. Actually, that's not true.

DM: No, they're actually very evident.

KS: They're quite visible.

DM: Yeah. Wait, no. I'm interested in—you said I have less than you expected?

KS: Well, how old are you?

DM: I am 28.

KS: Okay, I'm 30. I know that we go gray early.[41] But I'm expecting that everbody in my peer group would just have it.

DM: *(laughs)* Well, my brother started going gray at 17.

KS: Okay.

---

41 This is a racist crack on Kris' part. He means we Arabs.

DM: And first I kind of made fun of him, because, you know, when he was in his mid–early twenties, I was a young teenager, and so I was like, "Ha, ha. Old man. Old man." And my dad was snow white, you know, by his, like, forties or so.

KS: Yeah.

DM: Forties or fifties. But over time, as I've matured a little bit, I really anticipate this because I think it's cool.

KS: It's good!

DM: Like, I can't wait for the Mr. Fantastic...

KS: Because so many people are like, "Are you going to color it?" And I'm like, "No, I'm not going to color it." And they're like, "Well, don't color it. It looks so good." But who's—are there people who are still like, "I don't want to look mature and cool"?

DM: Well, I think it probably depends on the pattern. If you have some really patchy pattern, then you don't have the really dignified temples.

KS: You see, like the skunk. Where they've got the...

DM: Right, the stripe down the middle. Or, you know, that guys that have the beard but sort of on the sides—or it's the weird shape, where it sort of assumes, like snakes...

KS: It's like the word, "ass."

DM: *(laughs)* There's like these earthworms burrowing through a beard, and they leave a white trail.

KS: I just started getting them in my beard, and I think I'm gonna have an even coverage.

DM: Yeah, that's what I'm hoping. I've got a couple in my beard, as you can probably see.

KS: Yeah.

DM: And, uh, Nikki, my wife, is a little bit distracted sometimes, 'cause she'll see one in my mustache and she'll think it's like, "You've got something hanging out of your nose."

KS: Yeah.

DM: "Oh, it's just this bright white thing on your lip."

KS: "You have a strand of silver, metal, that you must have coming out of your nose."

DM: "Someone is trying to steal all the wire from your walls of your abandoned house."

KS: They've just draped a little of it across your mustache. As they escaped.

DM: They're just yanking it off your nose as hard as they can. But some of our friends are very gray.

KS: That's true.

DM: Like Dave. Dave Kellett.

KS: He must have gone gray really early, too. He's not much older.

DM: 31 or 32, I think.

KS: No he ain't.

DM: He's not? 33?

KS: He's at least like 35, 36.

DM: Oh, really? Okay. I thought he was in his early 30s.

KS: He's got the body of a 50-year-old man. But—

DM: Um, by which we mean *strapping*. A 50-year-old man. We mean like Richard Branson. In *such* good shape.

KS: Like a sea captain. Like a rugged man who has taken care of himself and had a good life.

DM: Um, but I definitely have noticed the gray coming in in the last couple of years, you know, and again: I welcome it. And my friend—this is the interesting thing—my friend, who's sort of early 30s, he says he used to work tech support. And he went very gray, he told me. This was years ago.

KS: Hmm.

DM: And now he is fairly gray. But he told me that he went back to black when he quit that job.

KS: What?!

DM: Like he *recovered.*

KS: No.

DM: I think he was like 24 or 25, just out of college, working at a tech-support job. And he's Chinese, so he's got naturally black hair. And then his hair went gray, or gray*er,* as he describes it. And then he was so relieved when he quit that job, that his hair recovered.

KS: Well, you've seen—I mean, I don't know about recovery, but it surprised me to learn that—like, they take those photos of the Presidents before and after their term.

DM: Right.

KS: They just look like corpses. Like they've just been destroyed by their work.

DM: Their skin is hanging off their bones.

KS: They are just miserable shells. Like the weight of the entire world, literally.

DM: Yeah, did you see those mock-ups of what Obama will look like in eight years? He looks like Bill Cosby, like, with the hair all spotty.

KS: Yeah.

DM: Um, but then I read somewhere else, it's like well yeah, that's eight years of age for a 50-something year old person...

KS: That makes sense.

DM: ...They just look eight years older.

KS: That's true.

DM: And it's accelerated, by that point in life.

KS: They'll never have a twenty-year-old President as they did in the DC series *The Prez*. From the '70s.

DM: *(laughs)* We've got @HUGPARTY here. Says: "Grey hairs are better than early balding." Uh, I agree with that.

KS: Yeah.

DM: I would much rather—I mean, if you would give me bald head versus snow white, I'll take—I mean, I *want* the snow white. It's not even a contest. It's not even a thing.

KS: Yeah, why would you—well, I mean, I figured if i were to go a little bald, I would just start to shave it. I would just cut it all the way down.

DM: That's kind of the thing that people are doing now. And I wonder what the threshold is for that. Like, I would be fine with some sort of higher temples, or some higher forehead. I wouldn't really mind that too much.

KS: Yeah.

DM: What I wouldn't want is the thin all over. Which I'm starting to get a *leeetle* bit of. And I wonder, how bald do you have to get before you just say, "You know what? Screw it. It's all coming off."

KS: The only one I can think of that's kind of in-between to me would be, like, Rob Corddry. You know?

DM: Oh, yeah, he's got the tufts.

KS: His hair is getting close to the front. Like he could probably still make something of it, but he's missing, like, off the sides, here on the top of the scalp...

DM: Yeah. It's—when it gets patchy, you need to do some trimming.

KS: It's time to start to get rid.

DM: Yeah, you've seen these guys, they've just got this dollop, this whip-cream spray of hair on their forehead.

KS: *(laughs)* Like Bob Big-Boy, or a Kewpie doll?

DM: Yeah, I think Rob Corddry has that too, kinda. There must be some term for that. I'm going to call it "the dollop." It's pretty ridiculous. But here's the other thing.

KS: Huh?

DM: I was in New York. I was on the subway, and I was with a friend, and we were looking at this guy. Looked like, I don't know, 40, 50-year-old Asian man, like solidly middle-aged. And he had this *epic* combover. That started here—I'm putting my finger right by my ear—

KS: Yup.

DM: ...Wrapped all the way around the top of the head to the other ear. This hair took the polar route. Right? It just did this.

KS: It went all the way. Yeah.

DM: The rest of his hair, fairly short. He had these select strands that were, like, 18 inches long, wrapping all the way around the head, and here's the kicker: Behind the two-inch coverage of hair, his crown and everything: totally cue-ball bald.

KS: So it's just enough for him to see in the mirror.

DM: Exactly!

KS: "I got a *little* hair."

DM: Exactly. His driver's license photo. When he's in the mirror, he's like, "I look good."

KS: Yeah.

DM: "I got it pegged. I got it fixed."

KS: "Everybody looking at me from directly straight on, I'm looking pretty nice."

DM: As far as he knows, every morning it's like, "Look at me. This is one handsome guy."

KS: At the early stages where you're not ready to feel bad about it yet. You're like, "It's *going* to be a problem." Like he's never bridged into "it's a problem."

DM: Right.

KS: It's still "going to be a problem" at some point.

DM: Well, I remember, after seeing, you know, horrible combovers for years and years and years on everyone, I remember, in high school, there was this teacher—I ddin't know him, but he was walking around the hallways. And I had no interaction with him at all, but I respected him, because he didn't even bother to try with the combover. He was like, "Yeah, it's kind of thin, it's kind of floppy, it's hanging off in strands. It is what it is." There's no artifice about it.

KS: Yeah. Speaking of artifice, @ERTCHIN writes: "David Letterman definitely has a dollop." I would say I think he's totally bald up front, and he wears a piece. Is that—I know he's not doing it as much.

DM: Well, his hair has been really short the last couple of times I've seen him.

KS: Yeah.

DM: I haven't noticed in particular.

KS: I'm wondering if he has a toupée that is a dollop.

DM: *(laughs)* Yeah.

KS: You know?

DM: Just so it's not cue-ball.

KS: Just so it's not bald in front. He's got a little puff.

DM: Well, this actually raises an interesting question. Like, here's the thing about balding: I think balding is one of the things that people feel worse about internally than other people project onto them.

KS: Yeah.

DM: Let me give you an example. I know you understand what I mean, but this is a funny story so I'm going to say it anyway.

KS: I'm gonna laugh.

DM: I was at the pharmacy—right, get ready to laugh. And there was a long line. There was a kid at the register—it's like one of these things where it's like one line and three registers, and you go to the register—and there was this kid who was at one of the registers. And there was this girl, you know, 20-something year old girl, like three people back in the line. This middle-aged guy comes over to the kid, and this girl said, "Excuse me, sir, there's a line." And he looks at her and he goes, "I'm with my child. Is that okay? Can I stand here with my child?"

[BOTH HOSTS LAUGH]

DM: And she goes, "Oh, okay. I'm sorry. I didn't know. It's all right." It was one of those things where he just kept pressing the point, 'cause he knew he could. He's like, "Really? It's fine? I can stand here? With my child?" And she's like, "Oh. Yup. It's fine. Totally." And she's turning beet red. And then ten seconds of silence pass, and she's just sort of...

KS: Looking at the magazines?

DM: Yeah, she's feeling in the spotlight and she goes..."Now I know!"

[BOTH HOSTS LAUGH]

DM: So this is the thing: I felt bad for her. I didn't think, "Oh what an idiot." I thought, "She must think, 'Everyone thinks I'm an idiot.' "

KS: Right. She gets on the P.A. and she's like, "I'm sorry. Attention."

DM: "Attention shoppers. To all who witnessed—in fact, let me explain what happened. And then let me explain how I was not at fault."

KS: It's like Missed Connections in the *PennySaver*. It's like, "If you saw me accidentally call this man a line-butter, I'm sorry."

DM: But I think that's the same thing with balding. When you're bald, you might think, "Oh man, I hate how I look bald. Everyone thinks I'm an idiot." But when I see someone who's bald, I don't think, "Look at that idiot." I think, "He probably thinks everyone thinks he's an idiot."

KS: Yeah, I think if you look at that guy with a combover, that's much more laughable than if he was just bald.

DM: Right.

KS: You're not going, "Look at baldy!"

DM: Right, 'cause the combover is something—is a choice.

KS: Right. Nobody's mad at him for being bald. I'm mad at him for having a horrible decision.

DM: Right, and so this is the thing that I weigh. On the one hand, I think there is no shame in being bald. Like, again, I don't look at anybody and think, "That guy looks like an idiot because he's bald." That never enters my mind. However, I had a teacher once—this is in college now—and he had hair plugs.

KS: Oh.

DM: Horrible-looking hair plugs.

KS: Yeah.

DM: It was the sort of thing where it looked like, you know the LEGO flowers, where it's the three stalks that come up from the central point?

KS: Right.

DM: It looked like he had a bunch of those in his forehead.

KS: Yeah, yeah.

DM: I remember thinking, "Man, he got those horrible hair plugs." But then I thought, "What if he hadn't gotten them and he was just bald?" And I pictured him just regular bald, and it changed my perception of him. Not in a necessarily-negative way...

KS: But you thought of him as an old man.

DM: ...But I thought of him as an older guy. And this was a guy in his sixties. He could legitimately be an older guy, but I didn't think of him as....doddering, let's say.

KS: Right, so the decision to him was, "Do I look like an old man, or do I look like a vain, *possibly*-old man?"

DM: I mean, to his credit, he may not have known that the hair plugs looked horrible. Or, actually—my feeling of how it probably went for real was, he went *into* the hair plugs thinking they would look great. It's not like he can now just yank them out. Now that he sees what they actually look like.

KS: Yeah.

DM: So the guy doing the surgery is like, "Don't worry, totally natural, absolutely no problems." And then afterwards he's like, "Well, dammit."

KS: Yeah, "Look, I've done this a million times. Everytime you have to space the follicles in a little cluster, every millimeter and a half. It's gonna look great. If you're a doll."

DM: *(laughs)* So this is—yeah, that's an interesting thing. Imagine he went in there and he's like, "Yeah, listen. I've seen people with hair plants before. I know it looks horrible. Can we just avoid the horrible-looking?" "Totally. 100%. Absolutely. We've got this one pegged."

KS: "Have you seen my hair? I'm not going bald, but..."

DM: "It's going to look equally as nice, and full, and lush as my own hair."

KS: "You'll feel as good as my hair looks. Let's put it that way."

DM: But then once you have it, the surgery is over. The procedure is done. What do you do?

KS: You wash it and comb it just like it's your own hair. You have a great time.

DM: You just have to pretend that...

KS: You just have to live your life.

DM: You just gotta be like, "Well, I guess I got this now. Eh, no one will notice." It's like the guy on the subway with the combover: "No one will notice. Everyone thinks I look great."

KS: Like I said, he's never transitioned from—and that might be more of a willful thing. Like, that guy with the combover, he never made the transition. He's always gonna look at his completely clean head, like there is not even skin. It's just skullcap. And he goes, "Someday this is going to be a problem, but I'm all right today." But the guy with the hair plugs is willfully like, "I went bald. I'm going to get hair put in. Maybe it doesn't look great, but I'm going to ignore it." You know?

DM: Right.

KS: He didn't ever—he actually crossed over and now he's trying to go back.

DM: "There's a full 270 degrees that people can look at me and I look fine. As long as it's not the angle that reveals the LEGO-flower hair plugs."

KS: Right. Why don't they just stagger those plugs like theater seats?

DM: Yeah, that makes more sense. Instead of just having them lined up like landscaping...

KS: It's like rows of corn. It's like a plantation.

DM: @Deeloquet says, "I'm not going gray, but I am getting red hair." This is something I've never seeen. Like, "I'm going red!"

KS: Is it a bleaching action?

DM: Well, I know that when you have dark hair and you spend a lot of time in the sun, it'll lighten up. That happens a lot.

KS: Yeah.

DM: In fact, pretty much all the shades of brown and red and blonde, it's all the same pigment, it's just a different concentration of it.

KS: Right.

DM: So, like, I bleached my hair once, and it went to red. And then further, it went to blonde. It's not like I tried to bleach it red or yellow.

KS: Right.

DM: It's just less or more. So I'm interested to follow up, @Deeloquet.

KS: *(French accent)* @deeloquet!

DM: *(Imitating Kris)* @deeloquet. And tell us what's your initial hair color, and what's the circumstances in which it's going red.

KS: "I was born bald. I didn't have hair. I had red hair put in."

DM: "I had the hair plugs. I wanted red even though it wouldn't match my complexion or anything. But I just think it looks so sharp. Like an anime character with the bright blue hair."

KS: That's kind of a thing, now that we're talking about appearances, that shift over time. Which is a good enough topic. But the idea of somebody getting a tattoo that cannot be completed in one trip.

DM: *(laughs)*

KS: So you'll see, like, people with a tattoo on their arm, and it's all the linework. And it's like, "Well that's kind of cool, though." And they're like "Oh, well, it's not done. 'Cause he's gonna fill it in, color it, draw feathers on all the birds" or whatever. And I'm kind of like...

DM: So it's, like, skeletons of birds to start with?

KS: Yeah, "Build it up! I want the muscle groups, I want to see the bird's stomach." But I don't understand—it's like sometimes I look at that and, maybe it's just my aesthetic, but I think that I kinda don't want to see it filled in. I feel like you're gonna wreck it. Like it's gonna be just noise. And anybody can do that.

DM: I—that also goes to the feeling that, you get used to the thing that is.

KS: Yeah.

DM: You know, you're working on some kind of design, or you're working on some kind of project and it gets half-done. You're like, "That looks kinda cool." And then if you go further to where you were intending to go to, well, you got used to the half-done thing and now you're not even sure if it's any better.

KS: Now it feels bad. Yeah, yeah, no, absolutely.

DM: So with tattoos I think the—if you're gonna do it in stages, you want to make sure that you stagger it such that each stage is a legitimate—well, I don't know. You tell me. Do you stagger it such that each stage is a legitimate thing by itself? In case you cannot finish it, it still looks okay? Or do you purposefully go the other way, so you don't fall in love with the half-done one? You have to go all the way—you trick yourself so you have to go all the way to the finish line.

KS: No, I couldn't do it. I would do it in stages. I would never want to walk around with something visible and unfinished. Like where lines were not, you know, "the leg's not there. Her breasts are clearly missing."

DM: "We've got all of her fish scales, but her breasts are still to come."

KS: "I want to do a good job. I need to clear that afternoon."

DM: Unless you just put it somewhere that's not obvious. Then no one will see the half-done one. It's just you in the mirror. It's like, there's the one guy with the combover, or with the hair plugs saying, "It looks all right." And then you're just sort of lifting up your shirt, looking in the mirror, saying "Uh, someday I'll be able to get the rest of the horns put in."

KS: The other horns. "This devil only has two horns, but I want mine with three. Someday he'll put it in." Uh, do you think there was ever somebody who was a Neo-Nazi and then decided to leave right after he got the swastika tattoo? Where he was like, "Oh, I didn't realize this was about hating people."

DM: *(laughs)*

KS: "Now what am I going to do with this thing! It's on my entire chest."

DM: "It goes over my whole stomach."

KS: Ahhh.

DM: "There's Hitler sort of saluting, and you can see it if I wear a V-neck—you can see his fingers under the collar."

KS: "I thought that was a historical reference thing!"

DM: "I was hoping to get Napoleon on the other side. And, you know, all the other greats."

KS: He's got a tattoo of, like, Hitler saluting, and all the Hitler Youth, and three swastikas—and then under it he was gonna get "Never again."

DM: *(laughs)* On the back there's FDR, you know, squashing the Nazis. And that way he can show both sides of the story.

KS: Right, right.

DM: So it's a fair use. Er—equal time.

KS: And then the tattoo artist died. "Well, how are we gonna do it now?"

DM: Do you think there are skin head tattoo artists who specialize in skin head tattoos and they've got the sample book that's like, "Here we have the eagle clutching the bones of the Jew. Here we've got Hitler laughing. And here's Hitler at a birthday party, you know, for the kids."

KS: I was gonna say, a lot of them are probably like "Here's a nice one: a rose, and then on the leaf is a little swastika. Keep it soft for you, you know, going to work or whatever."

DM: "I think you would look really good with dolphins... Can you put a swastika in there somewhere?" "All right, all right, I do have a swastika dolphin. How about this: the dolphin—on the flipper he's got the armband."

KS: Okay, that's good. I like that. That's solid.

DM: It's sort of like—I hate to—I'm not making any sort of moral equation here, but it's kind of like Christian rock. Where it's—they're trying to do everything that rock does, but they also have to put Jesus in there as well.

KS: That's my complaint. I know I make a lot of fuss about ELO, but one interview that they had was like, "yeah, we're Christian." I think it's because they put stuff in one of their songs backwards, and everyone was like "that's automatically Satanic." And they're like the *least* Satanic band. Probably less offensive than Christian music, because they're singing about spaceships they can't find.

DM: *(laughs)* Right.

KS: But, they were like, "We're God-fearing. I mean, we're not *Christian music,* but we are all Christians." But Christian music is like, "All right. I'm gonna write a song about getting to see my baby at the airport, except that Jesus is there..."

DM: Right, so there is also an element—or it's like, everything about it is, uh, "I'm trying to make it as heartfelt as, you know, my baby left me, and everything, but it's got to be about how Jesus *never* left me."

KS: *(laughs)* Which is difficult.

DM: So there is a little bit less melancholy in there? So maybe you have to talk about the life you left behind that Jesus saved you from. So you have this really great verse about all the drugs you did, then you gotta rebuke that. So...

KS: It's like, "why didn't Jesus—hold on a second—why didn't Jesus keep you from doing all those drugs?" "Well, all right, I guess I can't talk about the drugs. I'll just segue right into being saved."

DM: Or it's like the *Left Behind* books, or books kinda like this. where it's horribly—I haven't read all of them, but they're all horribly violent. There's vultures picking eyeballs out of people; there is flesh burning off of people's bones. You can't say "damn," though. I mean, that would be...

KS: In the book?

DM: ...Cursing is bad. And any sort of sexual references are very sinful. But it's Jesus doing the flesh-burning, or whatever. Or it's evil, it's in the context of the Antichrist burning people's flesh off their bones, so that's totally fine.

KS: They had a *Left Behind* game.

DM: Oh yeah, where you had to blow up all the unbelievers?

KS: Where it was just as violent as *Command and Conquer,* where you see all the units exploding and their guts flying out, but it's like, "Well, we're helping to purge—these are the disbelievers.."

DM: It's the *Quake* engine but it's just palette-swapped, you know.

KS: Right. There's just an explosion of holy light instead of blood.

DM: Right. Or it's just—back in the...

KS: Instead of viscera, can we put doves?

DM: Well, remember when *Mortal Kombat* went to the Super Nintendo? It's like, "Well, we can't put blood, so they're sweating. It's sweat."

KS: Yeah. It's just white sweat. Gouts of sweat.

DM: They're so—when you rip his head off he's exerting himself.

KS: He's panicking a little bit, because his head is gone.

DM: Got some flop sweat there, just like in the old cartoons.

KS: "I was hoping I'd do better."

DM: 'Cause his shirt is soaked through.

KS: "'Cause I lost my head!"

DM: "I'm so nervous. I have this performance anxiety with the spine being ripped out of my body."

KS: Yeah, they did that in a lot of games, but I didn't realize that—I know they turned it white, but I didn't think they were like, "Uhh, sweat." I thought it was like, "if it's not red, it's fine."

DM: Well, I remember reading in *EGM* or something like that—maybe they called it sweat sort of pejoratively, or I don't know if it was the real—I think it was actually the real intention.[42]

---

42 *EGM*, of course, being the now-defunct *Electronic Gaming Monthly*. Or perhaps the equally-popular-in-1995 *Elephant Gunner Monthly*. Hard to recall.

KS: I've got a story about this. My brother and I, when we were younger and *Wolfenstein 3D* was new, and we were playing it—and my dad does not like games. He thinks they are a big waste of time. Like, he would especially not appreciate a violent game.

DM: "You should be out geocaching!"

KS: No, that's not my dad either. But he sees us playing it, like we're trying to play it when he's not in the room. And he catches us playing it where it's like, you know, "Pow Pow" and the Nazi is like...

DM: *(knocking)* "What are you doing in there?!" "Nothing! Nothing!" "Are you playing *Wolfenstein?*" "No we're just masturbating." "Good!"

KS: "Eh, we're just exploring! Our sexuality; we're in puberty." No but he comes in and sees the Nazi guy blow up, he's like "bleugh!" and his head falls backward. He's like, "What're you playing?" And we were like, I remember saying, "Oh, yeah, they're Nazi *robots*, that's oil..."

DM: "Transmission fluid."

KS: Yeah. "That's coming out of him." And he's like, "no, not good enough."

DM: Oh, so he didn't buy it. I thought that—"it's historical..."

KS: He wouldn't have bought it anyway.

DM: "In between, there's..."

KS: You know the part where Hitler is in a mech suit and you have to beat him on the 6th floor of the building?

DM: It's school research. It's a clip from *The Greatest Generation*. From the cut scenes.

KS: They had that in...what? *Call of Duty* or one of those? The most recent one, there's clips, there's footage, and I'm kind of getting uncomfortable. I'm not playing anymore.

DM: Right, they're trying to make it so realistic and so tied in with the...

KS: That was my big, my big complaint about that game. That they were like, "We're gonna try and make it more real." And the other games, like the earlier—what is it? Not *Call of Duty*, but one of the earlier ones.

DM: *Medal of Honor?*

KS: It was *Medal of Honor*. There's not even blood. There's people on the ground, and they're going "aauugh" but they're just laying there. It's like a high school play.

DM: Right, they're like, "Let's make this game as unpleasant as possible."

KS: Yeah, but the most recent one it's like, "It's real!" And you can shoot off anybody's limbs and it's like, I don't know how much—I'm sure that some of that happened, but maybe not to the degree that I'm seeing it here.

DM: Well, it seems like some of those games are, "We're gonna make it super real with the photorealistic CGI and there's all the sound design on the 5.1 channel, but there's also 25 Nazi snipers that take eight bullets to kill each.

KS: Yeah.

DM: It doesn't seem like it's quite—now I haven't played the game so I don't know. Maybe it's a thing, but is that the impulse for these games? Where it's like, "I don't want to have fun doing it. I want to be horrified by it."

KS: I don't know. But the thing is, I would say you were having more fun that way rather than being horrified, because if it was horrifying, yeah, you could get them in one shot, but you'd die in one shot. You know? The big thing in games now is to not give anybody health. You don't have health anymore. If you take enough damage at once, you die. But f you're like, "Uh, I've been riddled with bullets!" You've just got to lay back, have a sip of water, then the damage just like fades, and then you're fine again.

DM: Oh, right.

KS: Like, there's no more healing.

DM: Oh right, yeah. Because you have that recovery period. And that way you can just keep playing a little longer.

KS: Yeah, because it's not fun to scrounge for health, or whatever.

DM: Right, so um...

KS: And it makes sense. Like, that's just as artificial a play thing as "You've achieved more health points!"

DM: "You've found a big white box..."

KS: "You're body is whole again!"

DM: "...It has something magic—it has Superglue in it that covers up this gash in your intestines."

KS: Right. "Bullets don't do anything, they just make a number go down."

DM: I think it would be interesting if there is a game, and at the end of every level it's like, "You survived! But died of gangrene. You got a tetanus infection. You were gutshot, you made it back to base; however, you got blood poisoning."

KS: *(laughs)* Right. And then you play the next round as another guy. Like, your friend. You know? There's plenty of—there's no shortage of infantry.

DM: Fighting as fine young soldiers. Now, do you think in that case, that *Contra* was the most realistic game? 'Cause that is just one shot, you're dead.

KS: Yeah, 'cause one shot, you're dead; you could freaking tumble in the air, and the spread gun. Like, you're shooting tomatoes at everybody, I don't know what the hell those were? Energy balls?

DM: I guess the—the mythos, to keep *Contra* fitting into the realistic framework: you get shot, you're dead, and then there's like a helicopter hovering just off-screen that's just, "All right, that guy's down. You go in, Bob. You're next." He just jumps down, picks up where the first guy left off.

KS: Yeah. I like that better than the guy blinking then coming back into existence. You know?

DM: Yeah, right, exactly. As soon as they land they've got to go, "Hold on. Wait 10 seconds. I'm invincible. Totally safe."

214

KS: "No, no, no, no!"

DM: "Ah, ah, ah!" *(scolding noise)*

KS: You go ahead and shoot. I'm gonna get in a position over here. I'm getting right next to you.

DM: It's in the Geneva Conventions.

KS: I want all three shots to go to the eyeball, so I'm gonna get right next to the head. 'Cause I almost killed him with my last two lives.

DM: Right. I got incrementally closer.

KS: Yeah.

[ACCORDION STING]

KS: All right, new topic.

DM: So, going back to the toupées, do you think if the hair...

KS: That's an old topic. *(laughs)*

DM: Yeah, well, I just remembered something I wanted to bring up. If you wanted to—if you didn't want to get the hair grafts, you didn't want to get the toupée that's all sliding around and looks gross, what are your options? What are other things you can do? Wear a bandanna. Some kind of crazy hat all the time.

KS: Crazy hat. You'd probably go with a hat. Bandanna's kind of a gang thing. I don't know.

DM: Gang thing and/or cancer survivor.

KS: Probably couldn't get away with that. Yeah.

DM: Do you think there's a lot of cancer survivors in gangs? They're like, *(interesting accent—probably racist)* "Hey, man! Odelay, homes. You've been to chemo, man. You gettin' all skinny."

KS: *(yup, definitely racist accent)* "No man, I'm just trying to lose weight. *Dat* guy's been in chemo!"

DM: "Oh dang, man, he said you been in chemo!"

KS: *(laughs)* Yeah, that's a very ineffective gang.

DM: Those guys, they kind of shave their heads anyway, you know.

KS: A lot of them might, yeah. But you know what, there's probably not a more effective way to get rid of all that unwanted hair...

DM: Than chemo.

KS: Right, than those chemicals, which you can probably buy on the Internet.

DM: Some Canadian pharmacy.

KS: "Forget Nair!"

DM: Or you know what? Here's the market for it. The guys that have resigned themselves to being bald, right?

KS: Yeah.

DM: They have the big, sort of, bald crown, but they have the fringe still thick, you know?

KS: They have the Picard.

DM: Right, the Picard. So they say, "You know what? I'm going to shave the whole deal." That's fine. That's the standard thing to do. But they have to keep that up. They can't let that fringe grow out. So, then, the one solution might be: you then need some product to clear off all the rest of that stuff. To bring the fringe to the level of the crown. No stubble, there's no sort of weird, two-tier...

KS: You're talking like a permanent—like electrolysis. But maybe faster than that.

DM: Yeah, 'cause electrolysis, you have to do, like, every hair, or some kind of deal.

KS: Why not—how about... well, no...

DM: So here's the pitch: "Have you resigned yourself to being bald, but you still have to shave your head every three days, otherwise you end up looking like some kind of crazy monk? Just—here's this permanent hair mask." Maybe it's a thing you wear when you're sleeping? It goes around your head...

KS: Wait, it's like a depilatory, but like *really* strong.

DM: Right.

KS: It just kills the follicles. And you wear like a hat while you're in bed.

DM: Yeah, maybe it's like a waxy thing. It's not hot wax, 'cause that's painful, but it's just sort of canvas wrap around your head. It's got a thin layer of paraffin inside of it. And then, as you sleep, the warmth and pressure of your head slowly softens the wax...

KS: Melts it into your head.

DM: And then it gets into—then the hairs get embedded.

KS: Literally melts onto your head.

DM: Right. And then what you do, you know, once you wake up every morning, or every week—once a week, or however often you do this—and then you just have to rip it off your head.

KS: Yeah.

DM: That part's maybe the part they don't show in the ad.

KS: That doesn't hurt though.

DM: Yeah, it's...

KS: They can put an anasthetic.

DM: Yeah!

KS: To help you sleep, and...

DM: It eases into your scalp, you pull that guy off. You get strips of flesh hanging off of it, but you're like, "Yup, feels great. I've had Novocaine pressed against my head all night."

KS: I think this is actually a great idea. Because you've got a whole cottage industry that can sprout up around it—no pun intended. But think about this. All right, how about this: "Your Hair, Your Way." You put this wax thing on your head. It melts at night. Then, when you wake up, you stick your head into a bag of loose hair, it sticks to the wax, you can just brush out the excess, clear that off, whatever you need to, shave it in the morning...

DM: Looks good.

KS: Looks great. Natural.

DM: And that way, it's sort of like you give away the razors, sell the blades. The money comes from selling the bags of hair.

KS: Right, we've got to find—there's enough hair.

DM: There's hair out there!

KS: There's hair to be found.

DM: Everyone's got hair.

KS: Look, you can go into any Supercuts, they're throwing away *bags* of hair every day.

DM: They're throwing that stuff away!

KS: You're like, "Can I take it, please?"

DM: It's like the guy in the biodiesel car going around the back of the Chinese restaurant and gets the—they were gonna have to pay to get rid of that grease.

KS: Right.

DM: He puts it into his Mercedes and drives around.

KS: And now this guy—exactly—this guy's gonna make million-dollar deals.

DM: Same deal with Supercuts, but here's what you'd have to do. Have you heard of those places where they take your leftover, like, half-empty paint cans? And they take them to Africa and they paint schools with them and stuff?

KS: Oh, really?

DM: Yeah, they put them in, like, shipping containers and they...

KS: What do the schools look like?

DM: Eh, they look all right.

KS: You know they look at the schools and they're all like, quilted, and you're like, "Ha ha. Stupid kids."

DM: "I enjoy having so much color in my life!" I don't know why that's Italian, but here's how they get around the weirdo colors. They group them in like three families. You know: whites, mid-tones, dark tones. And then they mix them all.

KS: Oh, so you end up with a brown, a beige, or something.

DM: Exactly, you end up with some neutral mid-tones. And then, they make 100 gallons at a time, or whatever it is, of the basic...

KS: To paint the school.

DM: Yeah, you get a school's worth of all one color.

KS: That's smart.

DM: And so that's what you would have to do with the Supercuts leavings. You sweep them all up and you sort of mix them all together, so that way you get...

KS: Uniform.

DM: Otherwise you'd get some different colors and different textures. You have to sort of sift them all—you segregate them in certain ways...

KS: Batches.

DM: And then you have some sort of an agitator that mixes them all together. So that way the hair that you put on your head into one of those mixed batches is roughly, you know, within one standard deviation of the same type of hair.

KS: Go one further. Go one further. Imagine: Instead of them doing that, and you stick your head in the bag, there is like a room or a chamber in your house where you put the bags of hair, you turn the air on, it circles throughout the room. And the only thing that's sticky on your body is the wax on your head.

DM: Right, so everything—well, except if you're, I don't know. If you have a haircut, those flecks of hair stick to you. They stick to your neck; they stick to whatever.

KS: Ah, that's true, maybe some sort of a hair-dryer thing.

DM: But that's fine. Maybe to product just doesn't work. You can still sell it...

KS: Yeah, we're not talking about making a *good* product.

DM: In college I got so... over time, do you remember the commercials for Epil-Stop and Spray? Do you remember that?

KS: Yeah.

DM: They got so pervasive that me and my friends were like, "All right, we've got to try that Epil-Stop."

KS: "I've got to stop my hair!"

DM: And it's like $12 or something, but it's like $9 shipping. And we were like, "You know what? We're going to outsmart these guys. We're just not going to pay the shipping." And so there was a store in the mall that was an "As Seen on TV" store. You could buy all the Flowbees and the OxyClean and all that stuff. And so we got the Epil-Stop from there. In the commercial, as you may recall, they show, like, an arm. And they spray the spray on there, and then they have, like, a rag. And they literally wipe the hair off.

KS: And it's just gone.

DM: It's just gone. It could not be portrayed any simpler. So, when you get the thing there's all this fine print that says, like, you know, procedures, you have to let it sit for twenty minutes and burn out the hair follicles...

KS: Yeah, yeah.

DM: That kind of thing. So my fairly hairy friend was the first to try it. I think he went into to bathroom or something 'cause he was gonna try it on his chest. And he sprays it on. And about 5 minutes later we hear this sort of, "Ahhhh, ahhhh." 'Cause it had just started burning.

KS: Yeah.

DM: Just burning and burning. So he's trying to wipe it off, you know—before starting to rinse it, he's trying to get the actual use out of it, and just nothing. Zero. Zero effectiveness. Maybe three hairs. Like, you could have just used anything—used white glue and you would have had a better ratio.

KS: And it wouldn't have burned. Yeah.

DM: So it was such a letdown!

KS: They have this product now that is a plastic—it's like a tongue scraper almost, but it's plastic. And then you—it's just like, here: check this out, take the hair off. You just scrape it across your skin. And the idea is that the plastic is sharp enough to get rid of really fine hair.

DM: Hmmm...

KS: Like women's leg hair, was the point. It's like, "If you need to touch it up, then you can use that. You don't have to go razor on the whole deal."

DM: Well, Nikki, my wife, has some stuff like that. Not for herself, but for her makeup work. They make these little tiny touch-up razors.

KS: Oh yeah?

DM: They look kind of like a toothbrush, except instead of bristles they have just sort of a very small razor blade. And it's meant to be applied without cream or anything. And it's such a small surface area, you can just get into weird corners and stuff, and for doing things like touching up beards or something.

KS: Like taking care of a stray hair.

DM: Right, like a stray hair here and there, or you're going around some weird corner on some part of your body, she can use that. On anybody. On me, on...

KS: You could shave the inside of your bladder.

DM: You could do it. Just get that endoscopic shaving. Where they go in through your bellybutton with the snake thing, and take care of whatever.

KS: "Eh, there's a bit of patchy hair."

DM: "We've got to scrape some of this stuff out." Uh, we've got @GUGGER_FANE who says, "Is dyed hair a problem with the Supercuts idea?"

KS: That's a good idea, though. You could dye the hair and then give it to people.

DM: Yeah, that way you could get it all consistent. That's really smart.

KS: I would say that is a problem, because it drives our costs up. I'm more interested in just getting hair from Supercuts.

DM: Well, maybe you could offer the premium. Like, maybe you get the people who are like, "I'm just gonna get the cheap one." And then they realize there are many inherent problems with the plan. But you phrase the ad copy such that the problems in the plan get blamed on them buying the cheap hair.

KS: You know what? If the problems with the—if the theme, if the slogan of this product is "Your Hair, Your Way," here's what we do. We don't need to really overthink the dying. We just have two vats. One for black hair, just dark, just throw a bunch of hair in there and everything that comes out is just going to be pitch black.

DM: Right.

KS: And then the other one is bleach—you throw the hair in there and it's just gonna come out snow white hair.

DM: Right.

KS: You get that snow white hair, you dye it to whatever color you want. You dye it to your old color! Then you're going to look just the same as you ever did.

DM: 'Cause then you have to get the kit of the dyes and the whole color chart. It's like a Pantone chart, where it's, like, 3 drops of brown, 1 drop of red...

KS: Right, we send you the little Pantone, little handheld device. You take a, you know, look at a photo of yourself, get that exact color combination, put in as much dye as you're gonna need. You go to town, buddy, you're gonna look great. You're a hero.

DM: *(laughs)* So, is the hair scraps being different lengths—is there a problem there?

KS: I don't care. For the people? Let's see...

DM: Oh, yeah, because if you have a big vat of leftovers, there's gonna be some short, some long. For cancer hair, it has to be like a foot, or 18 inches long or something.

KS: That's true. Ah, shoot.

DM: 'Cause you're gonna end up with a lot of the things that are left over after you shave. Like, little tiny...

KS: Loose fragments.

DM: So there has got to be some sort of centrifuge that spins out the pieces below a certain threshold. So the hair would have to be dried first, so it's not sticking to each other...

KS: Yeah, yeah. No no. You could just use grids. You could just use meshes. And you'd blow the hair through, and of course the largest pieces would get stuck and you could just go up, up, up, up. And then, the larger pieces you could have—if some guy was like, "I'm just having a crew cut." Don't worry, buddy, just sprinkle on these tiny shavings. Maybe they're all lying down. It's not quite the same, but it's all right. It's not like...

DM: It's a good thing...

KS: You're only a little damp. It's like you took a dip in the pool.

DM: So the, um—I'm thinking about the meshes though. If you have the big hair, it's going to clump on the mesh itself and the little hair is not going to be able to get through. So there's got to be some sort of a...

KS: Like an agitation? Like one of the meshes is kind of going like this *(rubs hands together)*. Kind of rotating next to each other.

DM: They're moving, or there's some sort of a squeegee that kind of peels them off each layer. I think the centrifuge idea is probably fairly solid, though.

KS: Yeah, maybe the centrifuge will work better.

DM: Maybe there are two rival companies that are like, "Well, these…" Here's the other thing I love: when you get two companies or products that are in the same field, and they each spin their method or unique way as better then the other guy.

KS: And they both make a product that is just retarded.

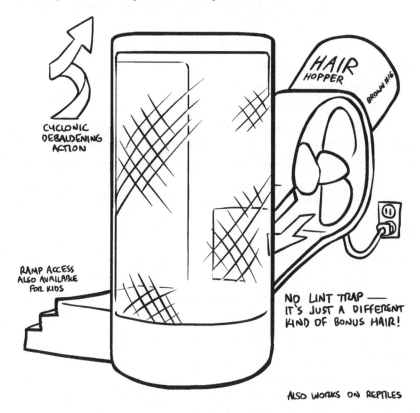

DM: Well, yeah, in this case, for sure. But it could be something like, "We use the centrifuge method. It's so superior to the mesh method because we—we're able to keep our costs down. We don't have—there's fewer moving parts, and that means a better product for you, the consumer." And then over, across the way there are the other guys going, "We use the mesh method. Those guys with the centrifuge…"

KS: "Tired of uneven, centrifuge hair?"

DM: "Our method is—it costs more, but that's because it's the better process." And it's not even general. It's like exact, specific things.

KS: "We're talking about your appearance here. Why not spend for the best. This is your livelihood."

DM: Right.

KS: "I used to use the mesh method, and now I'll never go back."

DM: "Here's a picture of me looking horrible." And it's just, bleughghgh. He's got hair all stringy and everything.

KS: And in the background you see his wife, with her suitcase just out the door.

DM: Right, the door is half open, she's like stepped into the hallway.

KS: There's a time element, like she's looking at a watch. And look—you can see a checkered cab in the background.

DM: And she's packed her suitcase so fast and so full and it's bulging...

KS: The socks coming out, or whatever.

DM: The scarf hanging half out the suitcase.

KS: And he's just frowning.

DM: And this flat, harsh lighting, just this glare shot against the wall from the camera flash, and he's got this stained T-shirt and knocked-over bottles on the coffee table.

KS: There's prescription medicine, clearly being abused, on the coffee table.

DM: Right, there's a newspaper sitting on the kitchen table and the headline says, "Economy in the toilet." Outside you see storm clouds. There's a car hitting a lamppost. There's a fistfight.

KS: Yeah, he's got a poster of 9/11.

DM: *(laughs)* A poster *of* 9/11...!

KS: It doesn't even say, like "Never Forget." It's just a poster that says "9/11."

DM: "Remember what I look like? Remember this?"

KS: "Remember how sad you were? Oh man."

DM: It's a collage—it's one of those *Truman Show* movie-poster collages, but it's all pictures of like...

KS: Where people are like falling down and crying.

DM: Or like one of those things that were really popular in like '97, where the tiny pictures make the mosaic of the big picture.

KS: Oh, yeah, yeah, yeah.

DM: And it's all video screenshots from 9/11, making the giant picture of 9/11. Photo-mosaic, I think they're called.

KS: Yeah, that's what it is. The "after" picture is just that that poster has been removed. That guy's life is otherwise the same.

DM: His hair is marginally better.

KS: His hair looks a little bit better.

DM: Marginally different.

KS: His wife left, though. I mean, what do you want? She's not going to come back because his hair is a little more even in length.

DM: *(laughs)*

KS: Clearly they had more problems than that.

DM: There were some deeper-seated issues in the marriage.

KS: This guy's got a lot of issues. I don't know why they got married in the first place.

DM: She thought she could change him.

KS: She thought she could fix him.

DM: And he thought the things that she complained about were just not as serious as she was making them.

KS: Well, you know, when you love somebody, you end up—like those things become kind of sweet, like, cute little errors or flaws in the other person.

DM: Right, right, yeah. And he always figured those things that were really bedrock, fundamental principles, like "We need to spend some time with my family." And this kind of thing...

KS: "You know a lot of people talk about 9/11, but I keep thinking about all the pets that died." And she's like, "That's uh, no. That's just you. That's why I love you."

DM: This guy, he loves animals. He really loves animals.

KS: "I mean, I personally, I don't care that they're dead, but what a tragedy. Just think of what kind of cleanup that would be. All that rotting, you know—dog carcasses, and what-have-you."

DM: "Do you think they segregated them? Like, imagine the people that have to move those tons of concrete. Like, they have to collect the body parts, obviously, because that stuff has to be identified, but what about the dogs?"

KS: "Oh my goodness, that is just adorable. I love you, but I can't take you anywhere."

DM: "Yeah, um, so we've been married for 6 months. We've stopped going to cocktail parties. We've stopped going to family gatherings. We've stopped going to the dog park, Lord knows."

KS: Can you imagine the—that just calls to mind the generic jackass at the theater going to see the movie like *2012*, and some tectonic plate is rotating and about to crush the White House and he's just going, "That's not how it would happen. That's B.S. I'm going to leave."

DM: "No one answered my letters. I wrote a lot of letters to the film company."

KS: "I saw that in the trailer. They had a lot of time to change it."

DM: Right. "I sent that letter certified."

KS: "It was the teaser. Four months out, they could have easily..."

DM: "I know they got that letter. Someone signed for it. 'B Strongburt' signed for it. I got the verification."

KS: "It wouldn't be a big stone sheet lifting off the—there would be a lot more magma. And maybe it would get cool, you can only see a little red glow for a moment, but no, all I'm seeing is…"

DM: And then his wife is like, "He has a lot of theories about—he wanted to be a geologist. He wasn't. We had to sort of—well, the schools didn't quite… well, he just decided to go another way."

KS: "Well, look. I think this whole thing is a side effect of the Chinese running the special-effects industry and I don't care for it. They're—they've got their pro-tectonic plates moving around, and they put it in the program that my children are going to have to watch."

DM: "He's got some really interesting theories about the geopolitical situation, and he's always—he loves to keep up on the news. He really likes to keep up on the news. He always knows exactly what's happening."

KS: "And I just get furious when I go into that theater and there is anybody else in that theater. Like what are they? They shouldn't even be there."

DM: "He's not a people person."

KS: "This is MY movie. I paid $10."

DM: "He definitely—he's frugal. He like to get value for his money."

KS: "God, I'm just so furious, I could urinate."

DM: "We're working through some sort of personal problem—he had a kidney disorder. Brought on by getting some blows to the kidney after an altercation in a movie theater."

KS: *(laughs)* "He has a urological disorder…"

DM: "He's seeing a very good urologist. He's seeing—I mean we found him… he had the biggest ad in the whole Yellow Pages."

KS: "He had a—whenever he feels displeasure, he express that, by you know, voiding his bladder. He doesn't really care who he's in front of."

DM: "We found some very good catheters. They have some really—you know the bags they make now, you can't even see them!"

KS: "They go all around the leg."

DM: "The straps are so secure. And they're machine-washable."

KS: "Honey, my bag's full."

DM: "I'll be right there."

KS: It's like, "What are we talking to these losers for?" "I'll change your bag in a minute, sweetheart."

DM: "Who're you talking to? You still talking to those guys? You still talking to that guy?"

KS: "Get in the car."

[ACCORDION STING]

DM: So, have you ever been—have you ever seen a contest where there's four… maybe there's fourth place, grand prize, second place, third place, but the winner of the contest is so horrible at whatever the contest is that you think, "They must have only got four entries." So it's like, "We *have* to give the grand prize to this guy, 'cause there's…"

KS: And in fact, there's so few entries that there isn't even a distribution of quality. Where it's like, "I don't know. Let's just randomly assign them because they are all pretty bad."

DM: Can you think of a contest that…

KS: Children's contests.

DM: *(laughs)* Well, yeah, I guess there is some sort of a threshold of how good that stuff is ever going to get.

KS: When I was in Cub Scouts I won a trophy—I won third place in the Pinewood Derby.

DM: Right.

KS: For my car, for my little racer car that I had painted. And I won it for Humor.

DM: *(laughs)* Wait, what? Third place in the Humor category?

KS: In the Humor category.

DM: Wait, so two people were funnier than you?

KS: They were funnier than me, and what had happened was I had painted the car to look like it had, you know, racing endorsements on it. I was not going for the humor category. I was going for just a race car.

DM: Verisimilitude.

KS: And uh, they were like, "Well, that's funny."

DM: "That's so cute that he actually did that instead of just a stripe. He made a little NASCAR, like a stock car."

KS: Right, and so no, I don't know if we have the car at home. I don't think I did a very good job. And I think I knew it. I think I was like, "Ah, I'm just going to put dots and dashes all over this thing."

DM: Oh, so it was just blots of color?

KS: Yeah it was blots of color to simulate, but I don't think it ended up that great.

DM: It wasn't like "I'm gonna make a 7Up logo really intricately?"

KS: No, so I think that they award that thinking like, "Oh that's creative. I like that."

DM: What were the other categories besides Humor?

KS: Uh, well, you know what? I…

DM: Was there like a "General Non-Humor But Creative," or this was the closest?

KS: I don't know, maybe? I actually don't remember; I was too young. But, given that there was a Humor category, I would be surprised to learn that there was a speed category. Like, maybe they didn't even judge—like, "It doesn't even matter whose car was faster. Let's just all look at these cool cars that we made and we'll have a good time."

DM: It's like an art show. "Here's all the craft projects."

KS: We have watermelons; the families will take pictures.

DM: Apple juice.

KS: And it will just be a lot of fun.

DM: So, um, what this reminds me of is the doll, or the scale model, like, props. You go to the hobby shop, and they've got like the little rocking chair in the 1/12th scale, or whatever it is, that you can paint yourself. And then they have all the accessories to go in your dollhouse that are actual brands.

KS: Oh.

DM: There's a miniature 7Up can, with a 7Up logo. There's a Coke logo. There's Lay's potato chips. So I wonder how? Is that licensed? I wonder if that's licensed.

KS: It has to be licensed.

DM: There's got to be some sales rep out there that's like, "We're gonna get our logo on doll merchandise!"

KS: Well you know what though, they're probably like, "Look. Teach your kids to always have 7Up in the house. Why not? You know, at a young age. Get them started." I think that would be very effective. Like, "Oh, my Barbie always has to have 7Up."

DM: @ALPHAJAMMER says, "For my Pinewood Derby car, I shaved it all the way down so that it looked like a skateboard and put a Bart Simpson toy on it."

KS: He won the speed.

DM: Yeah, he won. It was just like, "Well no one ever realized, this is actually…"

KS: "All you need is one wheel, and that thing is going to move faster than any car. You don't have any friction. It's basically…"

DM: "It's really a unicycle car and there's a tiny gyroscope in there. It's the same principle as the Segway."

KS: Right. "Are you familiar with the vehicle that General Grievous drove?"

DM: "Are you familiar with Gizmoduck?"

KS: "There are plenty of examples of this."

DM: We've got @DEELOQUET saying, "I always won the humor category by putting a cutout of Calvin driving, and putting tiger stripes." So you clearly have a recollection of this, so I would like to…

KS: Of gaming the judges.

DM: So fill us in. What were some of the other categories? 'Cause this is something I never did personally.

KS: I actually don't remember any of them now.

DM: And he was also responding earlier, too. He was going with the red hair. He said, "I'm going red." He says he probably just thinks he's going gray very slowly.

KS: Oh. Like a gradual gray.

DM: Right.

KS: Well, there were plenty of gray-haired people at this Pinewood Derby. I'm trying
to mix them together.

DM: @EMVASSEUR also said something earlier about listing all the melanin chemicals
in your hair, and it was really long so I'm not gonna read it. Thanks, Em, we
appreciate it.

KS: We are on cars now.

DM: Now we are talking about Pinewood Derby cars, and winning with bad stuff.
So yeah, children's contests in general, they're never going to get better than a
certain thing, no matter what the thing is. So the categories have to be relative.
It has to be, like, Best Effort and Most Improved. I remember getting Most
Improved in band in seventh grade and it was like...

KS: That's painful.

DM: Well, I knew I was horrible at the beginning, and so maybe—it's the sort of thing
where going from 1 to 10 is a thousand-fold improvement. Or what is it? It's a
ten-fold improvement.

KS: Yeah, yeah.

DM: And going from 90 to 92 is like a minor 2% improvement.

KS: Well, which one did you get then?

DM: Well, I just got a little trophy that said "Most Improved." I think I was in, like, the
10s. And I went up to like a 25.

KS: See, I would hate to get that one, just 'cause it's like, "hey, evidence!" This proves
that you were bad at the start. You were not good. They're not giving it to the guy
who was awesome, and who now is incredible.

DM: But they give him another one. They give him, like, "Best Performer" or
something like that.

KS: Yeah, I know, but I'm embarrassed.

DM: But here's the thing. Most Improved, at least someone acknowledges, "Hey,
you're not actually that bad."

KS: "You tried really hard." That's what I take away from it.

DM: But it's not just effort. There must be evidence of improvement.

KS: Growth, I would say.

DM: You must have actually gotten better, I would say.

KS: Yeah, I guess actually, like, "Most Effort" would be more insulting.

DM: Yeah, Most Effort would be good. If nothing else...

KS: "Most Labored Execution."

DM: Oh, @EMVASSEUR is talking here, she's some kind of a hair expert. She says, "Red is stronger than all the other colors. Is that simpler and shorter?" Yeah.

KS: Wait, so red is stronger, as in, it will stand out more?

DM: Well...

KS: Or is it stronger just as in it's better?

DM: I think...

KS: I think we lost the length, but now the ambiguity has stepped in.

DM: Stronger? I think she means that if you have red hair, it makes you mighty. All the Vikings had red hair.

KS: Oh yeah, there you go.

DM: Who else? Arnold Schwarzenegger is a redhead.

KS: Is he?

DM: Yeah.

KS: Well, he doesn't look that way anymore, but...

DM: He dyes it now.

KS: He's going gray very slowly.

DM: Okay, so, uh, I've entered art contests before. I've entered—I did get an honorable mention in an art contest, where they put my drawing up at the mall. That was kinda cool.

KS: Well, there you go.

DM: I entered an art contest at the Otis School of Art and Design here in L.A.

KS: Oh yeah.

DM: I was in high school at the time, but they had a contest. So I submitted my work, and I got an honorable mention, they put me up in the gallery. And my work was a pencil drawing. It was 8½" x 11", and I think I had it mounted on a piece of matboard or something. And I went to the gallery show with my parents, you know, to the opening reception. And there's my thing on the wall, just, like, mounted on its matboard. 8½" x 11". Next to these giant framed oil paintings. Everybody else had like framed it and they had all this, like, whole hardware around it—and mine's just this little thing that's kind of "eh, over there."

KS: Oh, no!

DM: But you know, at art school, there's always people trying to be weird for the sake of weird. And so we're looking around the rest of the exhibition. I'm with my parents—kind of elderly, older parents.

KS: Yeah.

DM: And it's like, "Oh, let's check this out." And there is a wall-sized painting, I kid you not—the size of a wall—of a woman giving birth. You know: spread-eagle, looking right at the business center, and coming out of her is a football player in full football gear with the pads and the whole deal. And I understand that there is some commentary to be made here about, you know, kids, whatever it is, but...

KS: I mean, depending on the age. If it's undergrads, the commentary is "I thought of it! And you decide. And I'm intelligent."

DM: But it was a really interesting kind of—and I'm like 17 by this point, and I'm always embarrassed by my parents, because my parents are very conservative.

KS: No one wants to see your parents see a vagina.

DM: And in retrospect, I realize they have, you know—they're much older than I am. They've seen their share. I'm 17. @CRAZYCSTUDIOS says, "We never had those everyone-wins categories with the Pinewood Derby cars in my Scout pack. Everyone got Participation ribbons." Yes, the Participation ribbon!

KS: Oh, I'd just throw that away. If I see you walking down the row and handing one to everyone, I don't want that.

"the day I saw superman naked." Maki! age 17

DM: It's purple.

KS: Yeah. "Congratulations for your dad buying the car."

DM: I remember in elementary school... how much are those kits?

KS: The ribbon says on it, "Your dad had $20."

DM: That's what I was gonna say. It's like, "yeah, good job!" In elementary school they used to give out these awards that were like—there's a Citizenship award, I remember.

KS: Yeah.

DM: There was, like, the Academic award. There was some kind of a—there was the Presidential Academic Fitness award, which was signed by George Bush the First.

KS: Those sound like really classy things. You're not talking about the yearbook categories, like Most Clowny.

DM: No, these were actually fairly academic. I had no idea what citizenship meant, like the word, in second grade, besides being a citizen of the country. You know, you're nice, you're a good sportsman, that kind of stuff. So I never won that, because I was a horrible child. And then there was also Perfect Attendance. Perfect Attendance was always—I *always* missed out on Perfect Attendance, except maybe one quarter my entire elementary-school career. And I remember my friend got it every single time, because his mom was a teacher at the school.

KS: What? Oh, 'cause he couldn't get away with it.

DM: Right, she'd drag him to school every single day. So he had 5 quarters' worth of Perfect Attendance awards, and he's like—this guy is King of the World. He's like, "I am the king of perfect attendance. No one can touch me." He's like Cal Ripken of the third grade.

KS: Oh God, that's sad. But, like, he's doing better than you now, is what you're saying? He's now the CEO of some Fortune 500 company, because of that. Because that shows the drive that you need.

DM: It's on his press kit, you know, his bio on the official corporate website. It lists all of his achievements. You know: 2009 Clio-Award-winning marketing campaign, all the way down to "1984 Perfect Attendance—4." All four quarters.

KS: Then underneath that one: "Finished all my milk."

DM: It's all described in a very...

KS: "Let me attend to your needs."

DM: *(laughs)*

KS: "They call me The Attender."

DM: "And you'll call my service to you Perfect." But it's like "had artwork prominently displayed in neighborhood home. Not *just* on the fridge—on the *primary* fridge. In the *downstairs* kitchen."

KS: *(laughs)* Yeah, I was gonna say, "on the Frigidaire DT20, with built-in door icemaker."

DM: "The General Electric FE44 EnergySaver. For 4 months. Superceded by even larger achievement: we got an even *bigger* fridge."

KS: "References: Mom, Dad, and Mr. Bear, my imaginary friend. He likes..."

DM: Then you click on Mr. Bear. He's got his own profile on the CEO website. His awards are, like, "Most Snuggly," and every now and then mixed in is a really disturbing one, like "Most Disturbing Interpretation of My Dream."

KS: Yeah.

DM: "Best Performance in the Context of a Nightmare I Had."

KS: Right. "Most Needed to Be Comforted on My Behalf after the Bad Dream That I Had."

DM: And then there is, like, National Honor Society. Bear's also a member of the National Honor Society.

KS: Junior Varsity, just one year.

DM: But the guy, the actual main guy, he couldn't get that. The bear...

KS: The bear won.

DM: He was helping the bear so much—he was tutoring the bear after school so much, that his own studies were lacking. He couldn't finish his essay, because he finished the bear's first. At which his teacher was like, "Why is this kid turning in two essays? One for him and one for the bear!?" No—the teacher reinforces it, like, "This Theodore F. Snugglepuss, he's not on my attendance sheet, but he's turned in every..."

KS: "He's writing better papers!"

DM: "He's turned in every assignment this whole semester."

KS: "I'd ask his father if he was helping him, but I don't think he's real."

DM: @Mʀʙɪʟᴅᴀɴɢᴏ says, "Mr. Bear: Sexiest Eyes That One Night."

KS: He would never do that to Mr. Bear.

DM: Come on!

KS: That's an imaginary friend! That is a *friend*. How about imaginary girlfriends?

DM: All right, imaginary girlfriends? "Most Number of Imaginary Girlfriends at One Time." And that award...

KS: "I have literally one in every county of the United States."

DM: "I have the whole list."

KS: They're all named Heather! After the girl I had a crush on in second grade.

DM: There are subtle differences. "Um, this one is just like the real Heather, except she didn't turn me down. This one is just like the real Heather—she *did* turn me down—but her hair was a different color. I thought I liked that one better."

KS: "She did turn me down, but she died."

DM: "She was hit by a car..."

KS: "Her parents were really upset. They were like, 'Why didn't you ask her out!' "

DM: "In this one she had cancer, but she recovered, but she needed me after that. Because I helped her. I came to her. I brought her soup."

KS: "I can't do any of those, except being dead brought her around."

DM: "I put wax on her head, I put her in a chamber to get hair blown all over her."

KS: "This is my love! This is my love for you. I bought you this system. It's a centrifuge, nothing but the best."

DM: "I dyed it so it matches your—not the hair color you have, but the one I would prefer you have."

KS: How about that commercial, where it's like, "Has this ever happened to you? Sorry you have cancer. Check this out. 'Oh my God, the Wax Hair Kit!...*Mesh* System?! *Wah wahhh*. Get out of my house.' "

DM: Chasing him in her wheelchair down the driveway, throwing the box after him, "And, don't come back!"

KS: The gravestone is like, "Thanks for the stupid mesh system."

DM: And the guy in the suit steps in from just off-camera and is like, "What you need..." And the girl still like—he's trying to pick up the stuff off the lawn, out of focus in the background...

KS: At this point they're just miming. At this point they're just like *wah wah wah*.

DM: Right.

[BOTH HOSTS LAUGH]

KS: Oh, God. There's a lot of dark paths that's going down in my head. I can't go there.

DM: I'm gonna file a bunch of trademarks this afternoon.

KS: Okay, we can do that online.

[ACCORDION STING]

DM: So this has been Tweet Me Harder, the world's first, best, only, and last talkback-enabled interactive audio podblast. I've been David Malki !

KS: I have been Kris Straub.

DM: This has been a fun hour of us in the same room, sharing laughter and joy with all of you out there on the Internets.

KS: Well, they just heard it. You don't need to wrap up.

DM: Yeah, but this is for people who came in late. What they've missed.

KS: Oh that's true. I forgot about that.

DM: Our next show is going to be probably in about, I'd say 8 or 9 days. Probably middle of next week.

KS: It's going to be hectic.

DM: Yeah, we've got a big week coming up. You can come and see us either at Comic-Con, or if you can't get into Comic-Con but you're still in San Diego, you should check out the TopatoCo/*Dr. McNinja* book-launch party. Wednesday night the 22nd, at the Rock Bottom brewery in San Diego, starting at 9 P.M. I think. We're gonna be—it's free to attend...

KS: We're gonna do a live podcast by sneaking into the booth and just commandeering whatever P.A. system they have.

DM: Right, no one is going to give us permission...

KS: It'll probably be about 20 seconds long, before they throw us out.

DM: Right, they hustle us off the thing, but we hope that you can—if you send us any tweets or something on your cell phone, we'll talk about them. You know, time permitting, in 20 seconds.

KS: A guy just approaches you with a card with a tweet on it, and somebody has to fetch me so I can stand next to you and talk about it.

DM: Right, don't give people ideas, 'cause that sounds horrible. Someone's gonna do it. @MRBILDANGO is gonna do it.

KS: If anybody does that, I'm just gonna rip the card up and not talk to you for the rest of the night.

A Secret Isthmus

KS: Hey everybody! Welcome to Tweet Me Harder—the world's first, best, only, and last talkback-enabled interactive audio podblast. I am Kris Straub.

DM: I am David Malki !

KS: And we're your hosts today, for the ninth episode.

DM: Welcome. This is a wonderful Wednesday morning.[43] Thank you for joining us. It's a beautiful day.

KS: I love it.

DM: I am so glad that you could join us. We are back with—Is it Wednesday morning?

KS: No it's, uh, it's Friday morning.

DM: Friday morning.

KS: Yeah.

DM: Yeah. Perfect. Um, welcome everyone.

KS: *(laughs)*

DM: The sun's kind of on the wrong side of the world for it to be Friday morning. I'm just noticing, looking out the window. Shadows are kind of pointing the wrong direction.

KS: Oh, really? All right, well you know what? It might be Friday afternoon.

DM: I think it's Friday night. I'm pretty sure it's Friday night because, yeah, I think... well, no, 'cause there's the sun. The sun is a thing.

KS: Shoot.

DM: I'm totally mixed up, guys.

KS: Do we have an arbiter? Can we just, can we get a ruling?

DM: You know what, here's the thing about time zones: it's *every* time right now. You know, every single time in the world, it is right now.

KS: *(laughs)* That's beautiful.

DM: We're all one. It's all "We Are the Children."

---

43 The joke is that it was really Friday night. I know! *Hilarious.*

KS: You are a Buddhist.

DM: When I first started to grasp the concept of time zones, I thought that if you drove like 100 miles to visit your uncle, you would move like 4 minutes. Like the time zones were prorated?

KS: Yeah, they're continuous. They're not discrete.

DM: Right, exactly. Now, obviously, I understand that every time you cross a time zone you move 3.5 hours. But back then I thought you could move, you know, 4 minutes per 100 miles, or whatever, if you drove east *or* west. It was all the same. It was just based on distance. It didn't have anything to do with the cardinal directions.

KS: So you could travel north and south and travel to some alternate plane of time.

DM: Right, I thought time zones were radial, based on where you were.

KS: *(laughs)* So, like, the Canadians' experience of time is completely different from like a Mexican time experience.

DM: It's utterly foreign.

KS: And it kind of informs the culture and, you know, that might be why, you know, in Mexico you've got, like, the Day of the Dead and stuff like that, and in Canada you've got, like—I don't know, moose and stuff.

DM: That's why you have so many comedians come from Canada. You know, you've got your Bill Murrays, you've got your Dan Aykroyds, and all this kind of stuff, or whoever it is. Is Bill Murray from Canada? I don't think so. Um, but you get your...

KS: *(laughs)* He could have been.

DM: But you've got your Stuart Littles and your Salmon Rushdies and all these famous Canadian entertainers, and I think that's because to American eyes, their worldview is so impacted by this sort of alternate experience of how life works just on a very fundamental level. To us it seems very strange. All of their observations seem very very novel to us here in America.

KS: Now here's a question. You think that if timelines are radial and they go all over the globe in every direction, how about elevation? Is that going to affect your, you know, experience. Is that going to affect the drift?

DM: Elevation is not going to affect the time zones in the same way. When you add that third dimension you start getting into *perceptual* time. That's where you get—sort of special relativity comes into play.

KS: Ah.

DM: The higher you go, the slower that time moves. The problem is you can never really measure that, because as you go up, time moves slower, obviously. When you come back down a mountain or wherever, time moves faster. So you catch up to where you were.

KS: Oh, exactly like a roller coaster!

DM: It's exactly like a roller coaster.

KS: No wonder I'm bored on the mountain. You know, have you ever gone up—have you ever gone hiking?

DM: I've never done that.

KS: That's freaking boring, dude. Don't go hiking. You know why? It's because you are experiencing a slowed version of time. Meanwhile, on the ground, or in a submarine, people are just, you know—5 hours, they're dead. That's like an entire life cycle.

DM: It's sort of like maggots, or fruit flies or something. People--the reason they put people in submarines is so they can study the accelerated lifespan of a human being from a scientific perspective. You know, the way they can give mice cancer over 14 generations. That's what submarines are for. Submarines are just experimental...

KS: Let's be honest. You can only do so much with mice. If you poke a mice with some drug. Yeah, whatever, it doesn't matter. That's not going to help. That's why you have to get people in there. Dying. In a metal tube.

DM: That's why you always hear about these special submarines that have to go deeper and deeper into the ocean. You can't go too deep, because if you go too deep people age too quickly and they die. That's why we can only penetrate so deep into the ocean.

KS: That's why a lot of these nuclear subs have missiles on them. Because we are afraid that we are going to penetrate time so deeply that we are going to arouse the interest of some unknowable higher-dimensional being from outside of time.

DM: Right.

KS: We need to defend ourselves.

DM: I think that's probably true.

KS: I mean, I don't think that's happened yet, but...

DM: I think the argument that they give for it is: the deeper you go, the faster time starts moving, you might end up encountering other nuclear submarines from the future. In which case, if they want to be aggressive, you have to be able to defend yourself. It's sort of a mutually-assured-destruction sort of situation, where you have to be as well-armed as they will be in the future. Which means you have to have the most horrible weapons possible, because in the future they are going to be even worse.

KS: Right, so, like, everything on board those subs literally has a built in H-bomb.

DM: Right.

KS: Like chairs and cups.

DM: Yeah.

KS: 'Cause you may need that. You don't know. If you get boarded...

DM: That's why everything is so expensive. You've seen those things where it's like, "Oh, well, NASA or the military has to pay $48,000 for a toilet seat." That's because it's not a wooden toilet seat you get at Home Depot; it's a toilet seat with an embedded bomb.

KS: Oh! To defend you. In case boarders from the future try to invade your bathroom space.

DM: And the *liberal media* is gonna say things like, "Well, the more horrible you make your on-board submarine time weapons, then you are essentially creating the worst weapons that they will have in the future," because you are trying to out—you can never out-arm yourself against the future, right? Because they're always going to have what you have, plus more.

KS: Sure.

THE LAST LINE OF DEFENSE

DM: So the solution, in my opinion, is that you just have to go high enough so that you go *back* in time, so that the people you encounter then are always going to be worse off than you are now. Hence, the space program.

KS: Oh, I get it now. But you know what makes a lot of sense to me?

DM: Yeah?

KS: The liberal agenda, as put forth by the left-wing media, is actually a positive thing. Because by promoting peace and socialism? What we're doing is *disarming* the future, so we can kick their asses right now.

DM: Right now. And that's why, this whole thing where it's like, trying to go back to Mars or trying to go back to the moon? We already *went* to the moon. We *conquered* it. Do you remember when we went to the moon?

KS: Yeah.

DM: There was nothing there. That was the *past*. The moon is full of the past. And obviously we're—maybe there is some kind of, you know, some lesser microbes or something that haven't yet evolved into humans, and we just stomped them. Neil Armstrong just stomped them with his moon boots.

KS: Yeah, we don't need that. We don't have to put up with that. We're done, man.

DM: We're already done.

KS: We own the moon.

DM: If we go back to the moon now, or in 2020 or some time in the future, we are going to encounter the moon landing from 1969.

KS: Yeah. It's always there. And he is always stepping on things.

DM: We don't want to kill those guys, those guys are *us*. We don't want to undo what has been done in the past, because it causes a *Back to the Future*-style paradox.

KS: I was gonna say that's why going to the moon is such a big deal, because then we are going to affect our present by—you know, if I accidentally knife Neil Armstrong on the moon, then that's gonna cause a problem. But when we go deep into the sea, we basically have the run of the place, we can kill anything we want. We can kill anybody form the future, blow up their cities. Did you know that the Marianas Trench is a network of metropolises from the future, just teeming with alien life?

DM: Teeming?

KS: Yeah. I don't care, just bomb it.

DM: Yeah, 'cause we can just rebuild it.

KS: Yeah, and we'll make it ourselves.

DM: We're going to, because we have to rebuild it. Otherwise it won't be there for us to bomb in the first place. *Obviously.*

KS: *God!*

DM: So this is why I think oceanography is a much much better use of our scholastic dollars than astronomy. There is so much ocean to explore. The future is infinite. The past is very dangerous to meddle with, as science fiction has taught us for decades.

KS: I know. You want to study the future, you want to study physics and time? You point that Hubble—point that at the sea.

DM: Right.

KS: Why are we looking at galaxies? That's nonsense, guys.

DM: And you know why? To be honest, I think it's a cop-out. It's because, what's in space, right? Nothing. It's just vacuum, right? So of *course* the Hubble...

KS: You can tell me about it. I heard that, brother.

DM: Of course the Hubble can see light-years and, you know, whatever...

KS: Big deal!

DM: ...Because there's nothing in the way! Right.

KS: Oh yeah.

DM: If there wasn't a door in my way, I could see across the street. No big deal. But the ocean is full of little microbes, and planktons, and water, and all *kinds* of stuff. And it's *hard* to see through that stuff because that stuff is *there*. It's *physical*. And so I think it's just a cop-out. It's like, "Yeah, we can see through clarity, but we're not gonna try to work and see through all the waters and stuff because that's harder."

KS: You know what it is? It's that kind of Marxist hand-waving that is putting America behind. That's why our kids aren't learning.

DM: Yeah.

KS: It's not because of schools. It's because we're not going into the sea more, with the telescope.

DM: Now, do you think the Chinese have a secret oceanographic exploration program?

KS: God, why *wouldn't* they? I bet they've been doing it for a—I mean, hell, they're probably colluding with themselves from the future. Which just shouldn't be done.

DM: Do you think that's why there's so many of them? Because they are actually— 'cause you can't grow that many people.

KS: No.

DM: You'd have to go—unless it's like I said: the life cycle moves faster under water. They have secret breeding laboratories underground, or under the water.

KS: *Just like that dream I had!*

DM: Just like that! Exactly! And so they're growing these huge vats of people. Or they're going so deep—I can't even bear to conceive of this—*so* deep that they've opened up a time portal to the future and they're *looping back*. They are getting *their own population from the future* to come back into the past to swell their current ranks, so as to outnumber the rest of the world. This is horrible!

KS: Hey, you want more proof?

DM: This is unbelievable!

KS: You want more proof?

DM: Yes.

KS: Japan, right? Surrounded by the ocean—best technology in the world.

DM: Right.

KS: Right? 'Cause they are mining the sea!

DM: And how'd they get so many people on that little island? They're an *island*. They can't swell their population by that much. How're they gonna *get* there? They would *have* to be using secret underwater technology.

KS: We've *seen* islands. You know what's on an island? Freaking palm trees and sand. That's all there is. You ever been to Japan? It's incredible. They're not getting that from palm trees, let me tell you that much. I don't think Japan is an island. I don't think so. It's at least a peninsula.

DM: You think there are secret bridges?

KS: There is a secret underwater connection to the mainland.

DM: A secret isthmus.

KS: *(laughs)* Exactly. That's why we need to go under Japan.

DM: All right, so let's see what we got on the Twitter. @DRBAMTASTICO says, "I would just keep a couple narwhals outside the submarine for protection." Do you think narwhals are evolved humans from the future?

KS: Yeah. I mean they *are* hard to find. And it makes sense that—well, let's think about this. Narwhals are typically found near the poles...

DM: Right.

KS: ...And under the water. So they have experienced accelerated time, and probably went toward the poles to push that acceleration even further.

DM: Because of the magnetic poles?

KS: Right.

DM: Of course.

KS: Because of sunspots.

DM: Right.

KS: So the narwhals are definitely an advanced breed of human. Now the question is: would they be friend or foe? I'm not sure if you could harness their fearsome tusk to defend...

DM: They are so far in the future that they have developed an alternate form of language. They have been trying to communicate with us—or to warn us. We have been sort of lax in holding up our end of the bargain. It's like when you get two guys trying to make a tunnel under the English channel? They have to start from both sides, and then they meet in the middle and they trade little flags.

KS: Right.

DM: That's what the narwhals have been trying to do with us with their communication. And we have just been saying, "Oh yeah, narwhals, great. We can grind up their tusks to get a boner. Fine." And we haven't been trying to actually hear what they're trying to say to us about the future.

KS: You think people in the future have boners all the time?

DM: Well, that's what the narwhal is all about. Look at that thing.

KS: That's true. You know what? Why are we trying to fight the future? It doesn't sound so bad all of a sudden.

DM: You get to swim around.

KS: Yeah.

DM: You have a perpetual boner.

KS: You have a really cool, twisty boner.

DM: Yeah. And you get to be the best guy around, because everyone else around you is from the stupid past.

KS: And the coolest part is is that your boner is on your head. You can swim forward and it's literally, you know—like you can probably swim fast enough that you get cavitation effects at the front of that thing. And you are swimming *so* fast—I mean, forget Michael Phelps, son.[44]

DM: Right. Oh, yeah.

KS: Your future whale erection--you're going to break the water speed record, like, instantly.

DM: Because you know why? And at the risk of getting a little too blue here.

KS: Yeah.

DM: People-boners are a drag-inducing force.

KS: Literally! They are a bummer. I don't like them.

DM: The more you're trying to swim, the more it's going to hold you back, because it's not as streamlined. Whereas with a narwhal: right there at the front.

KS: No trouble. No problem.

DM: It's like a delta-wing jet.

KS: Yeah, and not only that but, it's socially assistive too, because, like everybody knows you're down. You know what I mean? There is no question why you're at the party. It's freaking right on your head.

DM: Yeah. Everyone can see it.

KS: Yeah. It's not even an issue.

DM: We've got @JOHN7DOE7 who says, "What's super messed-up is the fact that creatures underwater are so developed that they get food from something else other than the sun." I don't know why we have to think that the sun is the boss of all of us. Of *course* people can get food from something other than the sun. Look, we've got plants, right?

KS: Yeah.

DM: Plants get sunlight, and plants get food from the soil. There's two food sources right there. How about people? I get my food from Vons, and I also sometimes

---

44   Note for future generations of readers: Michael Phelps was a famous 2000s narwhal.

get it from Albertson's depending on who's got the sale. Two different sources right there. Narwhals can get their thing from the future, and also from all the boner-sex they have.

KS: Well look, I mean, you've got to admit: if there is so much future under the sea, they've probably solved the energy crisis and they are generating—and are able to create food, and they are just sending it out into the environment.

DM: Right.

KS: To restore the ecosystem that we destroyed during the Robot Wars.[45]

DM: It's sort of like Dubai, where there's so much money from the oil that they just disburse it to all the people.

KS: Yeah, they don't need it.

DM: Right. In the future there is so much food that it's just floating in the miasma environment. Which is water-like.

KS: Yeah. I mean, at that point it might not even be—it might not even be water, when you get down deep enough.

DM: Right. It's probably—it's got milk.

KS: It's like a gel. It's like a nutritive colloid.

DM: Right, and depending on where you are maybe there's some sort of Frosted Flakes in this side of it. It's like a giant cereal bowl. The world is a giant cereal bowl. Over here, maybe you get your Cinnamon Toast Crunch.

KS: Sure.

DM: Back there you got your "Oops! All Berries" variant of Crunchberries.

KS: *(laughs)* Because travel is so fast underwater in the future, people are like, "You want to get Mexican?" They go to Mexico to have the Mexican food-water.

DM: Right. The Mexican cereals. Which you can get here, sort of in 99-cent-stores, but they're not very good for you because we haven't evolved enough to be able to overcome all the contaminants.

KS: We don't know how to—right, in the future those narwhals are eating as much Mexican cereal as they want, because their liver can filter that out.

DM: Right. It's a massive liver. I mean *massive*.

KS: It's basically all of their internal organs. They don't even need the heart anymore.

DM: Think about the shape of the liver, right? Do you think—this is going to sound crazy, but bear with me.

KS: Okay.

DM: Do you think Africa is the world's liver?

KS: Uh, you know, that's interesting. I didn't think about that, but could the future

---

45 Note for future readers: *The Robot Wars* was a television program on a channel called G4 (Gears For [the Conquest of Earth]), which was secretly funded by advanced robots from under the waves.

have infiltrated continents to the point where they're actually converting the Earth into a living thing?

DM: I'm a little bit afraid because this is the sort of thing that starts to make you sound like a racist. Where you say, "all the impurities of the world are filtered through Africa."

KS: Well, but they're making it better. It's not like they create it. Everybody else is dumping on them.

DM: That means at the top is all the horrible stuff, like all the Egyptians and stuff, right? And at the bottom it is filtered down to the glory of the South Africans.

KS: Right. That's why it's so awesome down there. I don't know if you've ever been, but it's really rad.

DM: It *sounds* good.

KS: But, so, I don't know if we can assign the other organs. I mean, I like this Africa-liver theory, but I'm not sure what else the Earth needs to survive as an organism.

DM: Right.

KS: Obviously, any living creature is going to require some means of filtration.

DM: Obviously.

KS: So he's going to need a liver. But a heart? Apparently he doesn't have a circulatory system, so I, as a West-centric person, would say that America is the heart. Just like Chevrolet is the heartbeat of America. But clearly I don't think it works that way.

DM: Well, it depends on if you define the oceans as the world's circulatory system, in which case all of the oceans—all that protein-rich miasma we've already proven earlier, is circulating around and sort of feeding all the continents in turn...

KS: It's going—yeah. From beneath.

DM: ...All the tributaries and all the rivers and all the seas and oceans of the world are like the veins and arteries of the world, as an organism. Which means that the flow of that—in the way the heart pumps blood through your body—the flow of the water is determined by heat currents, right? And so that comes from underneath. Geothermic energy. So the heart is probably somewhere in the core of the planet, if I were to make a guess.

KS: Okay. No, that makes a lot of sense to me. The idea that the heart is pumping narwhal boners into the Mexican cereal, and it's basically making our civilization possible at this point in time.

[ACCORDION STING]

DM: Kris, I am very excited to reveal for the very first time on this program, that I have unlocked a new skill in my life.

KS: What?!

DM: You know how, when you go through life, you know, you're doing something enough that you reach a threshold where you level up?

KS: Yeah, like the little meter fills up, and goes over.

DM: Yeah. The meter fills up, and then you gain the level and then you sort of have a new threshold to meet. But for the time being, you're stronger, you can wear better armor, and you have more hit points.

KS: Yeah, unless you were on the evil path, and then you start getting scars and your hair is turning gray.

DM: Yeah, it gets all sorta pointed in different directions.

KS: Yeah.

DM: All right, so let me ask you this. How many times in your, just, daily life, have you had to repair something in your home?

KS: Ah, none. Because I have refused to own anything of complexity.

DM: Right. That's the case with most people. Most people like to have things, or a box that when you hit the button a little green LED comes on—the thing is now functional.

KS: I don't even trust that though. I have a pulley. That's about as far as I've gotten.

DM: Oh, I see.

KS: I have a ramp.

DM: Oh, simple machines.

KS: Just real simple. I like to keep it simple. It's utilitarian.

DM: You have an inclined plane.

KS: Yes, I can push—I've pushed my pulley up that one time. Worked out great!

DM: You have some sort of a fulcrum.

KS: Yes, and I haven't been disappointed yet. I found out you can use the edge of the inclined plane as a fulcrum. So it's sort of like a two-in-one kind of a deal.

DM: Oh, that's great. So how many simple machines are there? Like seven?

KS: I think there's seven.

DM: So you've learned to combine them into actually being, like, three.

KS: Yeah.

DM: You've got an inclined plane that you can put a rope over, make it into a pulley.

KS: I think whoever came up—you know, whatever philosopher came up with that, they're just padding the list. There's literally only two simple machines.

DM: Oh you know what? It's like those Internet sites. Where it's like "Top Ten, you know, whatever." It's like "Top Seven Simple Machines," but I can only think of two so I'm going to break these into some components.

KS: Yeah, and can I be honest? One of the simple machines is a lever. Oh, wow, how long did that take you to think off? A long stick. Yeah, look at that. Going up and down. Okay. All right. Hey, nice job.

DM: Monkeys use that to get ants out of a log.

KS: Yeah. I mean, whatever, so.

DM: I think that one's a gimme.

KS: Whatever, Ancient Greece. —But you've got a skill.

DM: I've always been worried that my house is not full of enough things—not full of those simple machines that work easily. It's full of electronics that I don't understand. I have no idea how a circuit works. I have *no* idea. Some sort of magic electron comes on all these little square things on a green card and eventually it turns into TiVo. This is not a thing that I can comprehend.

KS: No.

DM: So I have always been reluctant to have these things in my home, because if they were to break there is nothing I can do to repair them. I wouldn't even know where to start.

KS: Yeah, that's impossible.

DM: And on a longer-term timeline, like when you look past the fall of civilization, those things are not going to have any utility left in them. Versus your inclined plane-pulley combo, which is always going to work 'cause they're...

KS: They're classics. They're classics!

DM: Yeah, exactly. So this is what I discovered recently. I thought that if I can replace everything in my home with something that I know how it operates on a fundamental mechanical level, then I will never be worried, and I will level up in the level of control I have over my world.

KS: Sure, yeah. That makes sense.

DM: Obviously, I don't want complexity in my life. I don't want to have ten expensive consumer products that all duplicate each other's function.

KS: Yeah.

DM: I want to simplify everything. I want to use as few devices as possible for every application. For everything I want to do.

KS: Sure. Yeah. No, I like that. I mean, clearly, that is what I have tried to do as well.

DM: With your inclined planes and so on.

KS: I threw the lever away. I don't need that.

DM: Right, 'cause you can just pick up a stick.

KS: Anything I want. Yeah, exactly.

DM: Or maybe you can use your pulley sort of as a lever, if it's long enough.

KS: It's pretty small. It's not a very effective lever, but you know what? How often do I need to use that?

DM: Not terribly.

KS: So are you saying—are you talking about replacing objects in your home with simpler variants?

DM: With the simplest *possible* variant that will still accomplish essentially the same result. And it is a diminishing-return sort of thing, where if the thing is 1% as complicated, and even if it delivers—not 100% of the same functionality, obviously, but there is a threshold whereby if it delivers 70% of the same functionality with 99% less complexity, I count that as a win.

KS: I see that. That makes a good—eehhh, why not!

DM: So here's what I've done: my television, I have replaced with a dry-erase white board.

KS: Oh, yeah. For you to make your *own* shows.

DM: Yeah, just draw stuff on there.

KS: Just make your own fun.

DM: Right! And so with the loss of the television, that means I do not need the TiVo. That means I do not need the DVD player. That means I do not need the Nintendo. It means—all those things are replaced by different-colored white-board markers.

KS: Ah, so it's sort of for yourself. Where you can say, "Red is the television." No, I'm sorry, I guess red would be the Nintendo.

DM: Right, if I'm trying to replicate the experience of watching something on the TiVo, I'll use the green marker. For example. If I'm trying to watch a DVD, I'll use the blue marker. And so on, in like fashion. I'll tell you, man, my life is so much simpler.

KS: How's that working out, though? I mean...

DM: It's great!

KS: Are you getting informed, though? I mean, I can see how that would work for entertainment being generated *by you,* but what about, like, information which you cannot produce?

DM: Right, but here's the thing. How much of that information was coming through my television to begin with? I posit, less than you'd imagine. There is a giant construct that takes on the *shape* of information, but yet has no core of information. This is sort of like a drug you take that latches on to a receptor in your brain so as to mimic the actual biological receptor and sort of fool your body into releasing, you know, whatever the resultant chemical is. It's a *false* thing of the same shape, that has none of the actual content within it.

KS: Okay, and so you decided to eschew the falsity, and just have the shape.

DM: Just the shape. And that way, not only do I satisfy the same urge, it latches on to the same receptor. But also I can make up whatever—if I need some information, I'll just make it up. And the dirty secret there? It affects my life *just as much* as whatever the real or pseudo-real information was. Obama's economic policy? Guess what, I'll just make something up. And you know what? In terms of when I go to the store, prices are still the same one way or the other whether I know what Obama really said or whether I just make up something that he said. It doesn't change what I pay for gas.

KS: Yeah. And then also, what you pay for gas doesn't change because unless you bother to remember if it changed, then you're fine.

DM: Right. So the television was the first thing to go. And I was a little bit nervous about that, but I figured a television typically is a non-essential. Like, you can live without the television. So I thought it would be a good first step.

KS: Yeah, I like that.

DM: So, the next step was the microwave.[46]

KS: Oh, yeah. How do you go without that?

DM: Now this was a little bit trickier. The microwave, as everyone knows, was first invented in the mid-20th century, and it was a huge revolution in terms of cooking, right?

KS: Yeah.

DM: Instead of cooking a cake in 6 hours, or whatever it was, now you can cook a cake in the microwave in 30 seconds.

KS: Yeah.

DM: Right? This was a big deal.

KS: Let me guess—let me take a stab at it, though. If I were you, using this set of logic, I would probably try to combine a white board with, say, my pulley. Because the white board—I mean, TVs look like microwaves.

DM: Right.

KS: And I think that's no accident. I think they want people to look at that food rotate.

DM: Yeah, I think they are definitely trying to present it in terms of something that is familiar and entertaining and rewarding.

KS: Well, you don't want to scare people.

DM: Yeah, you don't want to introduce a whole new strange—they're not going to put *spikes* on a microwave, for example.

KS: Yeah, energy is scary enough. I mean, it's cooking your food. *It's burning your food.*

DM: Yeah.

KS: Instantly. *Literally* instantly. Faster than light. But anyways, you've got a microwave, now you don't have one anymore. What *have* you got?

DM: A cardboard box with a sheet of plastic over it. Now, if you remember any of those old stories you may have read as a kid—I remember one where it's like, "Lost in the desert."[47]

KS: Yeah.

---

46 Note for future readers: we're referring to the microwave *oven*, the common kitchen appliance—not the microwave *horse*, which is probably much more common in your time.
47 *Lost in the Devil's Desert*, by Gloria Skurzynski (1993)

DM: And the person always seems to find a sheet of plastic. Right?

KS: Oh, yeah, so he can get the water.

DM: He digs a hole and he puts the plastic down, and then puts a cup or something under it. Then he puts a stone on the plastic to make a little point, and then all the dew condenses from the ground and beads on the plastic, then runs down the point and drips into the cup and he gets some water, right?

KS: He can take a bath.

DM: Right, he can take a bath.

KS: He can wash his car.

DM: He can make some Kool-Aid.

KS: Whatever he needs to do.

DM: Anything. He can shave.

KS: Literally any of the things you can do with water.

DM: Yeah, I mean, absolutely anything. 'Cause water is just—it's water. It's not like, you know, Mexican Coke, where the formula is different regionally. Water is pretty much just water.

KS: Yeah, and you can use it anywhere.

DM: Right.

KS: Okay, so you've got a cardboard box with a plastic sheet.

DM: Cardboard box with a plastic sheet. And here's the part that makes it really effective: just like they do in the desert, you have to put the stone in the middle of the plastic so it comes down and forms a point.

KS: Oh. Okay.

DM: So what it does is it captures geothermic energy, runs it down the point into whatever you have underneath it, cooks it up, *bam!* Microwave.

KS: I see.

DM: With none of the cancer-causing side effects.

KS: Man, that's smart. But wouldn't—the plastic sheet, in order to catch the water, you just put the stone in the center of the sheet...

DM: Right.

KS: ...So it uses gravity to, you know, buckle that sheet down and make a kind of a funnel, right?

DM: Right. Exactly.

KS: But if you're trying to capture energy from the Earth, wouldn't you need a stone that, like, behaves reverse to gravity, so that it would push the sheet *up* and the energy would funnel in from the bottom? 'Cause right now I'm afraid that you're just going to end up with a lot of different soups. Because you're going to collect water into that box.

DM: Well, no, that's the point of the box. Because when you're in the desert...

KS: Oh.

DM: ...You just have the Earth. The dirt. So you get that dew that comes up from inside the ground. The box prevents anything from coming up from underneath.

KS: Ah, okay.

DM: It's the same way that glass will transmit light, but not air. You can't blow through glass, but you can shine a light through glass, right? A cardboard box blocks all the moisture, but the geothermic heat still comes up from the bottom.

KS: You get that fresh-cooked taste.

DM: Right, it takes a little like sulfur.

KS: Well, it's from the Earth.

DM: It's natural.

KS: That's what we were meant to eat. You know what I mean?

DM: Yeah, exactly. It's all this sort of—all those shamanic religions where it's like, all the dancing and all the berries and all the nutmeats and so on that prevent all the diseases, and all the witch doctors that are doctors to witches, and all the witches that need doctors. All that kind of stuff? It's all based on natural principles.

KS: Right, and that's why I trust them. And that's why I like this idea.

DM: That's why I'm trying to—that's the direction I'm trying to take my life. Because I want everything to still work even when the economy collapses. That's the main thing. It's self-sustainability.

KS: And frankly, who doesn't like dancing and berries?

DM: Yeah.

KS: You know?

DM: I love it.

KS: That's just a good time.

DM: Right. Which brings me to the third thing that I've replaced in my home. All right?

KS: All right, I'm ready. I mean, I'm already—I got cardboard boxes aplenty, here.

DM: Yeah.

KS: I might make a microwave this weekend.

DM: That's great. It really is—I mean, your electric bill and the whole deal. So, instead of—you said "dancing and berries"?

KS: Yeah.

DM: Well, normally when you want to dance in berries, where do you have to go? You have to go into the shower or bathtub, because you don't want to get your carpet all messy.

KS: Yeah.

DM: You have to pour a bunch of those guys into the bathtub, you can dance all you want, then you can rinse it all down the drain. This seems to me like it's a big waste.

KS: It is. I mean, who are you feeding? The pipes? They don't need food.

DM: Right.

KS: They're not living things, David.

DM: Right, exactly. That's what I'm saying, Kris.

KS: Oh, okay.

DM: The whole idea of this sort of shower-in-the-bathroom, in a separate room of the house, has always been strange to me. It's like, "I'm gonna go take a dump in your house, in this special room set aside for just that purpose."

KS: Yeah, that makes—you know what? That's true!

DM: It's a little strange.

KS: Yeah, I mean, you *live* in your house. Why do you have to take a dump in *another part* of the house.

DM: So when you think about all of those people throughout history, before they had indoor plumbing, what was it before that? It was outhouses, right?

KS: Sure.

DM: You go back a little farther, it was chamber pots. You go back farther than that, it was people leaning their butts out their windows. You go back a little farther than that—the vast huge majority of human history is, what? The caveman age, right? Before the discovery of agriculture.

KS: Yeah.

DM: Where did they poop? *Where are we evolved to poop?*

KS: Wherever—wherever you want.

DM: *Exactly.*

KS: Ahhh.

DM: Here's the thing: we have only been civilized for a tiny sliver of human history, right? Evolution does not work so fast that we are now adapted to civilization. It's just been too sudden. So we get the best, the most natural, the most organic results when we just follow what our bodies want to do instinctually.

KS: Right. Like right now, literally right now, I have to go to the bathroom.

DM: Right.

KS: But I'm not going to be able to for another 20 minutes, because I don't want to get my pants dirty and my chair dirty.

DM: Right, because you are wearing pants. And because you are sitting on a chair. Neither things of which cavemen had.

KS: And here's another thing: maybe a little, just a tiny portion of my concentration is on my bowels right now.

DM: Right.

KS: And you're probably not getting the best show.

DM: Yeah, this is horrible.

KS: I could be a little funnier. I could be a little quicker.

DM: But you're distracted.

KS: But I'm distracted. I can't focus.

DM: You're trying to hold that in. Because you're trying to conform your body to society, rather than conforming your behavior to your body.

KS: It's taking a great deal of my concentration.

DM: Right, okay. So here's the thing.

KS: Increasingly!

DM: The reason that things have gone this way—it's a factor of the economy of scale.

KS: ...It's getting gross.

DM: When you have so many millions of people, billions of people in the world, you cannot have everyone just pooping everywhere. That is why indoor plumbing was invented. Out of necessity. I'm not saying that there's a problem with this. Right?

KS: Yeah, sure.

DM: It's the sort of thing where if everyone did this, our society would grind to a halt because our society has grown—like, we have to have these artifices in place in order for society to be sustainable. But on the individual level—you, me, the people listening to this show, are together, what? Less than 5% of the population of the world, I would say. Five or six percent.

KS: Oh, easily. Ten, but yeah.

DM: Ten, max. That's fine. If the 10% of the population of the world that is you, me, and the rest of the show can go back to nature, it's not going to cause a big problem. It's the same diminishing-returns thing. You're going to get a little more problem for a lot more benefit.

KS: I see. So you're saying that we should espouse on this show that behavior, and just try and see how that works out for everybody. Save them some time, as thanks for being faithful listeners.

DM: Right. So already everyone knows that you got the whiteboard television. That's a given, right.

KS: Sure.

DM: I just came up with that one day. I didn't even have to read a magazine or anything. Like, that was just easy.

KS: That's like a self-proof that it works—you didn't need the television to create that.

DM: Right.

KS: So why do you need television for anything?

DM: Exactly. Number two is the geothermic microwave. That's my gift to you guys. Now here's the thing. Because this is an audio program, it's hard to describe exactly—the dimensions are kind of precise; there was some experimentation. If it doesn't work for you right the first time, you may have some of the measurements off. It's hard for me to describe exactly the shape it has to take. But, you know, you just have to trust me. This works. This really works.

KS: There is literally too much information to convey to anybody.

DM: Right, there is a lot of...

KS: There is a sort of experiential thing that you have to do yourself.

DM: If you saw it once, you would kinda grasp it a little bit better.

KS: Yeah.

DM: And then number three is the—do you remember those games where you have, like, the big scoop and then you have a ball and you throw the scoop, you know, and the ball flings out and you catch it in the other scoop? Is there a name for that thing?

KS: Oh yeah. Jai alai.

DM: Yeah, so you take that scoop and you turn it so the handle is facing forward. And you simply clutch it between your thighs.

KS: Okay, yeah. Right.

DM: And then...

KS: I'm visualizing it.

DM: And then you have a little scoop, and then anytime you need to go, just go. And then you can just take that scoop and you just throw it... at your convenience.

KS: Where does it go? Like where... where should I throw it?

DM: Just anywhere. I mean, not in your house, but this is the one concession to civilization. You don't actually wanna just go on the *ground,* or anything. I mean, that's just ridiculous. But you don't let yourself be preoccupied, like you said, with, "Now I gotta find a special room in the house." And I use my bathroom now for storage. It's excellent. I don't have to rent a storage unit.

KS: That's smart. I like that. That's good stuff.

DM: If I have anything wet, like any barrels, I can put them in the bathroom because it's got a drain. No storage unit has a built-in liquid drain.

KS: But this one does.

DM: Yeah. Exactly.

KS: It's like your shower now.

DM: So you've got the little scoop deal, so you just kind of carry that around with you, waddle around, however you want, and then when you get to a convenient, you know, resting spot, or you get to some sort of—you're walking around, you get to a place that doesn't have a lot of buildings or something, you take that scoop out and just *WHOOP* fling it, clean it off. It just takes sort of a little wicking action.

KS: Yeah, you just probably tap it on the ground and that will take care of it.

DM: Right. Back to square one.

KS: Yeah, that's not bad. And you know what? You could probably come up with a way to kind of hold it down there and continue walking, so you could literally not miss a step on your busy day.

DM: Yeah, it just takes practice. Exactly. And we are so conditioned to holding that in as we walk, you know, it's like we figure we have to either walk or poop, you know. We cannot do the two together. But it's just—it's a learned behavior.

KS: Let me present to you a doctor's opinion.

DM: Okay.

KS: As a doctor.

DM: Right.

KS: The idea—we know about the human body. Clearly all of us do.

DM: All experts.

KS: We are all experts. Now I'm talking about the heart. You know how they talk about the heart as a different kind of muscle?

DM: Right.

KS: From the rest of the body?

DM: Smooth muscle.

KS: It's smooth muscle, and can contract over and over again. It keeps you alive.

DM: Yeah.

KS: Whereas if you were going to do the same thing with your arm—pump your arm over and over again? Your muscle would waste away. You would destroy it.

DM: Lactic acid.

KS: Exactly. Only the specialized muscle of the heart can permit it to beat for your whole life.

DM: Yes.

KS: Well, what kind of muscles are in your bowels? Not smooth muscles—it's just regular old muscles. So the act of holding this waste in is shortening your life.

DM: Yeah, oh yeah. I've been saying this for years.

KS: Yeah, it's damaging to you. So my problem was: I just didn't know how to—where to take it.

DM: Yeah. There was no solution, was there?

KS: I had to keep moving, you know? You lose the deposit, but now I see there is a better way.

DM: Yeah, you just, you allow—the relaxed state of the muscle is the natural state of the muscle, right? When you're sleeping, you're not tense. You're relaxed.

KS: Right.

DM: So the more you let those bowel muscles relax, the healthier they are. It's like they're resting all the time.

KS: And the more you'll be able to devote to thinking, and creation, and conversing, and all kinds of different things that you need to get done in your day as a modern man, or woman.

DM: Exactly.

KS: Although I don't think women should do this.

[ACCORDION STING]

DM: You're listening to Tweet Me Harder, the world's first, best, only, and last talkback-enabled interactive audio podblast. I'm David Malki !

KS: I'm Kris Straub. I don't know if we can say "best" anymore.

DM: *(laughs)* No, we are hanging on to that. It's a trophy that we can never let go of. Because otherwise... what do we have left? Just first and only?

KS: Someone else will make a mad dash, and I don't want that. I don't trust them.

DM: Let's look at the Twitter right now. We've got some interesting things on the Twitter. @WENDELLDOTME says, "the real answer is sloped flooring in every room that lets all the waste content flow down into a drain."

KS: Oh yeah...

DM: This seems to me like *additional* complexity, not *less* complexity.

KS: Well, I mean, I think there is overhead. But basically, what we're talking about is living inside an inverted cone.

DM: Right.

KS: And that is one of the classic solids. So that is a simple...

DM: Right. I mean my worry in terms of just the technological complexity is, where does that drain go? You're back to square one.

KS: Oh yeah.

DM: You might as well just go back into your bathroom. Drain goes to the same place.

KS: You could live near a cliff.

DM: I guess *some* people could live near a cliff. That's not really a solution that scales.

KS: There is a way to make it work for some people. Yeah. No, you're right. It's not a good idea, Wendell. I'm sorry.

DM: Another thing that we actually spoke about just the other day, in terms of simplifying our lives, was the idea that you could have a—you could have something like a can with a string, right?

KS: A can with a string...

DM: Like the old-timey sort of talking-into-two-cans and they are bound with a string.

KS: Okay. I don't know where you're going with this.

DM: Well, remember. If you want to simplify your life, you will have to somehow interface with the rest of the world, right?

KS: Right.

DM: So we need to have an adapter. If you don't want to have that cancer-causing cell phone up to your head all the time, you'll want to use that can with a string. It's all natural, it's regular ingredients that you understand how they work, but everyone else has a cell phone. So what do you do? You have to have an adapter.

KS: Oh.

DM: That goes *between* the can with the string, and changes the signal into a regular cell phone signal.

KS: You could put a megaphone up to your cell phone, using—and you wouldn't even be leaving the arena of "phone." Because that's *also* a type of phone. And then you would be able to listen to it at a distance. I mean, granted, a lot of other people would be able to listen to it as well, but at least you wouldn't get cancer in your head.

DM: Okay, so you're talking about having your cell phone off on some sort of a stick or something, where it's held away from your head.

KS: Right.

DM: And then you have a megaphone sort of attached to it. And then...

KS: That's pointed at your ear.

DM: Pointed at your ear, okay.

KS: And you could have a friend carry it. To increase your safety.

DM: Right.

KS: A stupid friend.

DM: Well, that seems like it's increasing the technological complexity. I think we're talking about simplifying.

KS: No, I don't agree with you! I mean, here's my thing: We've got a lot of this stuff lying around. We may as well create a couple of new simple machines.

DM: Oh. Right.

KS: And, like—so one of them is a megaphone. 'Cause that—we literally don't need to make anymore. We have enough.

DM: I understand. So instead of inventing something, let's just repurpose what we already have. That's good conservation policy: reusing existing inventions and existing materials rather than having to go back to the drawing board and saying, "well, all right, how am I going to do this thing from zero," you are going to generate a lot more waste in the process.

KS: Right. We've got a lot of this stuff right now that we can just assemble. I mean, think about the granularity of this. We've got cell phones today.

DM: Uh huh.

KS: We don't need to do better than that. Here is a tiny device that you can talk to somebody through.

DM: Right.

KS: You can—as an atom, you can do all kinds of stuff with that in other inventions.

DM: Yes, okay, so a tiny device that you can talk to someone through. What are some other applications for that particular—you know, as a component of another thing.

KS: Uh, talking to birds.

DM: Yeah, okay, you could give birds a cell phone.

KS: Sing cool songs to people at a great distance. You know what you need? Everybody's got to have it on speakerphone. At this point we all agree that having the thing next to your ear is a bad idea.

DM: Right, that's cancer.

KS: So let's just get over the whole idea of privacy. Let them be left on speakerphone the whole time.

DM: Right.

KS: And let's just have an open and free society.

DM: Well, and that way it's just like when you're talking to someone in public, a passerby can hear both sides of the conversation. How is that any different? How do you get different rights when you're on a cell phone, somehow?

KS: That's right, exactly.

DM: It's more confusing because the people walking by don't know. "Is he talking to himself? Does he have a Bluetooth?" No, you just have both sides of the conversation. That way everyone understands the score. When I say "hi" and the guy goes, "Sell! Sell," he's talking into his phone, he's not schizophrenic.

KS: Right, and that is something we can do right now.

DM: We can solve this problem.

KS: We know that.

DM: Just go onto speakerphone. So then with cell phones, if everyone is on a speakerphone, what do you think about the extrapolation, in terms of like repurposing the existing practices and the existing technology—you know, like when there is a hostage situation and the negotiator has a robot take the guy a cell phone?

KS: Oh yeah.

DM: So what if we sort of break that out into the world in general. Where it's like, let's say that your friend is across the street. You don't want to have to shout to him. Or let's say there is a lot of traffic, and he can't see you, can't communicate. So you have a—your cell phone has, like, an extension module, and then you just shoot that over to him, and you can talk to him. And so that way, you always have the ability to talk to someone else, even if they are out of shouting range, or you don't know their own cell phone number. You just have a little sort of attachment on your thing that's a little tube with compressed air that just—*boop*—pops it into your cell phone.

That way, if you want to go back to talk to birds or something, you can just shoot them a cell phone.

KS: Yeah, so I like the idea that you would shoot the cell phone to your buddy. He grabs it and is like, "Hey, what's up?"

DM: Yeah.

KS: And then he shoots it back to you and everything is fine. But imagine, as this develops and becomes cultural, it won't be saying "Hi" on that phone that's the greeting. Now it's just shooting that phone to you. You don't even need to say anything at that point. If I shot a phone at you, I'm your pal.

DM: Oh yeah. You could just skip the whole salutation. This is a time-saver.

KS: Yeah. So I mean, clearly there is a lot of room here.

DM: Now, do you think skipping that salutation as a cultural thing—like if everyone skips the "Hi, hello," and just the *boop* of the cell phone being shot across the street becomes the default salutation—do you think that will engender a greater intimacy between friends? Because we—the subconscious assumption is that we don't need to waste time with formalities because we are already that close.

KS: Yeah.

DM: Your brain will be fooled into thinking, "I know this person very well." Is that a good thing or a bad thing?

KS: Um, I think it can only be good. I mean, as the world gets closer and closer— that's the aim of this technology anyway. Why don't we just take it one further.

DM: All right.

KS: Why don't we stop trying to cram the email and all these different things into the phones, and let's just make the phone the method of greeting. So...

DM: All right, I've got it.

KS: Yeah.

DM: If every time we are going to be speaking to someone we are in range such that we can shoot them a cell phone, right? We'll take this as granted. We'll take this a given, right?

KS: Yes.

DM: So we'll want to have practices in place as humans, such that even if the economy were to collapse, our lives can continue unabated. That's the whole idea of the white-board television and so on, right? We want to be able to have lives that do not rely on the artifice of civilization.

KS: Yeah.

DM: Right, so, stage 1: we integrate this shooting-a-cell-phone-at-somebody as the default way of communicating via phone. This seems obvious. Stage 2: we just drop the technological part and put it back to cans on strings. It's a two-parter.

So you see the guy. Now you're used to shooting a phone back and forth, right? You understand; you've got the sort of muscle memory where the thing comes flying at you, you just snatch it out of the air. This is already taken as a given. You see him, just shooting him that can. *BOOP*—catches it, "Hey, what's up buddy?"

Then, this is touted as a step *up* in technology because you have now the tether of the string! You can reel that back in. In reality, we've just kind of taken the whole concept of interpersonal communication back to the fundamental and sustainable level.

KS: Ah, that is nonsense. I don't like it!

DM: All right, what's the problems with it?

KS: My problem is that that's *dumb*. Like, I've already said that we've got to do something with the technology we've already got. We are sitting on millions of cell phones. If we reduce it to cans and strings, we are going to have to be making cans and strings. Which are *finite*. Cell phones are *infinite*. I got one sitting right here next to me. I've got two in this house. I don't even use the other one. Why can't we just stick a cell phone in a jai alai launcher that we poop in, throw it at a friend, and just use it that way? Why do we have to develop *strings and cans?*

DM: I don't know. I mean, look. I'm not a savage. I'm not saying that we should be throwing cell phones in the same jai alai launcher that we use to poop in. I think you're going to ask people to carry around *two different* jai alai launchers, and to try and differentiate between the two?

KS: Just make—put them together and make just two of them that are near each other, and you just have to remember to poop on the left.

DM: This is a real recipe for disaster.

KS: I disagree.

DM: If you want your phone launcher to be similar in design to your poop sleeve, fine. If you want it to be situated nearby, or the same color or something, fine. But not all of them *together*. If they are both the same color, the same size, if they are both held by your thighs in the same position—but one of them you poop in and one of them you use to throw a phone to your closest personal friends? This is going to be a big problem.

KS: This is a classic problem that can be reduced to problems we have *right now* in culture. So, I don't see what recycling cell phones and using these jai alai sticks— why that's a problem. I don't understand how that makes things worse. That can only make things better.

DM: No, I agree that the actual slinging of the phone is an improvement, but you have such a potential for confusion...

Oooooh... unless! *I* get what you're getting at. What *you're* saying is, you want us to be so *close* as citizens, as fellow travelers on this spinning heartbeat globe of life, that we are so *bonded* together as individuals, that it's *okay*—even *if* you accidentally, every now and then, reach up to grab a phone from your closest friend and you get a handful of poop, it's all right! You just laugh it off. This is something that we sort of look past.

Like, it used to be that you couldn't go out in some civilizations with your ankles showing, right? 'Cause that is very vulgar. But we want to be so familiar and comfortable with each other that we can just catch *anything* that is being thrown at us, whether it's a cell phone, whether it's some sort of waste product, and it's all fine because we're all just—we get *past* that obsession with, "I don't want to touch my friend's waste product."

KS: No! *No!* That is *wrong!* That is *gross!* Why would I ever want anybody to touch poop? Can you not just keep one on your left side—that's the west side—and keep the other one on your right side. Then you *know*, the left side is poop and the right one, that one's for your phone. Why can't we have two? We have two legs. We are biradial creatures.

DM: No, no, you are making these decisions *for* people. When you are saying that we have to have a consistent cultural convention, that your right hand is the one that you throw phones at; your left hand is the one that you fling poop with—what you're saying is that the right hand is superior. You're discriminating against a whole class of left-handed people.

KS: No.

DM: You don't want to reinforce this idea that you have to be—you know, the right hand is the good hand, the left hand is the bad hand. This is the thing that we're trying to get *past*. I'm trying to bring everyone *together*, I'm trying to *solve* all the problems...

KS: I'm just saying, why don't we use these as an extension of our bodies. We *already* have to manage left and right hands. It's not that much harder to manage left and right poop/phone slinging devices. Just do it.

DM: But I use my left and right hands to do the same things. I don't *have* to keep them separate. I don't think they *should* be separate. I think we should be ambidexterous.

KS: What are you—are you left-handed or right-handed?

DM: I'm right-handed.

KS: Okay, but do you ever pick up a pencil with your left hand and go, "Oh, whoops!" *No.* You *always* pick it up with your right hand because you *know*. And *that's* all I'm saying. And if *you're* suggesting otherwise, what you're doing is *insulting* people. You're saying that they can't figure it out. And I have a lot more respect for people than that.

DM: I just think, why would you unnecessarily harm people by putting this artifice onto them?

KS: No.

DM: We're trying to improve society. We are trying to *improve* interpersonal relations.

KS: Hey.

DM: And what you're doing is adding obstacles to that whole development.

KS: *(sighs)* Hey, you know what? The jai alai thing—that was not my idea, that was your idea. Remember that?

DM: For poop, not for *phones!*

KS: No, no.

DM: Okay, look, here's the thing...

KS: You said a compressed-air device for the phone. I'm just saying, use two slings. You know why? Because we can't throw that far. You want to be able to talk to a friend, you want the distance of the object thrown to carry the same distance that your voice would carry, were you yelling. That's *all* I'm trying to say.

DM: But there's a *lot* of other ways that we can throw the phones. We can throw them in, like, a bolo situation. We can throw them...

KS: Ugh!

DM: ...They're tied to a boomerang, perhaps.

MAN, CIRCA 2013

KS: Talk about *racism!* What *happened* to you? What is going *on* with you today?

DM: With *me? You're* the one that's going to break society down into *classism* with your overly-naïve presumption about the dexterity of your man on the street flinging poop at his friends. You're going to get a lot of faces smeared with a lot of poop, if your worldview comes to fruition.

KS: You know what?

DM: What?

KS: I don't want to have this argument with you. Clearly we can not settle an argument like this.

DM: I don't understand why you are being so willfully dense about this. I'm...

KS: I don't understand why *your stupid face.*

DM: *(sighs)* All right. I think there is only one way to settle this.

KS: Yeah.

DM: We have to have a rap battle.

KS: I agree. I think we have to have a rap battle.

DM: I think we have to take the same beat, and I think we have to each write a rap of 60 seconds or less.

KS: Yeah.

DM: And we have to play them on next week's show, and then we have a celebrity judge tell us which one is better.

KS: Yeah, well, you know what? That's the smartest thing you've said all day. I like that. I think we'll take a week, and on the next show, we'll put together our own individual raps—and I don't think I'm gonna let you listen to mine before.

DM: Oh, I'm absolutely not going to let you listen to mine. We're going to play them for the first time live on next week's show.

KS: Fine. Then *that's* how it's gonna be. And then we will have somebody say who's the winner.

DM: This will determine the superiority of our relative arguments. *You're* saying everyone needs to have two jai alai slings for poop and for cell phones. *I'm* saying keep the one for poop, use a different method for cell phones. Rap battle will determine who is the winner.

KS: Well, let me ask you this, though.

DM: Yes.

KS: I don't want our raps to have to focus on that idea. I think that we know the argument at hand. I think that we should be able to rap about something else.

DM: Sure. How would we try and—I mean, we are so incensed about this issue, how will we know, how will we come up with some impartial subject to rap about?

KS: Wait, I don't know. We'll have to have people come up with it and tweet to us, I guess.

DM: I guess.

KS: To use one of these modern contrivances. They could tweet #TMH9 and say, what should you and I have a rap battle about? That's what we'll write about.

DM: And we'll figure this out. We'll do it. We want them to tweet right now, I suppose. We'll have to look at their tweets in these last five minutes of the show.

KS: Yeah.

DM: And we'll settle on what the subject of our rap battle will be.

KS: You know what, I'm glad that we are having this argument. Because they say that no good relationship can just avoid disagreement, forever. I think we've been of like mind for a long time, and now we're going to come out of this stronger.

DM: Yeah.

KS: It doesn't mean that right now I don't think that you are stupider than me. I mean, I really do.

DM: Yeah, I totally think that you're just willfully retarded.

KS: I'm starting to remember a foul odor the last time I was near you.

DM: Yeah, and I shouldn't have thought that we were close enough friends that I could just poop in your presence.

KS: Well...

DM: I should have held that back, because I thought that we were closer friends than we are, apparently.

KS: Well, you know what? All the pieces are starting to come together for me. Maybe it was a little much, but that aside—'cause that could happen to anybody—that aside, I think the larger issue is, how are we going to save society with these sling devices?

DM: Right.

KS: And how are you and I going to settle this difference with a rap battle?

DM: And save our friendship?

KS: And we don't even have a topic! Save the friendship. For the tenth episode.

DM: Right. The tenth anniversary episode of Tweet Me Harder will be next week.

KS: Yeah. So you know, I'm just hopeful that we get some ideas from our listeners.

DM: So here's what we have on the Twitter so far.

KS: Okay.

DM: @LymanAlpha says, "Rap about Ben Franklin."

KS: Okay.

DM: @Jwcovell says, "Rap battle concerning simple machines." That's not bad.

KS: I kinda like that one.

DM: I like that. @stevenfc says, "Either that, or Objectivist philosophy. An Ayn Rand rap may be the perfect decider."

KS: Oh yeah.

DM: I don't know anything about Objectivism so I'm not going to rap about that.

KS: No, but you should actually read it, 'cause I think that's really funny. If I did it separate, I think that's cool, but right now I think the frontrunner is the simple machines.

DM: I agree, but we've got @DRBAMTASTICO, "Narwhal boners." I think we kind of put that subject to rest. Plus, we are in perfect agreement about that, so I don't know what there could be to disagree about.

KS: Yeah, I think that would just confuse this issue. I think we would come out saying, "yeah, I like these boners. There's nothing wrong with that."

DM: There's two separate issues here: the poop slings, and the narwhal boners. @KINOTU says, "Rap about friendship."

KS: That's so broad, though.

DM: Yeah, I think simple machines are the frontrunner. We've got a couple more here though. @OBDORMIO says, "Rap about the Age of Exploration."

KS: Wow, I don't know what that is.

DM: It's like a historical epic in rap form.

KS: Yeah, yeah.

DM: That seems like a large chunk to bite off just to settle one friendship.

KS: We only got 60 seconds, so I think that, you know—that is gonna be a bit much.

DM: Yeah.

KS: Plus, we might just get so fascinated that we might forget altogether what we were trying to prove.

DM: My vote goes for simple machines.

KS: Yeah.

DM: So, @JWCOVELL on Twitter has provided us with a subject for next week's rap.

KS: Let's do that. I agree.

[ACCORDION STING]

DM: Thank you for listening to Tweet Me Harder: the Internet's first, best, only, and last talkback-enabled interactive audio podblast. This is the end of Show #9, and we will join you next week for Show #10. We will be having our raps featuring a funky fresh beat by DJ MC Kris. We will be premiering our raps on the show next week. Neither of us will be listening to each other's until next week's show.

KS: It's going to be surprising. And eye-opening!

DM: I think we are going to be learning a lot about the nature of friendship. And we are going to either settle the dispute about poop slings—or tear open the wound and unleash a whole new bevy of disputes.

KS: *(laughs)* Well I was gonna say, yeah, then after that, maybe we just don't do the show again.

DM: That's the end of it. It just stops abruptly.

KS: We're going to see if there's an 11, yeah. Well, thanks for listening, guys.

DM: Thank you very much! You can also—at any time you can tweet to us @TWEETHARD. You can call us at, if I can remember it: 206-337-8560, 206-337-8560 to leave us a voicemail. And if you want to cheer either of us on, you can leave us a short voicemail and we'll play them all in sequence before we launch the rap battle. If you'd like to be our cheering section, we definitely appreciate that, and we'd like to hear what you have to say.

KS: I'd like that, because I think—you and I—we're both going to have to get psyched.

DM: Yeah, we are going to have to really pump ourselves up for this.

KS: Yeah.

DM: So, if you guys want to give us any, "Oooooh snaps!" or any of that kind of stuff, just send that via voicemail: 206-337-8560, and we will make it into a nice cool thing that helps us keep our spirits up during the epic throwdown that will determine the future of our friendship, and possibly the future of humanity's dealing with waste products and interpersonal relationships.

KS: *(laughs)* I think that that is succinct. I like that. I would like to live my life solving both of those problems.

10

Fireworks

KS: Welcome to Tweet Me Harder, the world's first, best, only, and last talkback-enabled interactive audio podblast. I am one of your hosts: Kris Straub.

DM: I am your other host: David Malki !

KS: We are doing the tenth show. Tenth episode.

DM: Welcome to Tweet Me Harder, Episode Ten. You can tweet anything to us using #TMH10—that's numerals one, zero—and we will be able to see what you have to say. A lot of people already on the Twitter are saying—they seem to be weighing in on some kind of subject, I'm not sure what that could be, but...

KS: Well, I mean, it's an exciting time in our nation's history, I think. It makes a lot of sense that people would be fired up in general.

DM: Patriotic fervor, and so on.

KS: Just day-to-day excitement, simmering away...

DM: There's a lot of, just, repressed—people just wanna lash out and just take hold of something.

KS: A lot of anger. *Lot* of anger.

DM: There is a lot of resentment, you might say, building up.

KS: Yeah, you know, I mean, big stuff happening. Big stuff. You know, causing rifts, causing "shisms," if you will, but I mean, not that you will, because...

DM: I believe it's *schisms*. I believe it's *schisms*.

KS: Well, maybe I grew up in a different part of the country than you!

DM: Did you?

KS: Yeah.

DM: No.

KS: Okay.

DM: We're in the same major media market.

KS: Well, culturally...

DM: We both had FOX 11. We both had KCAL 9...

KS: Well, it doesn't matter. KCAL 9—I didn't watch news on KCAL 9, for your information.

DM: Oh, I'm sorry. Were you watching KCOP channel 13 or KDOC channel 56?

KS: I watched KCOP because it was the best channel with the best news, so shut up about it.

DM: Well, I watched KDOC because they played lots of *Hogan's Heroes* reruns. All right? Is that so wrong?

KS: There was no news on that channel!

DM: Do I have to apologize for everything now?

KS: Oh, my God, well maybe that's why you learned to like a bunch of Germans, 'cause that's what you are, right? A Nazi?

DM: Yeah, that's exactly right. All the German blood coursing through my *half-Egyptian* veins.

KS: *(laughs)* I thought you were half something else! *I'm* half-Egyptian. *Kraut!*

DM: Oh yeah, you're the one that's all German with your...

KS: All right, all right, hold on, let's hold on...

DM: What?

KS: Let's try and back off. I know maybe we've got a little tempers flaring and stuff since the last show, but maybe let's go ahead and try and proceed with the show and have a little decorum.

DM: All right, all right. Welcome, everyone. Thanks for tuning in to Tweet Me Harder, Episode Ten. Clearly the best *so* far, I would say. Off to a *roaring* great start.

KS: It's a good show, or maybe as you would say, *skoh*.

DM: Uh huh, nice. Nice. Bagging on my accent?

KS: Well, all right, I didn't mean...

DM: I've got some funny personal ads. You wanna read some personal ads?

KS: No, you know what, I think we spent a lot of time on personal ads on this show, recently.

DM: *Did* we? Oh, did we?

KS: Yeah.

DM: No, I think we spent a lot of time on *advice columns,* but personal ads, I think, are an untapped resource.

KS: Oh. Okay. Well, all right. That should be good for a laugh. Let's go ahead and see some personal ads right now.

DM: All right, this is the *North Bay Bohemian*, the June 30 issue.

KS: Oh, sounds *hilarious*.

DM: This is one of those alternative weeklies, sort of a small market, and we get a lot of people—this is the interesting thing about these personal ads, I think—there's a lot of "nurturing, compassionate, feminine female in her 50s, seeking male, 50–69."

KS: Okay.

DM: "Single female in her 50s looking for male." "Seeking similar male in 50s for LTR." "Compassionate SF, 60, seeks similar man 60-plus."

KS: Okay, what's the point of this?

DM: Now here's my question: Is this some sort of community that attracts only elderly singles, or are the older crowd the ones still using the newspaper? Everyone else has fled to Craigslist and Match.com and so on.

KS: Well, what's interesting is that that also implies that it's the women—that seems to imply that it's the women who stuck around to use the *PennySaver*.

DM: Well, I'm looking here at Women Seeking Men, and we see "SF, 50ish, seeking gentleman 56–64." The women are always seeking older, of course. And then over in Men Seeking Women—which is a much shorter section, I will say—we get "WM, 48, trying to find an outgoing, good-looking woman to go out, have a good time with, 30–50." So 48 wants 30–50.

KS: He wants 30? That ain't gonna happen.

DM: 37 wants 23–58.

KS: That's ridiculous.

DM: 45 wants 35-plus, and so on. So, obviously, this is not really news. We have women who want someone older, and men who want someone slightly younger… but I never knew it was that *institutionalized* as far as their preferences. I just thought that was how it worked sort of subconsciously. But these people are specifically requesting.

KS: Do you think that would work right off the bat, 'cause the men want—wait, now hold on a second. It was the men who want younger.

DM: Right, and the women want older.

KS: Well, they should not be advertising in those sections, so yeah, you're right. I think they did move on, to maybe a pay service.

DM: Right.

KS: Or, where you can—that might be a proof in and of itself. The idea that you're using the *PennySaver* personal ads, then you probably don't have a lot of money, and you're probably not a balla'. Uh, so maybe you're not gonna draw a 23-year-old. Maybe that's a bad idea.

DM: Here's the strange wrinkle in the Bohemian Romance section: "To listen and respond to ads, call 1-900-287-1222. Call costs $2.19 a minute." $2.19 a minute? Really? 900 numbers on the personal ads? I was just remarking the other day, watching TV that the—it seemed like the 900 number had gone the way of the dodo, to be replaced by "make a text message and you will be enrolled in a…"

KS: Oh, yeah.

DM: …There's some commercial for, like, sexy ladies: "Hey, you want a cool screensaver? Text now to 4535," you know, whatever the number is. And then in really tiny print it's like, "you are enrolling in a $10-a-month service." It seems like that's the 900 number of this generation.

KS: Yeah. You know, Malki, as bored as I am with this topic you've brought up, and as much disdain I have for you, I do have to bring something up.

DM: Oh yeah? I can't wait to hear it.

KS: I have to bow to your skills of research. There was a show on—it wasn't a show, it was a commercial. It was one of those personal ads on public access. I was on vacation, I wish I could remember where, but it was some website—now I'm being super vague, but here's the point. You were supposed to text your number to their service and get in touch with the lady that you wanted. You know? And it was showing the ladies on TV, during the ad. This ad was a half-hour, it was an infomercial, and the way that the women were being presented was so incredibly robotic. And I couldn't understand the appeal of this program. It was like, I don't know, *Lovemates. Lovemates.com.* "Just text to 3147."

DM: This was recent then, right? Texting?

KS: Yeah, it was relatively recent.

DM: Okay, so what time of day?

KS: Oh, it would have been, like, 2 A.M. It would have been the wee hours.

DM: And what kind of channel?

KS: Uh, public access. It was public access. Or it was cable after everything had gone dark, you know?

DM: On the Twitter feed we have @FROSTYPLUM saying, "Honey, women ain't always seeking older, at least not for frivolous things like relationships." Well, this is what I thought. I didn't want to make that stereotype, but this is empirical evidence I have in my hand. And again, maybe it's strictly the *Bohemian* readers...

KS: What region is that—does that paper service?

DM: This is Napa Valley. "Serving Sonoma, Napa, and Marin counties."

KS: Oh, Napa, *how fancy.* Who's been to *Napa* recently?

DM: I had a friend get married in Napa just like a week ago.

KS: Oh, that is *lovely,* that is *wonderful.*

DM: And a lot of people go for a lot of different reasons. It's a lovely vacation.

KS: Oh, that must be *fun* to be able to take *vacations.* Not do any *work.*

DM: Uh, well, yeah. I thought it was a lot of fun, but that's because I'm not—I don't get to live in the exotic *middle of the country,* in glorious *Texas,* with your never-ending expanses of fabulous *desert* on every side...

KS: You know what? It's pretty great. It's pretty great.

DM: ...And every day of your life is *like* a vacation, when you don't ever even need to *take* a vacation because your life is *so grand.*

KS: Well, you know what? My life *isn't* grand. My life is pretty *rotten* here. So I'm saying maybe you should shut your mouth before you act like you've got it so tough.

DM: We're gonna have a rotten-life-off now?

KS: Yeah! Yeah! Teah, why not?

DM: Argue whose life is rottener?

KS: Sure. Why not? Go for it.

DM: All right. I've got some sort of mole on my foot. I don't know. It might be cancer. It's black, irregular, and it's been growing.

KS: Oh my God, my... *(sighs)* I wasn't going to say it. I wasn't going to bring it up on the show. It's too hard, it'll destroy you. I can't do it! Plus it's personal. It's in a personal area.

DM: My foot is a personal area.

KS: Well, I guess the definition of personal—well, I mean, I meant like not-allowed-to-be-touched-by-strangers area. Although I guess if somebody's touching your...

DM: You allow your *feet* to be touched by *strangers?* This is *disgusting!*

KS: Well, now hold on a second, you're putting words in my mouth, uh. But yeah, I do, so. What you wanna fight about it? There's nothing wrong with it. It's natural. Nature.

DM: All right, so, where is your mole now? I don't understand.

KS: I don't have a...! Okay, look.

DM: What's your convoluted story?

KS: *(sighs)*

DM: Yeah, get to the point!

KS: My point is, this show was on public access late at night and a robotic voice... These women were being displayed, being narrated about. And their interests, their likes and dislikes. And it was stuff like, "*(in monotone)* Meet Colleen. She's interested in meeting an older man who can take of her. She likes fruit and walks on the beach." And it was even more devoid of personality than that. And the entire thing was presented that way. And I was trying to understand what demographic that appealed to. And it wasn't like it was a voice-synthesis thing. It was like, "I'm scared by human inflection. I don't want any of the women I meet..."

DM: Was it a budget thing? Or was it on purpose? You're saying it was purposeful?

KS: I think it was purposeful.

DM: There seemed like there was some reason to choose the robot version of the narrator.

KS: Yeah, it wasn't like a lady sitting at a desk with a fern behind her, like a public-access thing. They had women lounging, and flirting, and twirling the phone cord and stuff. Like, any one of them could have delivered that in a sexy voice. But they didn't do that.

DM: Was it in the Mac voice? Was it, "*(robot voice)* Meet. Colleen. She likes, walk on beach."

KS: *(laughs)* It was like somebody had—yeah, it was like that was on the sheet when they hired the voice actor. "Can you do the Mac voice? How close can you get? That's what we need. I want—we're looking for men who get turned on by the default Mac text-reader voice, for the disabled."

DM: I don't want to hear about your seedy television experiences!

KS: Look...

DM: What's the audience? *You're* the one watching it!

KS: Well, you know it was late—look, I don't have to—okay. It doesn't matter. It doesn't matter.

DM: Are we going to be able to get past this? Are we going to be able to do a show where we can be cordial? Or do we have to drag this all out into the open so everyone can listen to it?

KS: Look, I think that if people are just tuning in, they have to be aware that Malki and I had a bit of a disagreement on the last show, and clearly...

DM: There is a little history behind this.

KS: ...Clearly, you know, getting beyond it like we'd hoped—it was harder, harder than it seemed at the start of the show. You know, I thought we could just roll in and do our usual, but...

DM: I thought we could be professionals, personally. I really thought we could...

KS: I thought—well you know what I thought? We could be professionals. So...

DM: Let's just put this behind us! I mean, let's...

KS: No you're right, that's true.

DM: ...Let's exhume this as much as we need to and do whatever we need to do to sort of settle this conflict...

KS: Okay.

DM: Because I care about the health of the show. I would rather we move forward.

KS: I'm with you there.

DM: And if we have to sort of cathartically do some sort of competition or whatever, to just definitively put this whole ugly issue behind us, I would rather just move forward with this show.

KS: You know what? That would help me settle. Unfortunately, I don't think there is anything that could achieve that. I mean, previous things offered on previous shows notwithstanding. I don't think there is really a solution. I think we should just bury our feelings deep down, roll them into a tight ball of hate, and just stick that down in your stomach and just let it fester. For decades.

DM: @Wendelldotme says, "Do the rap battle now. Ninnies."

KS: Oh wow, nice. Do you want some of this? Do you want some of this? *(sighs)*

DM: Are you talking to me or to @WENDELLDOTME?

KS: No I'm talking to Wendell now. I mean, we can't even—we're trying to get past doing a show here. We're trying to solve problems, you know...

DM: And he's telling us to rap like a bunch of adolescents.

KS: Right. Like we can't just settle our differences by discussing them.

DM: You know what? I think everything should be able to be solved with diplomacy. We should be able to talk our issues out, right?

KS: Yes. Look. You know what? I am willing to do that just to spite Wendell, you know?

DM: Yeah, exactly. We're not your monkeys, jumping around here.

KS: Yeah, we're not doing this show for your entertainment.

DM: We're doing this for court-mandated reasons.

KS: Yeah. We're—wait, hold on a second. *I'm* not. I was just doing it 'cause I'm bored and lonely. I mean, I've got a cool life.

DM: I have a thing on my ankle that says I have to do a show every week.

KS: Oh, really? Oh...

DM: Yeah. I have to pay, like, a bail fee, and I have to take, like—it's the equivalent of traffic school, but it's, like, for Internet.

KS: Oh, hell. Well, look . It doesn't mean that I don't think that you're an idiot, but I felt a pang of sympathy just now. That's kind of rotten.

DM: *(sighs)*

KS: Look, it's hard enough for me to do a show with this guy without people egging us on in juvenile ways.

DM: Here's the whole problem, @WENDELLDOTME: Lord knows I would *like* to have a rap battle, but I don't know who would decide it! I mean, we want to have something that is easily—a judgment can be rendered.

KS: Right, I think that we kind of—I mean, you and I got busy during the week. First it was back and forth with the whole, you know, the pranks that we were playing on each other. That kind of ate up a lot of time. And, I mean, I'm still getting those stains out. But, the point is we didn't really line up a lot of that stuff, so if we, I mean, if we had an impartial judge...

DM: If there was someone that we knew that could come on the show, then, I mean, it would be great, but—I just don't know who we would call.

KS: I don't know. I don't know what to do. But you know what? I don't care, because it's never gonna happen. There is no way that anybody else is going to get onto this show. It's not possible.

DM: Absolutely. Wait—is this one of those things on the sitcoms, where they go, "There is *no way* I am getting on that boat to Bermuda!" And then it just kinda cuts to—

KS: No! Like, and then the thing actually happens? That's nonsense.

DM: That's such an old...

KS: You've been watching too much *F Troop*. That doesn't actually happen. This show's on lockdown. Just you, me.

DM: There's absolutely no way that anybody will ever join us on this program.

KS: Yes.

DM: It's just you and I.

KS: It's just us. It's just us and our differences.

FSL: Excuse me, True Believers!

KS: What? Is that you, David? Because that is a terrible impression of Ernest Borgnine.

DM: No, that wasn't—I thought you were trying to be an old man or something.

KS: No, that's not funny.

FSL: I'm sorry, gentlemen. Did I stumble into something here?

KS: What—who are you?

FSL: What? You don't recognize me?

DM: This is—no. This is...

KS: This is *highly* irregular.

DM: Kris. This is Fake Stan Lee.

FSL: Yes, indeed, True Believers!

KS: Fake Stan Lee? How did you find out that we were having an argument?

FSL: Oh, well, I'm a big fan of your show. I listen to it every time you guys do it. And, I couldn't help but notice that the two of you were having a bit of a squabble.

KS: Squabble, to say the least.

DM: Yeah, that's a bit of an understatement.

KS: Yeah. He's a jerk. I hate him.

DM: Whoa. Yeah. I don't like him very much either.

FSL: Well, you know, this reminds me of a time when Ben Grimm and Mr. Fantastic—

KS: Hold on, wait a second. We're kinda not doing a show about comics or anything. We're kinda just doing a show about—yeah, you know.

DM: We were actually gonna—we were gonna have some sort of a competition and we were looking for some sort of impartial judge so we could...

FSL: Well, I could certainly be a judge. You know, I judged many things in the past. I remember one time when the Mighty Thor and the Incredible Hulk—

KS: Now hold on, hold on. It's not—yeah. That's not the kind of battle that we're referring to. It's more like—I don't know, some people had the idea that we were going to do a rap battle to kind of settle this.

FSL: Oh.

DM: We were each going to do a rap. And someone was going to be able to tell us, sort of, which one...

KS: Is better.

DM: ...Is the best. And then we could, sort of, solve this interpersonal thing.

KS: We would know who is better, at that point.

FSL: Oh, well, that sounds great but, you know? You guys are going to have to explain something to me.

Now...what exactly *is* a rap?

KS: Oh.

DM: Um, well, a rap—it's kind of like... what would you say, Kris?

KS: It's like rhythmic speaking to a beat.

DM: It's kind of singing, a sing-songy pattern.

FSL: I see. Okay. I get it. You know, this one time, the Colossus had to go to a jazz club—

KS: Well, no. Hold on a second. We don't...

DM: Yeah.

KS: I mean, unless he was in a rap battle, I don't really see how this is...

FSL: Well, it wasn't specifically a rap battle. What happened was, Charlie Parker challenged him to—

DM: No, no.

KS: I don't think that happened.

FSL: It was in an issue of *Marvel Presents*. Not a lot of people read it.

KS: Well, okay. That's fine. We could just go ahead and do the battle. I mean...

DM: I don't think that our audience is really going to understand some of those references, Fake Stan Lee, so, um... but if you *(sighs)*... if you think that you could... I mean, obviously you've been around for a long time. You've experienced a lot in your life. Would you be able to—hypothetically speaking, if Kris and I were to do some sort of rap battle...

KS: Extemporaneously. Just off the cuff.

DM: ...We'd just happen to sort of think of something...

FSL: It would have to be completely live. I mean, I think people can smell when something is prerecorded, of course. So...

KS: Yeah. That's true.

DM: I mean we would just find some kind of a beat, somehow. And then we'd maybe make up some sort of a rap, and to make it fair we would each have to do a rap about the same theme.

KS: Yeah.

DM: So that we could—we'd have to be on a level playing field.

FSL: You want to have the same topic, huh?

KS: Yeah.

FSL: Let me think about this for a second. Okay. Uh, how about you gentlemen make up one of your rappities about a, uh... about the time that Magneto and—

KS: I don't think...

DM: No. Wait, wait, wait. Hold on. I don't think that...

KS: Yeah, we probably shouldn't do it about comics.

DM: That's not something that is going to be relevant to this particular...

KS: They don't really care about that.

FSL: *(laughs)* Oh, okay. I understand.

DM: *Do* you? Because it's happening kind of a lot.

KS: *(laughs)*

FSL: Before we get into your rippity rap battle, um, I just wanna know. What exactly was going on between the two of you to make you get to this point?

KS: Hmm.

DM: Well, Stan, we were having a conversation on our last program, and we were talking—we kind of hit a lot of topics toward the end of it.

KS: Yeah, it's just kind of a blur. I mean, clearly it was bad, because it's lasted a whole week.

DM: I definitely remember all the rancor. I mean, I remember just gritting my teeth and sort of waking up with a sore jaw. But, what was it? I think we were talking...

KS: I don't know. Was it, like, the economy? Like stocks? Like, I thought there was something about money?

DM: It had to be something really, really, really...

KS: Really base, like religion or something.

DM: Yeah, were we having, like, a political....?

KS: I don't remember.

DM: I can't really remember what the actual...

FSL: It doesn't matter, because the point is, you guys are both at odds with each other and I want to make sure that we all end this program as friends. Does that sound like something you gentlemen would like?

KS: No!

DM: *(laughs)* I wanna *destroy* Kris!

KS: Yeah, I'm not happy with what happened. That I don't remember.

DM: I'm sure it was really bad.

KS: Yeah, I think—just based on how I feel right now—that there is some bad blood. Like, I can't identify it, but I don't need to, because it's in there.

FSL: Well, don't say that I didn't try. Sometimes you just have to go into battle. Like back when the X-Men went into battle against the terrible—

KS: Nah, I don't think...

DM: All right, all right.

KS: Yeah, okay. I don't know about that one.

DM: Well, I guess we're at the point where we're out of options.

KS: Sure.

DM: If we're gonna rap, we're gonna need some kind of a beat.

FSL: You know, I have a couple of songs and beats around my office here, just laying around from the time that I hung out with Michael Jackson. I don't know if you guys could use them, but I would be welcome to pass them along.

KS: Well, hold on a second. Yeah, I mean, let's... could you play a little bit of it?

FSL: Ah, yeah, well, I've gotta dig around here for a second, but I'm sure I would need to find something. Um...

[BEAT BEGINS PLAYING]

KS: That sounds pretty good. I like that. Is that it just there?

DM: I mean, provisionally—I mean, hold on a second. Before we just jump with both feet into this, I think there's a lot of, uh...

KS: I think we could use that one.

FSL: Okay, well you guys can use that one. And I have to admit: it's not actually me sending it. I have my nephew sitting here next to me.

[KRIS AND DAVID LAUGH]

FSL: Uh, he's a genius, he's fantastic. You know, he's like Professor Xavier. I just—

KS: Uh, yeah, wait...

DM: Uh, hold on, hold on. All right. But, okay, I'm on board. I think that's kind of a cool beat. I feel like I could—I feel confident that I could do something with this beat that would definitely show Kris that I don't have to be subservient to his ridiculous notions all the time.

KS: Well, ha, you know what? If you're confident, then I'm *beyond* confident. Like, I'm twice confident. Three, at least, four times confidenter than you seem to be not confident. You're not confident...

DM: We happen to have some folks out there in Internet-land that would like to weigh in on the subject of the conflict between Kris and myself.

KS: Well, that would be good to hear some different voices for a change. In my headset. I'd like that.

> *Good evening, gentlemen. Uh, I understand that there is to be a rap battle. That is excellent. I just want to call and say—well, you know, give you both my best wishes, and may the best man win. Let's see some fair play out there. It's not really whether you win or lose, it's how you play the game, so... yeah, I think this is going to be a great experience for everybody.*

DM: This is not amping me up for combat.

KS: I was gonna say: This is not a mumbling battle. This is going to be a rap battle.

FSL: I'd like to talk to that young man for a second. Now, young man, I was wondering...

KS: Whoa, Stan, Stan, Stan. He wasn't here. That was a recording.

FSL: Oh I see, okay. Well, my nephew didn't tell me that. I'm sorry. Go ahead.

KS: Yeah, let's hear some more...

> *Yo yo, what up, it's Fuzzy B. I gotta put my money on K-Strizzle in this particular altercation, cuz Straub got more beats than Doug Funny, cuz his rhymes is cash money. He's flowing like the Tigris and Euphrates, pleasing all the fellas and the ladies. Got more rhymes than the Wu-Tang Clan. Got more magic than the medicine man. Best of luck to you, Malki. I hope you're prepared. And everybody go read "Checkerboard Nightmare."*

DM: *(laughs)* Wow, that was...

KS: Fuzzy got my back!

FSL: Now was that one of the raps that you guys were talking about?

KS: Yeah, a little bit. Yeah.

DM: Sort of. It was very similar to that. Yeah.

FSL: 'Cause I only understood about three of the words in that entire thing.

> [KRIS AND DAVID LAUGH]

FSL: I think it's fantastic. If that's what you gentlemen are gonna do then I'm all aboard.

KS: That's good. I mean, I feel—I gotta admit. That one did kinda pump me up a little bit for my impending fight.

DM: A little bit. Let's see what else other people have to say.

> *Okay, so I'm calling to support Kris Straub, and I wrote this, but I don't have a DJ so I don't have a beat. I'm sorry. Hey yo, I'm Risque A and I'm here to say that Kristofer Straub is gonna win the day. You think you got it Malki? Oh hell, no way, cuz Kris is the sumbitch that makes the ladies say, "Hey-eh." Yeah, that's right. 5'6". 36-24-36. Kris Straub has a posse. We got your back, Sweetness. Peace!*

FSL: Oh dear.

KS: Wow!

DM: So, uh, sounds like Kris has got some fans out there in lady-land.

KS: I was gonna say, if the audience is just ladies, then I got this on lock. But, I mean, that's...

FSL: *(laughs)* You remind me of a young Reed Richards. Now—

[KRIS AND DAVID LAUGH]

KS: Now, hold on a second...

DM: Wait wait, let's not—let's just move on before Kris gets too overconfident, I think we have a little more...

KS: Oh, okay.

> I have confidence that Malki will dominate this competition, and Kris will be left completely destroyed.

DM: Huh?

KS: Wow.

DM: What do you say to that?

KS: That guy had a mean-on.

DM: He was pretty upset, I think, about the fact that you were trying to front. You trying to front?

KS: Yeah, well, I think it's pretty cool that you got your brother to call in. That's rad. I like that.

FSL: Oh, oh, that's—those are fighting words if I've ever heard them.

DM: Well, here's—we got a few more fighting words to sort of amp ourselves up, because I'm starting to feel a little adrenaline coursing through my veins.

> I don't even know what the contest is for, but I'm always pulling for my man Mr. K-Straub. Top dog of the webcomics, Internet, all right.

DM: Oh I see. Way to pull out the nerds—okay, so now we have two voicemails, two readers, talking about your Checkerboard this and your Internet that and your webcomics this, that and the other...[48]

KS: Well, I have a mailing list, and I happened to mention...

DM: ...I'm starting to feel like you and Fake Stan Lee might be in collusion, because I'm the only one sticking to the ground rules here, which is that this is *not a show about comics!*

KS: Yes, well, I'm...

FSL: Kristofer, do you draw comics?

KS: Well, I mean, yeah, but it's sort of not a thing that we really deal with on this— this is sort of a general-interest show that has to do with...

---

48   Kris is well-known outside the world of podcasting for his long-running webcomic "Checkerboard Nightmare," a retelling of *Crime and Punishment* with furries.

FSL: This is what I want you to do. I want you to send some of your comics over to me at the Marvel offices, and I will take a look at them.

KS: That—no, I'm good. I'm okay. We really don't need to talk about it...

DM: No, hold on, let's stick to the subject at hand.

KS: Let's just stick on—yeah, exactly.

FSL: All right.

> Yo, yo, yo, Malki. Word up! I heard you got this little thing going on with
> some guy named Kris. A name don't mean a thing if it ain't Malki !
> Thought I'd give you my support.

DM: Huh? Huh?

KS: Snap! Ouch, that hurts.

DM: One more.

> I don't know much about Kris Straub, but I do know that there is no way
> he's as good as Malki. Oh snap! And also, booyah.

KS: Oh snap... *(laughs)*

DM: ...And also, booyah.

KS: He got a booyah all up on there. Damn!

FSL: Now back when I was growing up, *booyah* was actually an ethnic slur. You couldn't...

KS: Whoa, whoa, whoa. Hold on a second, hold on a second...

DM: ...We're really, we're really—yeah I've got one more that I wanna play here.

KS: Okay.

DM: And I think it'll put the whole thing just into clear perspective. We'll be able to move forward.

KS: Great.

DM: All right, here we go.

> Yo, I'm giving a shout out to my boy, DJ Malki-Malk Malki ! Kris Straub,
> you better watch out because he's gonna kick your ass! Booyah!

FSL: Oh dear, there it is again.

KS: *(laughs)* Don't worry. In this day and age it's actually a positive thing, and has nothing to do with ethnicity whatsoever.

FSL: Okay. Fantastic.

> Get ready for Tweet Me Harder
> Where tonight they'll have a rap martyr.
> Will it be Malki? Or Kris? They'll fight and they'll dis.
> And if you resist, then you'll get the verbal fist.
> Cause they'll tweet while they battle
> And they'll battle while they tweet.

One will stand up, the other takes a seat.
Because Twitter will decide which of them will come to rise.
Who's high-tech and keen...and who's a simple machine?

DM: Oh, simple machines!

KS: Simple machines would be a great topic!

DM: Yeah! Fake Stan Lee, do you know anything about simple machines? Can you adjudicate a contest if it were to be about simple machines?

FSL: Simple machines!? You're talking to the man who invented ROM, the Metal Knight! Of course I know about simple machines.

DM: *(groans)* All right. Okay, you know what?

KS: Yeah, that's...

FSL: I would be happy to adjudicate this rap battle.

DM: All right, so how do you wanna do this, Kris?

KS: I don't know. Maybe, Stan Lee, maybe you should go ahead and...

FSL: Here's how we'll do it: It'll be a trivia contest. Whoever can answer the question correctly will decide whether or not they go first.

KS: I like that.

DM: Yeah, that sounds fine.

FSL: All right, a trivia question. This one's easy. Okay. In *Amazing Spider-Man* number 72, on page 5...

DM: *(groans)*

KS: *(laughs)*

FSL: ...There's a picture of Spider-Man hanging upside down. What is he hanging from?

KS: *(laughs)* Do you mean, like, a web? Or do you mean like a...

FSL: What's his web hanging from?

KS: Oh, I don't know...

FSL: Guys, this is a softball, everyone knows this!

KS: *(laughs)* Um...

DM: All right. Um, I'm gonna say... a girder.

KS: Okay, I'm gonna say he's hanging from a, uh... from the top of the high school.

FSL: Well, I hate to tell you, Kristofer, but Mr. Malki is correct.

KS: *(groans)*

DM: OOOooohhhhh!

FSL: Good work, True Believer!

KS: How did you know that?

DM: I just figured, every Spider-Man comic cover I've ever seen, he's hanging from a girder.

KS: Oh, he—that's right. He...

FSL: So David, now you get to decide whether you're gonna go first or second.

DM: I think I'm gonna let Kris go first.

KS: All right.

FSL: Okay, so, uh...

KS: (clears throat) All right, let me get up on the mic here. Hold on. Testing. Check check.

DM: All right, Fake Stan? Can you hear everything? Are you positioned?

FSL: I am ready. Let's commence this rappity rap battle.

KS: All right, gimme that beat in my cans.

[THE BEAT STARTS]

Let's do this. K-Straub 'bout to drop mechanical science
Like they'll make you change majors like a major appliance
But I ain't talking Frigidaire. I mean machines that crane beams up in the air
I've seen sh— like Egypt when they thought this
Walking blocks up the inclined plane, that's how they got this
Pyramid on up to ziggurats lean on the golden mean
Now how you figure that?
From sheiks to Greeks how the hell did he knew?
Archimedes saying to the water, hey screw you
These bros in togas ain't yet invented soda. Whatcha think?
Motherf—kers cranking on cranks just to get a drink
Pulley and rope converts strength to length up to high ground
Need a place to stand to move the Earth, I've got to lie down
To leave 'er, I couldn't see her no more
She told me I made her feel / Like a wheel the way you roll me!
Okay so now she transports her wares elsewhere, how harrowing
Mechanical advantage took care of everything!
Attached two levers—now she wheelbarrowing.
See the theme of simple machines I hold in high esteem
These machines don't scheme, or freeze the wheels of progress
or lock pod bay doors or kill Dave in protest!
Sim-ple machines...

[APPLAUSE]

That was amazing—Booyah—Woot—Oh no he didn't—I believe we're in
the hot spot—I'm gonna have to take off my shirt it's getting so hot.

KS: (gasping for breath) Oh yes, phew! Hey, thanks, guys.

FSL: That was very exciting. Wow.

KS: How you like me now, huh? How you like me now, Malki?

FSL: Kristofer, did you come up with those raps all by yourself?

KS: Yeah, I did.

FSL: Oh, that is great. That is fantastic. David, I don't know how you can follow that up, but I'd certainly like to see you try. *(laughs)*

DM: All right, Fake Stan. Let's see if you can give me that beat. I'll just do my best.

[*THE BEAT STARTS*]

Yo, listen up real good 'cuz this is coming at you fast.
MC Malki busting rhymes on the TMH podblast.
Empirical perfection from your boy Malki-Malk
A lyrical injection like my name was Jonas Salk.
But here comes a story about what happened yesterday.
I'm strutting out in my hood and this homeboy says, "Hey!"
He rises up real tall like a monster from a dream
Then he opens up a coat full of simple machines.
He sez "I got more pulleys than there's bullies at school.
Best believe I've got a lever you can use as a tool.
Take some Paxil cuz my axle's gonna cause you some stress
Until my wheel seals the deal because you know it's the best!"
He sez "If you think that's tight, well I got lots more still."
Then he grinned real big to show the pulley in his grill!
He said, "I got more screws than a prostitute all-nighter.
Got more wedges than you've got wingmen on your X-wing fighter."
I said "It sounds dope, G, but ain't there one more sort?"
He said "I've got more inclined planes than a sideways airport.
These goods are the best, they don't need no 'lectricity."
I said, "Eff that mess, I ain't into simplicity."
He tries to argue then. He says, "It's easy, it's proven."
Pull out my MAC-10, and his jaw stops moving.
He tries to work some spell like a creature from fantasy
I say, "Go to hell." And I empty my magazine.
He goes up in steam like a demon from Hades—
Fool, my simplest machine is my blinged-out Mercedes.

[*APPLAUSE*]

Wuh-hoh! Snap, no he di-int—That was awesome—Man!—Damn, that
Malki-Malk so fly—Go, Malki, booyah.

FSL: Wow.

DM: *(sighs)* Well, um, I don't know what to say, we've kind of put ourselves out there.

KS: That was—sheesh, that was pretty good.

FSL: Wow. That's—now am I the sole judge here or are the people out there in Internet-land also going to weigh in? Is that something that's going to happen?

DM: Uh, well, yeah, let's take a quick look here. I mean, Stan, we want you to be the final arbiter. We don't want to have this democracy thing going on. It's too hard to count the votes. But, we will have—we will let some people on the Internet weigh in with their opinions. @SUPRALIMINAL says, " 'More inclined planes than a sideways airport.' It's quality stuff." I will take credit for that one, seeing as how my rap was the one that was intelligible.

KS: Well, that's 'cause it was slow. All right, let's see here. You've got, uh—Wendell said, what? "Your rap has better flow than Polly Holiday." I don't even know what that means.

DM: *(laughs)*

FSL: Billie Holiday? She was fantastic back when I was growing up.

KS: Well, no. That's not what he said.

FSL: She was quite a sex symbol, I'll tell you that much. Boy...

DM: We also have, uh...

FSL: I'm sorry.

KS: *(laughs)*

DM: I will give @SHAMZAM here a word: "It is incredibly difficult to bleep yourself and echo yourself while rapping live. Kris Straub, you do have some hot flow."

KS: It's breath control. It is true. It is difficult. And then up here we've got @MALPERTUIS. Eh, that might be French. "Points for name-checking Archimedes." I'll take that credit, right? 'Cause I did say that.

DM: You did say that. Uh, @WENDELLDOTME says, "That was more fly than Jeff Goldblum on a bad day." Uh, Wendell may be causing more problems than he's solving here.

KS: *(laughs)* He's not helpful. Let's see, we've got a lot more coming in. Wow! Just rolling in now.

FSL: Now where are these coming from? That's what I'd like to know.

DM: This is from Twitter, Fake Stan. Are you familiar with Twitter?

FSL: Ah, Twitter. I'm gonna have to—I'm turning to my nephew, he's making... okay he's just making—I don't know what you're saying. Just use your words, Jeffrey. All right.

DM: We do have, "Kris wins for technique," says @VANPATTON, "but Malki had some pretty dope rhymes. Or something." I will take that. I will absolutely take that credit.

KS: I'll take some technique.

DM: Sure.

KS: That doesn't come any closer to solving this battle, though.

DM: Yeah.

KS: It seems like it's pretty evenly matched, from what I'm seeing.

DM: Well this is why it's best to have someone who is just. They're gonna just lay down the law. We're not gonna have votes. We're not gonna have everybody's opinion. Fake Stan Lee, who wins?

FSL: Well, gentlemen, first off I wanna say that both of you did a fantastic job. You know, it reminds me of the time that Mary Jane Parker decided she wanted to—

DM: *(groans)*

KS: No, that's...

DM: *For crying out loud!*

KS: ...That's fine, but we just kinda want to know who won this.

DM: Just stick to the raps, Fake Stan.

KS: Yeah.

FSL: All right, so back to your raps. Here's the thing about these raps. You know, I've been listening to your raps and everything like that. You know I like what the kids like. I'm still hip, right?

DM: Well yeah, Fake Stan, of course.

KS: You're the coolest guy.

DM: The voice of a culture.

FSL: And I think—maybe I can give this whole rapping thing a try. What do you think about that?

KS: ...This is highly irregular.

FSL: Well, you know. I've been inspired by what you gentlemen have done.

KS: Well, yeah. I don't have a problem with that.

DM: Sure, we'd love to hear what you have to say.

KS: Yeah, let's hear it.

FSL: Okay, well, then, let's start that beat there. Let's try this out.

[THE BEAT STARTS]

Check it, True Believers!

When you called me up and said, "Hey, Stan,
Come judge our epic throwdown."
I said, "of course," because I pictured a real titanic showdown.
I heard your songs, and I played along, and it's okay, I suppose.
But let MC Stan show you how a real story goes.
A young man's hit by cosmic rays, and gains the power of flight.
He vows to wear a Spandex suit and fight for what is right.
His mother's sick, his grandma's old, his uncle's lost his penision.
He has to write an essay, and if it's late, he gets detention!
Then a space invader lands! With designs on planet Earth.
Our hero skips out on a date to fight for all he's worth.
Then a gamma bomb explodes! And turns his bones to steel!
He's late on paying rent, but just look how fast he can heal!
Then he lifts the hammer Mjolnir and gains the power cosmic—
He fights a being who eats the sun—but then he has to rush home to deliver pizza—

DM: All right.

FSL: And his uncle becomes a loveable mailman that he always relies upon for advice—

KS: Okay, Stan. Hey...

FSL: Until he becomes enraged and discovers that he can shoot lasers from his ears! It's really quite a—

KS: Stan!

FSL: What?

DM: Stan?

FSL: Yes.

DM: Um...

KS: Nope.

FSL: I'm sorry, gentlemen.

KS: You didn't really stick to the theme of the battle.

DM: Yeah, we had a theme going on.

FSL: I'm sorry. But—did I not murder it? Did I not *murder* it?

[KRIS AND DAVID LAUGH]

KS: Yeah, you put it one foot in the grave.

DM: *(laughs)*

FSL: I absolutely think I killed it. I think I totally killed it.

DM: *(laughs)*

KS: I'm dumbfounded.

DM: I'm laughing. I'm laughing for the first time—I'm laughing along with Kris for the first time in at least a week.

FSL: You see there, True Believers? It all comes down to what you experience together. And if the two of you can laugh at an old man like me, then my job here is done.

[KRIS AND DAVID LAUGH]

KS: You know what? I'd like to laugh at an old man. What do you say, Malki?

DM: I could—you know what?

KS: Let's laugh at him.

DM: If there's anyone I'm gonna laugh at, it's gonna be an old man trying to do something hip.

[KRIS AND DAVID LAUGH MEANLY AT FAKE STAN LEE]

KS: What a dumb old man.

DM: What a jerk.

FSL: Watch it now. Watch it. Okay. Thank you so much for letting me judge your rap battle. I think I'm going to declare all of us the winners.

DM: Well, thank you, Fake Stan Lee. I will definitely accept the co-hand of victory with my good friend, once again, Kris Straub.

KS: I will accept a double win with David Malki.

DM: It's sort of like a church game where everyone—it's sort of a tie, so no one goes home in tears. But that's—you know what? I'll take what I can get at this point.

KS: Well look, I—you know what—this kind of opened my eyes to something. I think that this podcast has the freshest flow, you know?

DM: I'm thinking...

KS: I would challenge any other podcast to play—I mean, Tweet Me Harder is pretty solid.

DM: It definitely has the dopest rhythms.

KS: Yeah, as far as laying on the mic.

DM: Fake Stan, would you agree?

FSL: I definitely agree. I think we're all incredibly fresh and good-smelling.

[ACCORDION STING]

DM: Well, everyone. It's been Episode Ten of Tweet Me Harder.

KS: It certainly has. And I think we've learned a lot.

DM: We've come a long way. We started somewhere, and we've ended up somewhere else. And I think we all learned a little something about ourselves, about friendship, about the nature of competition, friendly at-each-other's-throat-ism, and about Fake Stan Lee. I didn't know he could bust out such dope rhymes.

KS: I didn't know he just appeared when called.

DM: He's sort of like Mr. Mxyzptlk in that way.

KS: Yeah. Oh, God, I love DC. Those are some great books.

DM: Batman, he's such an inspiration to me. The fact that he's not a superhero, but he goes out and he fights crime everyday.

KS: I know, but he can stand toe-to-toe with anybody in the Justice League.

FSL: Gentlemen, you know I'm still here, right?

KS: Oh.

DM: Oh.

KS: Hey.

DM: *(nervous laugh)*

FSL: Well, I'm gonna go, I—I wish you guys the best of luck with your show, and your rappity battles, and your hippity hops.

KS: Well, thank you, Fake Stan Lee!

DM: Fake Stan Lee, everybody.

FSL: Yes. Say it with me, gentlemen. Say, "Excelsior!"

ALL: *"EXCELSIOR!"*

FSL: Very good. All right, I'll see you next time.

[ACCORDION STING]

DM: I will say, this is sort of an interesting episode of Tweet Me Harder, because it is the end of our first season of Tweet Me Harder.

KS: Yes! Which I don't think we mentioned that we will do them in seasons. But…

DM: No, we never mentioned it before, or even to each other until just now.

KS: Yes, so I'm flabbergasted. I'm interested in learning more about this concept of seasons on this show.

DM: Well, Kris, we are doing this show in seasons of ten episodes, and we have reached the end of Season 1.

KS: That's nice.

DM: We are going to start Season 2 after a one-week hiatus. We are going to be off next week, then we are going to be back in two weeks with all-new, all-different, stupendous Tweet Me Harder.

KS: Singing and dancing. Mostly raps. Probably just all rap.

DM: It's going to be a lot of this stuff, guys. Moving forward. Expect 80%.

KS: This worked so well that I just want to sing. I just want to make songs that make people clap.

DM: It's interesting how the innateness of rhythym is such an important part of our human biology and makeup that…

KS: And it's really—it's something that we've ignored as a, you know, as a culture, as a species.

DM: This whole "talkiness" is—I mean, I could take it or leave it. It feels somehow lacking now, that I've been to those heights of music.

KS: Do you remember how at the turn of the millennium, there was a big countdown to 2000 and then it hit and then a bunch of shows showed up on, what channel? Like E! and stuff like that? It was all those top-ten, those countdown shows, like *Best Week Ever* and all that stuff?

DM: Oh yeah—on VH1?

KS: Yeah. I read a theory in some magazine that said the reason why those shows came up after the millennium was because we were so thrilled, as a culture, counting down to something, that when it passed we all got real down and were like, "Well you know what? Let's count to other things. Let's count to the ten worst celebrity dresses." You know?

DM: Really, I would say, those top-ten lists—okay, maybe not in terms of television, but top-ten stuff has been super-popular for a long time. Hasn't it?

KS: Right.

DM: Or has it just seemed that way because it's everywhere now?

KS: There were top-ten lists certainly before that, but after that, there was just a glut of them, because we had to count to things and feel a little bit more of that excitement. To see that odometer roll over.

DM: Because here's the thing: Our lives just progress without markers, right? That's why when you get out of school you feel aimless, because there's no more seasons, there's no more semester breaks. There's none of those things that let you mark your time.

KS: Right.

DM: And so you watch people go through their regular life, and kids who are still in school, and you're out of school, and it's like, "Wow. It's been another year already? Because I didn't even notice it go by." So I understand the importance of putting those milestones down, those flags along the path.

KS: Yeah, and I understand the idea of putting an arbitrary marker, say on ten shows, just to limit a season. I think that's actually a great idea. To get people pumped for the next ten shows.

DM: Right. For Season 2 of Tweet Me Harder. Starting with Show #11 in two weeks.

KS: Or perhaps we'll call it Tweet Me Harder, Season 2, Show 1.

DM: Uh, I don't think we should do that.

KS: We could denote it as 2-1.0 just to make sure. And then you could do a timecode there, after the period.

DM: Oh, I see. So we could do it like Mario levels. World 1-1...

KS: Yeah.

DM: 2-1...

KS: Because, I mean, if you think about it, this show really—Tweet Me Harder *does* take the format of a Mario level.

DM: Oh, yeah! There's all the mushrooms we have to step on.

KS: Well... I mean more generically. There is a challenge to be met, and then...

DM: Because of the flagpole at the end, where we slide down.

KS: We jump up it and...

DM: There are fireworks. Occasionally there are fireworks, if we've timed it right.

KS: *Emotional* fireworks.

DM: On our Twitter, @white667 says, "End Season 1 with this question: if you have the choice of living Kris or Malki's life, which would you choose? Both of you."

KS: Is that a question for us?

DM: It's a question to us. Of both of our lives, each of us, which would we rather live?

KS: I don't know. I think we should answer simultaneously, so as not to embarrass one of us.

DM: All right, ready? We're gonna go 1-2-3-answer. Ready?

KS: Okay I'm ready, yeah.

DM: 1, 2, 3... Malki.

KS: I wish I was David Malki.

DM: ...Hey!

KS: *(laughs)* No, it's true. You're a handsome man. So that's one for you. Clearly you can lay down that beat. And it's just, you know, strong. I imagine it would be a very full and enriching life.

DM: All right, let's end this show before everyone goes into a diabetic coma. Thanks for listening to Tweet Me Harder. Stay tuned to the Twitter feed, @TWEETHARD, to learn about our next program. We'll be off. Thank you very much for listening. And we'll see you next time.

Index

Notes

Listen to Tweet Me Harder

You finished the book and I feel like we're best friends now. But it doesn't have to end here, you know. Not like this.

Listen to the Tweet Me Harder livestream every week at *tweetmeharder.com*. Check out our blog while you're there, and catch all the past editions of the podblast, as well as video of our live appearances.

And if you tweet along during the show with hashtag #TMH, you might end up in the next collection yourself. After all, that's what a best friend would do.

We'll see you next time.

—Kris & David !

Made in the USA
Monee, IL
12 December 2020